THE MATERIAL CULTURE OF WRITING

THE MATERIAL CULTURE
OF WRITING

EDITED BY
CYDNEY ALEXIS AND HANNAH J. RULE

UTAH STATE UNIVERSITY PRESS
Logan

© 2022 by University Press of Colorado

Published by Utah State University Press
An imprint of University Press of Colorado
245 Century Circle, Suite 202
Louisville, Colorado 80027

All rights reserved

 The University Press of Colorado is a proud member of the Association of University Presses.

The University Press of Colorado is a cooperative publishing enterprise supported, in part, by Adams State University, Colorado State University, Fort Lewis College, Metropolitan State University of Denver, Regis University, University of Alaska Fairbanks, University of Colorado, University of Northern Colorado, University of Wyoming, Utah State University, and Western Colorado University.

ISBN: 978-1-64642-229-6 (paperback)
ISBN: 978-1-64642-230-2 (ebook)
https://doi.org/10.7330/9781646422302

Library of Congress Cataloging-in-Publication Data

Names: Alexis, Cydney, editor. | Rule, Hannah J., 1981– editor.
Title: The material culture of writing / edited by Cydney Alexis and Hannah J. Rule.
Description: Logan : Utah State University Press, [2022] | Includes bibliographical references and index.
Identifiers: LCCN 2022014506 (print) | LCCN 2022014507 (ebook) | ISBN 9781646422296 (paperback) | ISBN 9781646422302 (ebook)
Subjects: LCSH: Written communication—Social aspects. | Writing materials and instruments—Social aspects. | Authorship—Technique. | Writing—Social aspects. | Material culture—Study and teaching.
Classification: LCC P211.7 .M38 2022 (print) | LCC P211.7 (ebook) | DDC 302.2/244—dc23/eng/20220504
LC record available at https://lccn.loc.gov/2022014506
LC ebook record available at https://lccn.loc.gov/2022014507

Cover illustrations, clockwise from top left: courtesy of Kouji Hayateno; photo by Anne Mackay; courtesy of Austin Neall; courtesy of Cydney Alexis; photo by Emilie Merrigan.

CONTENTS

Foreword
Laura R. Micciche   vii

Acknowledgments   xv

1   Introduction: The Material Culture of Writing
    Cydney Alexis and Hannah J. Rule   3

PART ONE: WRITING IDENTITY   19

2   The Symbolic Life of the Moleskine Notebook: Material Goods as a Tableau for Writing Identity Performance
    Cydney Alexis   25

3   Black Ink, White Bodies: Gender, Race, and Writing Instruments
    Desirée Henderson   49

4   Indexical Heirlooms in Immigrant Literacy History Narratives
    Jenny Krichevsky   69

5   Material Motherhood: The Disconnect of Science and Consumerism from Nostalgia in Baby Books
    Emilie Merrigan   89

PART TWO: WRITING WORK   115

6   New Writing in New Spaces: "Social Writing" in an Interdisciplinary Academic Makerspace
    Deborah C. Andrews   119

7   "Every Convenience for a Man of Letters": Thomas Jefferson's Writing Suite
    Diane Ehrenpreis   140

8   Assembling the File, or, How Conservation Works
    Anne MacKay   170

    PART THREE: WRITING GENRE   **191**

9   The Victorian Visitors' Book as Genre and Artifact
    Kevin James   194

10 Gendered Letterwriting in Renaissance England:
    Genre as Sociomaterial Action
    Keri Epps   211

    Afterword
    Kate Smith   231

    Index   239

    Contributors   245

FOREWORD

Laura R. Micciche

Moleskine notebooks, ink and paper, heirlooms, baby books, conservation materials, visitor books, and personal letters: What do such objects reveal about writing practices and their sociocultural contexts? What relationship do objects have to one's writing identity? While exploring these questions, *The Material Culture of Writing* makes a compelling case for treating objects as capable of facilitating our literate lives in ways that may otherwise escape notice. It does so by focusing on ordinary objects like paper and desk chairs, part of literacy's "aboveground" (Deetz) composed of visible, expected objects that populate everyday writing activities.

Such ordinary objects are mined by the contributors, inviting readers to reflect on how exactly "writing and its practice [happens] *through* things," as Cydney Alexis and Hannah Rule contend in their introduction. More precisely, though, the collection asks us to take "things" seriously not only because they have agency and persuasive power, a claim familiar to object-oriented work in writing studies (WS), but because things like ink pots, filing systems, and writing furniture can serve as portals into writing culture, history, and identity. Jenny Krichevsky's life-history interviews with Russian-speaking immigrants, for example, attach transcultural significance to reference books, bookcases, passports, and military medals passed across nations and generations. And Emilie Merrigan's chapter illuminates how mothers use the materiality of the baby book genre, initially created to serve "scientific motherhood," to create "pathways to social power and individual agency" (Epps, chapter 10). Across this collection, the authors' attentiveness to discrete artifacts shows how people creatively use objects with and against their intended usage in order to construct identity, preserve connection to one's history, and articulate a future for oneself.

Attention to small artifacts is complemented by the authors' acknowledgment of the larger contexts in which objects circulate. To that end,

https://doi.org/10.7330/9781646422302.c000

Alexis and Rule write in the introduction that their collection aims to "trace sociocultural and sociopolitical resonances of writing artifacts." This focus is achieved through contributors' investigations of individual, communal, and sociohistorical identity work achieved by objects, a line of inquiry shaped by the material culture studies (MCS) dictum that "to be human is to consume."

But, as this book demonstrates, consumption only gets us so far in understanding how objects are used and integrated into our writing lives. While MCS scholars describe usage and adaptation of objects as a way to singularize or decommodify possessions, *who* has access to objects in the first place strikes me as an especially timely matter that is brought to life with thick description throughout this book. The term *access* is not emphasized evenly across this volume, but I think it's a useful lens for naming a significant contribution this book makes to WS. I was frequently drawn to the surprising ways in which mundane objects illuminate privilege in both the foreground and background of writing practices—a topic of urgent interest in WS and beyond as struggles for social justice grow across every sector of US society.

Who can imagine themselves as writers and gain access to objects that facilitate a writing identity? Moleskine notebooks, the subject of Alexis's chapter, are sacred objects to many users in part because they link to a history of esteemed artists like Vincent Van Gogh and Ernest Hemingway (Alexis points out that Hemingway's actual usage may be a myth). However, not everyone can imagine themselves in a lineage of such artists, nor, more practically, can everyone afford to spend $8.00 to $15.00 on a hardbound notebook. Writing objects are permeated with racialized significance in Desirée Henderson's chapter on depictions of white women writers in nineteenth-century fiction. Henderson explores associations between writers' inky hands and perceptions of these women as masculinized domestic failures "stained" by black ink, associations that impose racist connotations on "the visual dimensions and color contrasts inherent to the material objects of writing." In the second half of her chapter, Henderson describes African American authors' efforts to resist racialized associations with writing objects and challenge impediments to access through creative improvisation. Describing writing instruments as "emblems of white supremacy," Henderson shows how Frederick Douglass nevertheless crafted his writer identity from makeshift materials: "board fence, brick wall, and pavement; my pen and ink was a lump of chalk."

Diane Ehrenpreis's study of Thomas Jefferson's writing suite may be read in direct contrast to Henderson's. Jefferson could write in his suite while leaving "the mundane responsibilities of plantation life for others to shoulder." In material ways, slavery enabled Jefferson's writing life and identity as a writer. And because he owned property and had the means to secure his legacy, family members were able to preserve his possessions, creating "a nearly complete record of the material culture of Jefferson's writing practice." His private room with locks on the door, Ehrenpreis points out, allowed him a space that no one else on the estate grounds could claim. Cultural power in tandem with gender and race privilege are the conditions of Jefferson's life that made possible his writing life at Monticello.

No doubt my mind has gone to access and privilege because of the moment we're living right now. As a parent, I receive bi-weekly announcements from my kids' schools about access and writing objects. How and where writing can happen is a pressing issue for schools as COVID-19 surges across the United States. Where I live in Cincinnati, Ohio, the public school district is distributing thirty thousand digital devices to students in K–12 schools—iPads for second and third graders; laptops for everyone else—equipped with school-approved software. In partnership with local technology companies, the district is also providing free Wi-Fi access to all student households, as schools try to anticipate and address the inequity that online education lays bare. Writing assignments are to be completed in Google Classrooms, as they are for many during ordinary times when students meet face-to-face in classrooms. As of 2019, 68 percent of secondary schools in the United States reported usage of Google Classroom in their districts (Kajeet). When my thirteen-year-old son composes in a Google document, he does so with a knowledge of process and revision that astounds me. "Nothing is final," he tells me if I try to offer a suggestion. "My group members and my teacher will add comments. I'll make changes after that."

For him, and probably for other users who have grown up using this technology, writing is naturally mediated and changeable, a relationship that the field of WS has sought to cultivate for some five decades. This volume illuminates the fact that experiencing writing as a process (or whatever else) is due not only to persuasive research by writing scholars but also to the widespread availability and affordability of tools that have made process a material reality. In other words, a philosophy of writing becomes a practice by way of tools.

As suggested by my son's assurance that readers will offer feedback, he experiences online writing spaces as social. Within WS, however, the usual baseline for considering writing a social act is a face-to-face write-on-site model located in rooms and realized through peer groups and in-class collaboration. In this volume, too, physical proximity is the presumed condition of writing in Deborah C. Andrews's chapter on academic makerspace design. Yet, her attention to environment-structuring, involving choices of furniture, surfaces, and space-separators, offers a productive model for thinking about how to structure online writing environments to approximate a "neighborhood" that welcomes conversation, real-time collaboration, and "the mess that often accompanies innovation" within aesthetically and creatively inspiring spaces. Andrews's chapter encourages reflection on what constitutes a writing workspace and how such a space always responds to context-specific needs. While academic makerspaces are on trend because they materialize community-university partnerships that serve the economic interests of both partners, the surge in online teaching as the condition for education (not complement or last-resort) is driving new (old) conversations about the design of online spaces. Increasingly, these spaces are expected to serve the social fabric of learning as well as the delivery of content. For example, in the spring of 2020 when schools went online, my kids' teachers held weekly videoconference check-ins for students who wanted to talk about how they were doing or simply see other peoples' faces.

In short, COVID-19 is forcing online writing environments to address the social and material infrastructural limitations of brick-and-mortar schools designed for togetherness, not apartness. I kept thinking of this when reading Anne MacKay's "Assembling the File, or, How Conservation Works," where, among other things, she draws on information scientist Steven Jackson's concept of "broken world thinking" while discussing the wear, damage, and decay of conservation infrastructure. For MacKmay, analysis of "damage and deterioration . . . [creates] a pathway . . . back to an accomplished form of the object, which was unknown at the beginning of the process." Thinking of traditional school infrastructure as fragile and in need of repair has potential for rethinking what's required for maintaining schools in both ordinary circumstances (cracked plaster, nonworking toilets, unmovable furniture) and extraordinary ones: Should innovators in education partner with disease specialists? When is community and collaboration not a social good and how can material structures address that? What material infrastructure offers the most flexibility for learning and teaching as well as for public safety? Does thinking of education as a "safe space" end up endangering students and teachers?

***

As the above suggests, reading this book in the summer of 2020 made me look differently at the stuff around me. In addition to making me reflect on education in a COVID-19 world, I began thinking of *streets*, the ultimate "aboveground" of most US cities, as writing artifacts—large public canvases for personal and cultural expression. In the aftermath of George Floyd's murder by police officers and the newly energized Black Lives Matter (BLM) movement fueling worldwide protests for racial justice, my thoughts went to BLM street murals painted on roadways across the United States. Before reading *The Material Culture of Writing*, I'm not sure that I would have viewed the mundane surface of streets as ripe for *written* activism.

The first BLM mural appeared on Sixteenth Street in front of Lafayette Square, leading up to the White House, an area renamed Black Lives Matter Plaza by DC mayor Muriel Bowser. In fifty-foot all-capital yellow letters stretching two city blocks, "Black Lives Matter" commands the street and draws the attention of anyone driving, crossing, walking alongside, or flying over it. While some members of the DC BLM chapter have criticized the mural as motivated by the mayor's contentious relationship with Donald Trump, rather than by her support for meaningful political change, there's no denying that the mural is a defiant occupation of space. What the mural communicates is that the street—and the communities it borders—belongs to the city's inhabitants, a more than 45 percent Black population, and not to the government.

BLM street murals have since appeared around the United States, from Hollywood, California, to Raleigh, North Carolina, to Denver, Colorado, where artists painted a mural on Broadway near the state capitol building. In Cincinnati, a collective of seventeen Black project managers and seventy local artists known as Black Art Speaks, led by organizer Alandes Powell, designed and created a mural on Plum Street in front of City Hall (see fig. 0.1).

City Council passed an ordinance approving the project, demonstrating that mural installation is not a lawless activity but one that goes through established local government and city channels. And the cost of materials is not necessarily covered by local funds; in the case of Cincinnati, paint, materials, and artist fees were covered by a GoFundMe account that generated nearly $150,000.

Not adhering to the usual design of most BLM murals (yellow letters that stretch street-wide), Cincinnati artists designed a mural in which each letter, created with bold Pan-African colors (red, black, and green), is inspired by a line from Powell's poem, "We Want What You Want." Wearing facemasks, artists painted the mural in two days, enduring blistering sun and stifling humidity punctuated by short bursts of rain, in time to unveil the finished mural on Juneteenth. The artists designed each letter

Figure 0.1. Black Lives Matter! mural in Cincinnati, Ohio. Image from https://www.reddit.com/r/cincinnati/comments/hc4tv8/cincy_blm_street_mural/. Courtesy of Austin Neal.

of the mural with specific goals in mind, beginning with hand-drawings on paper that were the basis for chalk outlines on the street, which were then filled in with paint applied by brush and roller. Artist Michael Coppage describes the idea behind his "L" in "Black": "The fist punching through a pool of blood is representative of the resistance to barriers of institutionalized obstacles and how no matter what, Black people push through" (Rice and Haselhorst). Describing her design of the "K," Tamia Saunders chose to use "unrestrained, free-flowing" lines in an effort to "emphasize inclusivity" so that the mural can be meaningful to everyone, not just Black people (Rice and Haselhorst). In her "I," Hannah Jones features a woman with an afro and a transgender symbol, a set of images that she finds personally empowering: "Race is introduced to you from everybody else in the world. . . . They tell you where you do or don't belong. It is really important and cool that I'm involved in this, because my Black community saw me even though I am half white" (Rice and Haselhorst).

Powell has said that the Cincinnati mural paint is expected to last five years. If its message is not realized by 2025, she plans to fundraise to repaint it. Street murals are created with the expectation of material deterioration. Paint doesn't last forever, especially not in high-traffic areas where murals get lots of wear and visibility. Mural placement on streets near seats of power in cities around the United States emphasizes the potency of public streets for political messages, even if those messages fade over time or get vandalized, as has already happened here, nearly a month after the mural's installation. Several hours after someone poured red paint over large swatches of the mural, City Council members and artists began planning its repair. Defacement and decay are an inescapable material reality of street murals, and maybe that's nothing to mourn. The processes of creation and ruin are keeping conversations about race alive in Cincinnati in ways that a more permanent installation might not have done.

Another effect of BLM street murals relevant to this book is that they make us see and experience ordinary streets in a new light. Painted streets can't be seen as solely navigational, as enabling passage from one place to another. They are surfaces for challenging the commonsense of a place by proclaiming racial injustice a part of the everyday, the very ground we travel when moving through a city. The street is an often-overlooked utilitarian object that has been turned into a staging ground for seizing narrative control over whose lives matter during this tumultuous summer of 2020.

Alexis and Rule note in their introduction that material culture analyses help us appreciate "complex interrelations among human cognition, cultural-historical moments, scribal acts, and writerly identities." The editors' and authors' efforts to reveal those interrelations are refreshing and will, I think, make us look anew at seemingly mundane objects in order to tell diverse stories about writing artifacts, identity, and power. The book may also inspire us to pay attention to the creative possibilities that mundane objects offer us as composers, researchers, and citizens.

JULY 2020

WORKS CITED

Deetz, James. *In Small Things Forgotten: The Archaeology of Early American Life*. Anchor Press/Doubleday, 1977.

Kajeet. "Why Chromebooks Have Expanded in K–12 Classrooms." Kajeet Extracurricular, 22 Jan. 2019, https://www.kajeet.net/extracurricular/why-chromebooks-have-expanded-in-k-12-classrooms.

Rice, Briana, and Sarah Haselhorst. "Behind the Black Lives Matter Mural: Artists' Speak to Equality, Family and Hope." Cincinnati.com, 19 June 2020, https://www.cincinnati.com/in-depth/news/2020/06/19/cincinnati-black-lives-matter-mural-artists/3215684001/.

ACKNOWLEDGMENTS

We are indebted to Laura Micciche for bringing us together and suggesting to each of us that the other was interested in such a project.

This collaboration came to fruition due to the imaginative work of our contributors who have populated this collection with their visions of how material culture enriches the study of writing and vice versa. Similarly, this book would not exist if not for the vision and diligence of our awesome editor, Rachael Levay, who answers emails at lightning speed even in the middle of a pandemic and after recently having a baby. This book would not be the same without the constructive developmental and editorial feedback we received from our anonymous reviewers, as well as Utah State University Press and the University Press of Colorado's editorial board. It has been a great experience working with this supportive press. We are grateful to the English Department at Kansas State University and the College of Arts and Sciences at the University of South Carolina for grant support that aided in the finalization of this book.

A deep thanks to our friends and mentors within writing studies and material culture studies who encouraged our engagement with material culture and the materiality of the writing process and offered their guidance and insight along the path to this project, including Michael Bernard-Donals, Deborah Brandt, Amber Epp, Beverly Gordon, Byron Hawk, Matt Hill, Eric Leake, Christina LaVecchia, Laura Micciche, Kate Smith, and Morris Young.

Last, we would like to thank our husbands, Chris Swenski and Christopher Innes, for their conversation, encouragement, and support—and for helping us carve out time for intellectual work.

THE MATERIAL CULTURE OF WRITING

1
INTRODUCTION
The Material Culture of Writing

Cydney Alexis and Hannah J. Rule

This book originated out of two scholars' love for the material culture of writing—those objects, artifacts, possessions, and goods, animate and inanimate, we write with, on, and around. These goods support us and, at times, thwart us. We have been interested in the study of material culture specifically for its ability to reveal unknowns and complexities of writing identities, practices, and processes. In our home field of writing studies (WS),[1] it is impossible not to notice that objects are everywhere. How could they not be? Objects populate homes, writing desks, personal lives, offices, composing processes, classrooms, family rituals, writing centers, and other university spaces—in short, they fill or constitute every contour of historical, social, cultural, and individual (writing) lives. Along with being a cognitive, social, and cultural practice, writing is a material practice.

Three observations motivated us to create this edited collection. First, despite the proliferation of interest in the materiality of writing in writing studies in recent years, there remained a lack of qualitative research on writing's material culture. Second, the scholarship that did exist rarely explicitly engaged with the vast, interdisciplinary work in material culture studies (MCS)[2] that had proliferated since the 1970s and legitimized the study of everyday, vernacular artifacts. This includes work in a parallel field, consumer culture theory, that—while drawing on its own scholarly consumer research corpus—bears a similarity in purpose and interest to MCS.[3] Third, when we prepared to teach seminars on the material culture of writing, we could not find a textbook specifically dedicated to objects of writing and their sociocultural histories. We think writing studies is the perfect discipline to undertake this work (as opposed to, say, library studies/history of the book, art, or history). Writing studies scholars might, for example, study the objects that motivate their writing practices and populate their offices and classrooms. And we might study the history of writing artifacts, as Denis Baron did in his history of writing technologies that included a discussion of Thoreau's ten-year endeavor to improve the American pencil, and as did Laura Micciche in her short history of writing boxes, dating back to the seventeenth century, as a kind of mobile writing device. And we might expand on the study of rituals and habits of writers in context, as did Susan Wyche (who is no longer an academic) in both "Time, Tools, and Talismans" and her unpublished dissertation on writers and ritual, in which she studies two classes of academically "at risk" students at San Diego State University in order to discover more about their situated writing behaviors. Taking a psychophysiological approach, Wyche's work establishes the importance of qualitative investigation into the integral roles that objects, material environments, and rituals play in college students' processes and their senses of themselves as writers, foci that anticipate the field's interest in how writing environments, rituals, and time structure writing processes (Prior and Shipka; Rule).

While it may seem intuitively true that objects matter, and it might seem more true in 2020 than at the time that Baron and Wyche were writing, scholars of writing haven't very much or for very long noticed it, especially where qualitative, quantitative, and longitudinal studies are concerned. In some of writing studies' landmark scholarship from parallel disciplines such as literacy studies, such as Shirley Brice Heath's *Ways with Words*, Deborah Brandt's *Literacy in American Lives*, and Prior and Shipka's "Chronotopic Lamination," objects appear on every page (again, how could they not?), but they remain in the background. As literacy scholar Nigel Hall highlights, the study of writing (across disciplines) has always tended to overlook, or look through, writing tools and objects. In Hall's words:

> In the study of writing, particularly its history and development, the materials and objects people use to write (apart from those used by printers) have been studied much less than the meanings and products of the writing process, or their economic, political or pedagogical relationships. On the whole, little has been written about the materiality of writing and it is probably the very everydayness of such artifacts, and the fact that the mind of the user is mostly focussed [*sic*] upon what is being created by their usage, that makes for them being so taken for granted that they become virtually transparent to their user. (83)

Our collection, instead, wishes to foreground objects, as they are one key part of the situated contexts of writing.

We are often asked what is novel or important about a material culture approach and how it differs from other recent work interested in objects and materiality. Our answer, one we hope is evidenced in the chapters in this volume, is that a material culture approach foregrounds and maintains focus on the everyday artifact as meaningful and as a revealer of culture and history, as a way to account for the experiences and lives of particular people, as well as communities, in situated contexts. Again, in Hall's terms, an MCS approach prods the researcher to treat objects as material realities that demand historical accounting and research.

Such centering on the artifact is an approach in some contrast to recent material-focused work in WS that largely centers on theoretical approaches that disrupt humanist subject-object dichotomies and critique views of objects as inert, passive vessels of human will. This body of work, often engaging theories such as object-oriented ontology (OOO) and new materialism (e.g., Barnett, "Chiasms"; Barnett, "Toward"; Barnett and Boyle; Gries; Lynch and Rivers; Rickert),[4] has brought attention to writing's materiality by highlighting the ranging and interconnected materialities of writing, often conceptualized in large-scale metaphors like ecologies, networks, or complex systems (Edbauer; Hawk; Syverson). For as much as it pushes the field toward materiality, and though MCS itself has engaged some of these theoretical frameworks, when reading this scholarship, we have sometimes thought, *where's the stuff* and *where are the people*? As feminist critique of OOO emphasizes (Behar), the theoretical ambitions to sunset notions of human subjectivity through hyperfocus on nonhuman things is problematic when we live and breathe in material worlds where agencies and access are far from a given for all people. MCS emerged out of interest in real people and the life circumstances that brought certain objects to bear on, and to have meaning in, their lives. *The Material Culture of Writing* aims to connect writing studies to work in MCS and related fields as an effort to add to the intellectual lineage of material work in WS.

The idea of everyday artifacts being meaningful in themselves for their potential to reveal human cultures and histories is what motivated interdisciplinary scholars throughout the 1970s and 1980s to study how everyday objects mattered. These scholars, who included artists, art historians, folklorists, historical archaeologists, psychologists, and consumer researchers initiated a movement that validated the "low-art," ordinary, everyday artifact as worthy of scholarly study.

For emeritus professor of folklore Henry Glassie, the importance of studying material culture developed out of a concern that histories are incomplete without attention to vernacular artifacts. In *Folk Housing in Middle Virginia*, he writes: "a philosophically and socially valid history must come out of painstaking analysis of direct cultural expressions that the analyst can study at first hand. Many of these expressions will be documents, but when no documents are available, we must study other sorts of artifacts rather than consigning the great bulk of humanity to historical oblivion" (12). Historical oblivion would face, for example, those whose stories are not preserved in written records, those without the power or access to represent their histories through written texts or high-art artifacts of dominant cultures. Glassie stresses how "dreary" it would be if the only known histories were that of those who can read or write (or who have access to writing materials) (*Material Culture* 46). More aggressively, he asserts that "politically, the study of material culture confronts prejudice and seeks justice, resisting forces that deny art or history—excellence or significance—to human beings on the basis of gender, say, or race or class or culture. It demands the construction of an idea of art and an idea of history that can meet the needs of all people during their struggle to shape for themselves fulfilling and decent lives" (68).

Historical archaeologist James Deetz stresses similar concerns throughout his scholarly corpus. In his 1977 *In Small Things Forgotten*, Deetz defends his interest in the "aboveground," that which had been considered trivial objects and artifacts by archeologists and museums (7). He argues that while digging up belowground artifacts has its merits, the aboveground artifact—that which would have been considered "low" culture and therefore unworthy of preserving in a museum at the time he was writing and still, in many instances, today—has the power to reveal an enormous amount about human culture. While he acknowledges that what we find in museums is a small piece of the historical record, like Glassie, he questions the privilege, capital, and other sociocultural factors that favor "survival of certain objects and the disappearance of others" (8). Everyday aboveground objects are valuable for the rich(er) stories they tell. He writes:

> In spite of the richness and diversity of the historical record, there are things we want to know that are not to be discovered from it. Simple people doing simple things, the normal, everyday routine of life and how these people thought about it, are not the kinds of things anyone thought worthy of noting. We know far more about the philosophical underpinnings of Puritanism than we do about what its practitioners consumed at countless meals. But all left behind the residue of their existence, and it, too, is worth study. (11)

Scholars such as Deetz and Glassie were concerned that the high-art artifact, encountered in a scholarly text or museum, tells a fragmented, incomplete story and thus attention should turn to the "everyday" household structure (such as the vernacular house types Glassie studies in his landmark *Folk Housing in Middle Virginia*) or household artifact—objects some might even consider mundane.

Understanding everyday objects and how people use or consume them in context is what motivates Glassie, in his 1999 *Material Cultures*, to trace the journey of one carpet made by Turkish weaver Aysel Ozturk, from the animal, to the loom, to the market, to the buyer, theorizing this movement along the way. Glassie demonstrates the power of staying both focused on the carpet and also the different contexts that surround the making, distribution, purchase, and use of any artifact. Glassie provides three "master contexts" (creation, communication, consumption) and fourteen sub-contexts within these three (such as learning, collaboration, commerce, and assimilation) that a student or scholar could use when trying to understand an artifact's history. His point in suggesting this method is that in order to understand artifacts most completely, the historian must contend with many contexts not observable on the surface, such as its life before purchase, the collaborative skills needed to produce it (in Aysel's case, she was a master weaver taught by her family and with other makers she weaves near), and the way that families integrate the artifact into their lives. These are the dimensions of histories, lives, and cultures that focus on objects in context can make available, dimensions that might be cleaved away, even lost entirely in more traditional historical records, research methods, or museum curation.

Some of the other theoretical and methodological touchstones for our approach to material culture in this book come from canonized work in interdisciplinary fields. Like Glassie and Deetz, Yale emeritus professor and art historian Jules Prown penned a methodology for studying artifacts that has been hashed out in various articles, reprinted, and widely read and taught in material culture studies classrooms ("Style;" "Truth"). This methodology asks students and scholars to begin with an artifact and to study it extensively as a material thing, obsessively recording its features and potential uses and even relying on metaphoric association in order to uncover unknowns about an object's reach, potential, and history. With Kenneth Haltman, Prown published *American Artifacts: Essays in American Culture*, an edited collection each chapter of which features the results of a semester-long, graduate-level investigation of one artifact (these analyses were produced in Prown's Yale art seminar). *American Artifacts* presents essays on objects such as lava lamps, a lighter, and the telephone, and we could see the potential of such a collection focused on writing objects. Indeed, one of the chapters in this volume, Emilie Merrigan's, emerged out of a graduate class taught by coeditor of this volume Cydney Alexis and relied on Prownian analysis to unravel the tangled principles of scientific motherhood that circulated around early twentieth-century mothers and was presented to them through baby books, in which mothers created counter-narratives of their daily parenting practices.

Other touchstones for us of the power of object research is the work of Daniel Miller, through which he studies countless objects—including writing artifacts such as shopping lists (*Material Cultures*). In a fascinating piece on the shopping list, Miller demonstrates how women who grocery shop utilize stored memories of store architecture to organize their lists, leading to efficiency while shopping (*A Theory*). Csikszentmihalyi and Rochberg-Halton's *The Meaning of Things: Domestic Symbols and the Self* also tracks countless artifacts meaningful to everyday people throughout their lifespan; they demonstrate how attachment to particular types of goods changes from youth to old age. In consumer research, particularly generative is the work of Epp and Price. In their widely cited "The Storied Life of Singularized Objects," Epp and Price collect qualitative data on the life of one table in several generations of a family, and they use actor-network theory to expose how family practices are disrupted as the table moves from central locations and into storage. Epp and Price's findings (in this article and others) could have enormous impact in WS, as they demonstrate the importance of the ways that families construct identities around objects and practices, as well as the ways that objects facilitate certain types of family engagement. Writing objects and spaces in the home, at work, and in the classroom are ripe for study.

The prolific Russell Belk has detailed historical scholastic engagement with possessions from William James to the present day and qualitatively studied innumerable objects and artifacts with various contributors, including immigrants' possessions, shared possessions, and digital objects (Belk, "Extended Self" and "Sharing;" Mehta and Belk). In his canonical 1988 "Possessions and the Extended Self," Belk provides a theoretical framework for understanding how humans extend the self-concept to inanimate objects, often rating inanimate objects as more tied to their sense of self than certain parts of their body (such as the throat). He theorizes that people connect most intensely with objects they are able to manipulate and control; in WS, we might think of digital technologies such as the laptop, the phone, screen readers, and assistive technologies that help with writing and communication.

Coming out of literary studies, one of the most engaging books we have returned to frequently in defining our approach is feminist literary scholar Diana Fuss's *Senses of an Interior: Four Writers and the Rooms That Shaped Them*. Fuss pushes against the common notion that positions creativity, genius, or authorship as "unfettered imagination" that transcends "base materiality" (1). Fuss's "miniature biographies" (215) of authors' material spaces show, on the contrary, how writing is always a situated and contextual act, "a place animated by the artifacts, mementos, machines, books, and furniture that frame any intellectual labor" (1). Particularly generative is Fuss's chapter on Helen Keller, which reveals not only Keller's fascination with objects but the tight link between the design of her home, the objects within it, and her productivity, which declined when a fire forced her to move into a new space that was designed without a visually impaired person's needs in mind. This chapter resonates with recent work in WS and specifically disability studies, such as that by Jay Dolmage and Stephanie Kerschbaum, that interrogates ableist approaches to writing, teaching, and design, including the design of university spaces (and writing spaces such as Keller's for, as Fuss reminds, Keller was a prolific writer). The "stuff of great literature," Fuss shows, is nothing less (or more) than objects, sacred and mundane—"things as seemingly inconsequential as an open door, a broken relic, a warm hand, or a crumbly teacake" (Fuss 214). Though Fuss writes about four famous literary figures, her approach might be adopted to study the vernacular writing contexts of everyday writers and the artifacts they write with (such as Alexis' work on the Moleskine, in this volume, and the writing of enslaved worker Israel Gillette, referenced in Diane Ehrenpreis's chapter on Jefferson's writing suite).

The recent proliferation of interest in materiality in both popular and scholarly culture, including in writing studies, has led to much work that is sympathetic to our interest in this volume. This was the case when we read Gouge and Jones's groundbreaking and intellectually exciting special issue of *Rhetoric Society Quarterly*, titled "Wearable Rhetorics: Bodies, Cities, Collectives." In this volume, Gouge and Jones and their contributors expand the purview of what might be considered a rhetorical, communicative, or writing artifact. Each article centers on such an artifact, such as the breast pump, ostomy pouch, and cell phone. This special issue highlights the intellectual yield of honing in on artifacts to reveal unknowns of human life. Jordan Jack, for example, reads the wearable technology of the breast pump as an "idealized object" (202) preloaded with marketing, cultural, and social meanings, the promise of a seamless and simultaneous embodiment of the roles of mother and career professional. Undermining the control of those messages, Jack's study prioritizes everyday, "actual use *in practice*" (208) of such objects, a method that reveals how use "depends on performances of status and gender, policy frameworks, space-time arrangements, and the material design of technologies themselves" (208). The cascade of contexts of situated use that hover around this object, that emanate from and back to it, for us harkens back to Glassie's master and subcontexts. Maybe it's Jack's mention of the seventeenth-century invention of the air-pump or the editors' emphasis on what it means to "wear" an object in its small-scale, intimate, embodied, and rhetorical dimensions but, to put it plainly, we see a strong investment in material culture in this special issue. We read this kind of material work for its potential expansion of what counts as writing objects of study for our field, and we wonder about the many ways MCS (and consumer research) scholarship could help advance it.

MCS may also become an ally to literacy scholars calling for attention to the sociomaterial dimensions of literate practice. Generally, these efforts serve to ground the social and cultural situatedness of literate practices emphasized in New Literacy Studies. Focus on literate objects and materialities opens access to practices, meanings, behaviors, and interconnections not otherwise observable, as literacy and education scholar Kate Pahl emphasizes. "By seeing literacy as material," she writes, "I can recognize the ways in which literacy practices are linked to other practices. . . . By extending the lens of what is important, a much wider meshwork of symbolic practices come to the fore, instantiated within the material world" (19–20). And that meshwork is never neutral, as literacy scholar Lesley Bartlett reminds. In 2005, she argued that "the lifelong process of literacy learning relies, in part, on symbolic self-making through the use of cultural artefacts" (4). She gives the example of a Eunisia, a woman of African descent living in Brazil, who tells a story about going to get her voter's card and being terrified because she did not know how to read and write and was not sure she would be able to sign her name, a requirement for the card. Her friend had relayed a story of being called an epithet when she had to sign by fingerprint. In this story, Bartlett demonstrates how the inkpad used for fingerprinting, as well as the pen, are more than neutral, simple tools. They are social and political artifacts that reveal systemic issues related to how literacy is wielded as a barrier to access and representation.

Within WS, literacy scholar Kate Vieira similarly makes an explicit call for this "sociomaterial approach to transnational literacy" (423), one we align with. Her work on "writing remittances," material objects that travel between migrant and homeland, supporting literate and material development at home, shares a material culture spirit. It expands upon the work of scholars such as Brandt, who frequently references both the material practices of writing and writing's material culture, particularly as they serve as markers of points of access to or denial of literate resources.

This collection, then, takes its inspiration from a wide-ranging collection of sources. It aims to build connections to work in material culture and consumer culture studies, build on scholarship in WS that has called attention to the importance of writing materials, and build from literacy studies' call for sociomaterial approaches to writing practice. Its contributors zoom in on the material culture of writing—the everyday, often overlooked objects, tools, and artifacts that accompany writers and help them perform their work. They investigate a range of these artifacts—digital and analog, historical and contemporary, familiar and less so—situated in literate acts across ranging historical, geographic, and sociocultural moments. In our call for submissions to this volume, we asked: What can writing artifacts tell us about writing as a material practice? How do particular writing objects help us understand writing processes? What stories do writing objects reveal about writers enmeshed in their sociocultural moments, about cultural mores, about genres as sociomaterial practice, and about individuals' identities or professional practice?

We selected proposals from scholars across (sub)disciplines including WS, museum and conservation studies, literary studies, history, and technical communication. Of the approximately seventy proposals we received, we chose work centered on material culture artifacts, spaces, and contexts. We wanted chapters that kept their sights on material goods, mingling perspectives of MCS, WS, and contributors' own disciplines. We also wanted to expand what counted as writing or what could count as writing studies research. This is what appealed to us in chapters such as one on the conservator's file or the Victorian guest book. But looking across the collection now, we wonder why *wouldn't* their foci—the inscriptional practices of Victorian-era travelers; the gendered and racialized associations of writing tools in the nineteenth century; the writing practices of professional conservators or of Renaissance letter-writers; the desk innovations of a complicated historical figure—be of central and paramount interest to scholars of writing, and to those in WS in particular? Each chapter provides distinct methods to approach writing-related things across time, location, and culture, methods that intervene in questions in contributors' own disciplines while at the same time speaking to WS' interest in writers and writing practice. Toward the latter purpose, we have organized the chapters into three parts—Writing Identity, Writing Work, and Writing Genre—and for each, we provide a contextualizing introduction. We see these sections as porous more than delineated, as questions of identity, work or practice, and genre are at stake in some ways in nearly all the chapters in relation to writing objects and spaces. In addition to introducing the chapters themselves, the introductions imagine further possible directions for WS research facilitated by MCS frameworks and approaches.

Contributors focus us on notebooks, ink and ink pots, hotel visitors' albums, baby books, writing implements, and furniture, among other artifacts. They demonstrate how focus on such artifacts stretch our conceptions about literacy, workplaces, genre, curation, literary authorship, and access. Ultimately, we hope the chapters inspire readers to engage in studies of their own that animate the sociomaterial lives and histories of the writing objects that populate their and others' writing lives. The intersection of MCS and WS offers incredible potential scholarly space for those interested in understanding how everyday writers, now and historical, such as manual writers, ghost writers, activists, cookbook writers, mothers, fathers, soldiers, children, nurses, mechanics, politicians, and infinite others interact with the objects that sustain their work. In the same vein as Deetz and Glassie, we note the potential of material culture study to uncover structural inequities in access to literacy, education, and material goods that are built into the fabric of American society.

The Material Culture of Writing offers just some of the yields made possible by mingling work in MCS and WS. Our intent is to reveal unknown histories of objects significant to our field's research and history, trace sociocultural and sociopolitical resonances of writing artifacts, and give the discipline access to MCS frameworks and scholarship that can propel more such interdisciplinary research focused on things that animate writers and writing practices. We hope this collection builds conversation around and scholarship on writing's material culture within WS.

POSTSCRIPT: WRITING IN THE SPRING AND SUMMER OF 2020

We have been revising this book throughout the spring and summer of 2020, in the context of both a global pandemic (COVID-19) and widespread global antiracist protests triggered by police brutality against Black people in the United States. This cultural moment has once again pointed a spotlight on systemic injustice faced by Black Americans, as well as other people of color, in far too many sectors, such as policing and the justice system, healthcare, housing, finance, and publishing. These issues have always demanded reflection, response, action, and change. An academic book is far from direct action. But on the smaller scale that is an academic edited collection, as editors we have reflected on the choices we've made in this volume, those we didn't, and those we'd do differently if we could start all over. It has had us thinking about what actually matters in our call for attention to the material culture of writing.

As Glassie emphasizes, we can turn to material culture artifacts, as have so many material culture scholars before us, to understand the complex entanglement between material culture and systems of oppression and injustice. Some of these artifacts might be more obviously in need of study. One that comes to mind is the face mask. The mask recalls for us Gouge and Jones's expansion of what it means for an object to be an object of writing and raises a meditation similar to Micciche's on the street, in the foreword to this volume. The mask has become not only a political and personal symbol charged with personal identity values but also has highlighted problems of access and power. In terms of wearing masks in public, Black communities have called attention to how systemic racism puts them in jeopardy of being racially profiled as "criminals," a reality that has been documented as Black men have been targeted by police in disproportionate numbers when wearing masks and unequal penalties have been applied to white and Black communities for not wearing or having access to masks. At the policy level, corporate entities have placed frontline workers in jeopardy in the healthcare, retail, and food production sectors with unclear policies around masks, lack of access to personal protective equipment (PPE), and even the outright refusal to let workers wear masks because it conflicts with the company's branding (Alfonso III; Boyd; Cineas; Graham; Noor). The pandemic has evidenced the greater health risks Black communities face due to the disproportionate effect of systemic injustice and disparities in health care, which amplifies the potential impacts on such communities when white people protest wearing masks or Black people choose to refrain from wearing a mask in order to protect themselves from racial profiling (The Center for Disease Control; Oppel et al.; Saini).

Using everyday objects to reveal the systemic inequities that are either invisible or denied in American and global culture aligns with MCS's attempts to redress inequities in whose histories are told and which artifacts are used to corroborate and understand human experience. Glassie asks, "How can you study a society if you attend only to the expressions of a small and deviant class within the whole?" (*Folk Housing* 8–9). He was referring in this instance to the historical problem with studying only those with the ability to read and write, but this applies to current questions of representation, equity, and injustice as well. How can we document the material and literacy histories of those whose lives have not been as meticulously preserved as those of presidents,' or famous literary authors, or other privileged and powerful persons? This collection only begins to answer to this question. But we are reminded of Glassie's sentiment that it is an ongoing *aspiration* of material culture studies to reveal people's diverse ways and means of material meaning-making in the "struggle to shape for themselves fulfilling and decent lives" (*Material Culture* 68). We have more to do.

NOTES

1. We call our field writing studies, rather than composition studies or rhetoric and composition, to reflect current trends in naming (e.g., Adler-Kassler and Wardle; Harris; Moxley). But we also choose this name to push the conventional boundaries of our field's interests. In this, we follow after Charles Bazerman, who sees "the study of writing [as] a major subset of the study of the history of human consciousness, institutions, practice, and development over the last five millennia" (36). We take similar direction from Susan Miller, and her call for writing studies as "a way to describe the cultural work undertaken in any act of writing" (41). Writing studies investigations take an interest in "acts of writing and their products as evidence of a particularly crucial cultural work . . . [which] does not detach 'popular' from 'high' texts, nor does it separate 'ordinary' from 'creative' writers on the basis of relative revisionary talent or levels of access to the ethical and economic status requisite to authorship" (S. Miller 42; see also Alexis, "Stop"). For us, these perspectives make our field's purview plain and spacious: any act of writing, investigated as at once a cultural, social, material, and individual act, or in Miller's words, "what, who, to what ends, and especially, how people have written and do write" (52).

2. As a loose orientation rather than a defined field, work in MCS spans disciplines including art, art history, consumer research, historical archaeology, social psychology, and English, to name a few. Hence, much work that is significant in MCS might be produced by scholars who do not necessarily identify as such (including, for instance, consumer research scholars, who do work on how humans make meaning of the consumer goods they pull out of the commodity realm by purchasing and using them). We refer to the discipline throughout as MCS, despite this naming issue, to identify work that foregrounds an MCS orientation.

3. Consumer Culture Theory is a branch of the field of consumer research composed largely of marketing scholars. Its scholarship addresses the "cultural dimensions of the consumption cycle," including the "sociocultural, experiential, symbolic, and ideological aspects" (Arnould and Thompson 868). Rather than attempting to construct a "unified, grand theory," CCT "refers to a family of theoretical perspectives that address the dynamic relationships between consumer actions, the marketplace, and cultural meanings . . . within the broader sociohistoric frame of globalization and market capitalism" (868–869). For a broad overview, readers might turn to Arnould and Thompson's "Consumer Culture Theory (CCT): Twenty Years of Research" (see Works Cited). Much, but not all, of this research is qualitative, and the *Journal of Consumer Research* is a locus point for this scholarship. This research shares the spirit of much work in MCS, and many of its scholars utilize it in their teaching and scholarship. In no way do we mean to collapse into one term the dispersed, varied scholars who work in MCS and CCT; both of these research areas, however, provide context for the intellectual and material orientation of this collection. For the purposes of simplicity in this collection, although we do reference

CCT as a distinct field, we are also thinking of it as a component field when discussing MCS texts, concepts, and scholars.
4. We recognize in this "material turn" the efforts of cultural rhetorics scholars and others (e.g., Clary-Lemon; Grant; Powell et al.; Todd) who have detailed the much longer and non-Western lineages of ideas central to OOO and new materialism.

WORKS CITED

Adler-Kassler, Linda, and Elizabeth Wardle. *Naming What We Know: Threshold Concepts of Writing Studies.* Utah State UP, 2015.

Alexis, Cydney. "Stop Using the Phrase *Creative Writing.*" *Slate,* 6 Jan. 2017, https://slate.com/human-interest/2017/01/lets-banish-the-phrase-creative-writing.html.

Alfonso, Fernando, III. "Why Some People of Color Say They Won't Wear Homemade Masks." *CNN,* 7 Apr. 2020, https://www.cnn.com/2020/04/07/us/face-masks-ethnicity-coronavirus-cdc-trnd/index.html.

Arnould, Eric J, and Craig J. Thompson. "Consumer Culture Theory (CCT): Twenty Years of Research." *The Journal of Consumer Research,* vol. 31, no. 4, 2005, pp. 868–882.

Barnett, Scot. "Chiasms: Pathos, Phenomenology, and Object-Oriented Rhetorics." *Enculturation: A Journal of Writing, Rhetoric, and Culture,* 2015, http://enculturation.net/chiasms-pathos-phenomenology#footnote3_q5x6y6w.

Barnett, Scot. "Toward an Object-Oriented Rhetoric: A Review of Tool-Being: Heidegger and the Metaphysics of Objects and Guerrilla Metaphysics: Phenomenology and the Carpentry of Things by Graham Harman." *Enculturation: A Journal of Writing, Rhetoric, and Culture,* no. 7, 2010, http://enculturation.net/toward-an-object-oriented-rhetoric.

Barnett, Scot, and Casey Boyle. *Rhetoric, through Everyday Things.* U of Alabama P, 2016.

Baron, Denis. *A Better Pencil: Readers, Writers, and the Digital Revolution.* Oxford UP, 2009.

Bartlett, Lesley. "To Seem and to Feel: Situated Identities and Literacy Practices." *The Teachers College Record,* vol. 109, no. 1, 2007, pp. 51–69.

Bazerman, Charles. "The Case for Writing Studies as an Intellectual Discipline." *Rhetoric and Composition as Intellectual Work,* edited by Gary A. Olson, Southern Illinois UP, 2002, pp. 32–38.

Behar, Katherine, ed. *Object Oriented Feminism.* U of Minnesota P, 2016.

Belk, Russell W. "Extended Self in a Digital World." *Journal of Consumer Research,* vol. 40, no. 3, 2013, pp. 477–500.

Belk, Russell W. "Possessions and the Extended Self." *Journal of Consumer Research,* vol. 15, no. 2, 1988, pp. 139–168.

Belk, Russell W. "Sharing." *The Journal of Consumer Research,* vol. 36, no. 5, 2009, pp. 715–734.

Boyd, Rhea. "What It Means When You Wear a Mask—and When You Refuse To." *The Nation,* 9 July 2020, https://www.thenation.com/article/society/mask-racism-refusal-coronavirus/.

Brandt, Deborah. *Literacy in American Lives.* Cambridge UP, 2001.

The Centers for Disease Control and Prevention. "Health Equity Considerations and Racial and Ethnic Minority Groups." 24 July 2020, https://www.cdc.gov/coronavirus/2019-ncov/community/health-equity/race-ethnicity.html. Accessed 13 Oct. 2020.

Cineas, Fabiola. "Senators Are Demanding a Solution to Police Stopping Black Men for Wearing—and Not Wearing—Masks." *Vox,* 22 Apr. 2020, https://www.vox.com/2020/4/22/21230999/black-men-wearing-masks-police-bias-harris-booker-senate/.

Clary-Lemon, Jennifer. "Gifts, Ancestors, and Relations: Notes toward an Indigenous New Materialism." *Enculturation: A Journal of Rhetoric, Writing, and Culture,* 12 Nov. 2019, http://enculturation.net/gifts_ancestors_and_relations.

Csikszentmihalyi, Mihaly, and Eugene Rochberg-Halton. *The Meaning of Things: Domestic Symbols and the Self.* Cambridge UP, 1981.

Deetz, James. *In Small Things Forgotten: The Archaeology of Early American Life.* Anchor Press/Doubleday, 1977.

Dolmage, Jay. *Academic Ableism: Disability and Higher Education.* U of Michigan P, 2017.

Edbauer, Jenny. "Unframing Models of Public Distribution: From Rhetorical Situation to Rhetorical Ecologies." *Rhetoric Society Quarterly*, vol. 35, no. 4, 2005, pp. 5–24.

Epp, Amber M., and Linda L. Price. "The Storied Life of Singularized Objects." *Journal of Consumer Research*, vol. 36, no. 5, 2010, pp. 820–838.

Fuss, Diana. *The Sense of an Interior: Four Rooms and the Writers That Shaped Them.* Routledge, 2004.

Glassie, Henry. *Folk Housing in Middle Virginia: A Structural Analysis of Historic Artifacts.* U of Tennessee P, 1975.

Glassie, Henry. *Material Culture.* Indiana UP, 1999.

Gouge, Catherine, and John Jones. "Wearable Rhetorics: Bodies, Cities, Collectives." *Rhetoric Society Quarterly* (special issue), vol. 46, no. 3, 2016.

Graham, Renée. "With—or without—a Mask, Communities of Color Fear Unequal Enforcement during Pandemic." *The Boston Globe*, 5 May 2020, https://www.bostonglobe.com/2020/05/05/opinion/with-or-without-mask-communities-color-fear-unequal-enforcement-during-pandemic/.

Grant, David M. "Writing Wakan: The Lakota Pipe as Rhetorical Object." *CCC*, vol. 69, no. 1, 2017, pp. 61–86.

Gries, Laurie E. *Still Life with Rhetoric: A New Materialist Approach for Visual Rhetorics.* Utah State UP, 2015.

Hall, Nigel. "The Materiality of Letter Writing: A Nineteenth-Century Perspective." *Letter Writing as a Social Practice*, edited by David Barton and Nigel Hall, John Benjamins Publishing, 2000, pp. 83–108.

Harris, Joseph. *A Teaching Subject: Composition Since 1966.* Utah State UP, 2012.

Hawk, Byron. "Reassembling Postprocess: Toward a Posthuman Theory of Public Rhetoric." *Beyond Postprocess*, edited by Sidney I. Dobrin, et al., Utah State UP, 2011, pp. 75–93.

Heath, Shirley Brice. *Ways with Words: Language, Life, and Work in Communities and Classrooms.* Cambridge UP, 1993.

Kerschbaum, Stephanie L. "Avoiding the Difference Fixation: Identity Categories, Markers of Difference, and the Teaching of Writing." *College Composition and Communication*, vol. 63, no. 4, 2012, pp. 616–644.

Lynch, Paul, and Nathaniel Rivers. *Thinking with Bruno Latour in Composition and Rhetoric.* Southern Illinois UP, 2015.

Mehta, Raj, and Russell W. Belk. "Artifacts, Identity, and Transition: Favorite Possessions of Indians and Indian Immigrants to the United States." *The Journal of Consumer Research*, vol. 17, no. 4, 1991, pp. 398–411.

Micciche, Laura. "Writers Have Always Loved Mobile Devices." *The Atlantic*, 18 Aug. 2018, https://www.theatlantic.com/technology/archive/2018/08/writers-have-always-loved-mobile-devices/567637/.

Miller, Daniel. *Material Cultures: Why Some Things Matter.* U of Chicago P, 1998.

Miller, Daniel. *A Theory of Shopping.* Cornell UP, 1998.

Miller, Susan. "Writing Studies as a Mode of Inquiry." *Rhetoric and Composition as Intellectual Work*, edited by Gary Olson, Southern Illinois UP, 2000, pp. 41–54.

Moxley, Joseph M. "Writing Studies." *Writing Commons*, https://writingcommons.org/section/writing-studies/. Accessed 12 Oct. 2020.

Noor, Poppy. "A Tale of Two Cities: How New York Police Enforce Social Distancing by the Color of Your Skin." *The Guardian*, 4 May 2020, https://www.theguardian.com/world/2020/may/04/coronavirus-new-york-police-enforce-social-distancing.

Oppel, Richard A., et al. "The Fullest Look Yet at the Racial Inequity of Coronavirus." *The New York Times*, 5 July 2020, https://www.nytimes.com/interactive/2020/07/05/us/coronavirus-latinos-african-americans-cdc-data.html.

Pahl, Kate. *Materializing Literacies in Communities: The Uses of Literacy Revisited*. Bloomsbury, 2014.

Powell, Malea, et al. "Our Story Begins Here: Constellating Cultural Rhetorics," *Enculturation: A Journal of Rhetoric, Writing, and Culture*, no. 18, 2014, http://enculturation.net/our-story-begins-here.

Prior, Paul, and Jody Shipka. "Chronotopic Lamination: Tracing the Contours of Literate Activity." *Writing Selves/Writing Societies: Research from Activity Perspectives*, edited by Charles Bazerman and David Russell, The WAC Clearinghouse, 2003, pp. 180–238.

Prown, Jules David. "Style as Evidence." *Winterthur Portfolio*, vol. 15, no. 3, 1980, pp. 197–210.

Prown, Jules David. "The Truth of Material Culture: History or Fiction?" *History from Things: Essays on Material Culture*, edited by Steven D. Lubar and W. D. Kingery. Smithsonian Institution Press, 1993, pp. 1–19.

Prown, Jules David, and Kenneth Haltman. *American Artifacts: Essays in Material Culture*. Michigan State UP, 2000.

Rickert, Thomas. *Ambient Rhetoric: The Attunements of Rhetorical Being*. U of Pittsburgh P, 2013.

Rule, Hannah J. "Writing's Rooms." *CCC*, vol. 69, no. 3, Feb. 2018, pp. 402–432.

Saini, Angela. "The Data Was There—So Why Did It Take Coronavirus to Wake Us Up to Racial Health Inequalities?" *The Guardian*, 11 June 2020, https://www.theguardian.com/uk-news/2020/jun/11/the-data-was-there-so-why-did-it-take-coronavirus-to-wake-us-up-to-racial-health-inequalities.

Syverson, Margaret. *Wealth of Reality: An Ecology of Composition*. Southern Illinois UP, 1999.

Todd, Zoe. "An Indigenous Feminist's Take on the Ontological Turn: 'Ontology' Is Just Another Word for Colonialism." *Journal of Historical Sociology*, vol. 29, no. 1, 2016, pp. 4–22.

Vieira, Kate. "Writing Remittances: Migration-Driven Literacy Learning in a Brazilian Homeland." *Research in the Teaching of English*, vol. 50, no. 4, 2016, pp. 422–449.

Wyche, Susan. "Times, Tools, and Talismans." *Essays on Writing*, edited by Lizbeth A. Bryant and Heather M. Clark, Pearson, 2009, pp. 52–64.

Wyche-Smith, Susan Lee. *The Magic Circle: Writers and Ritual*. 1988. University of Washington, dissertation.

PART ONE

Writing Identity

The four chapters in this section all in some way engage with the idea of *identity*, whether the identity of *writer, mother, author,* or *literate person.* They highlight the tight connection between objects and self-concept around writing, literacy, and authorship.

For us, these chapters point to an exciting area of research, the development of writing (and literate) identity as it emerges with, around, and through material culture goods. The term "identity" is picked up by different disciplines and used throughout popular culture, and we know our readers will hear varied things in the term. In its many associations in writing studies (WS), identity might evoke work on the inseparability of language and identity, especially racial or ethnic identities (e.g., SRTOL; Villanueva). It may signal discoursal constructions of identity in academic work (e.g., Ivanic; Hyland) or the idea of identity as "voice" (or the critique of it) in written discourse (e.g., Hyland and Guinda; Matsuda, "Identity" and "Voice"; Matsuda and Tardy; Royster). But we mean to also signal through this term a narrower, more specialized sense.

In using the term "writing identity," we follow scholars in consumer research, the social and psychological sciences, and literacy studies who posit that just as a person might have an identity, persona, or self-concept as an athlete, musician, or scientist, people also develop an identity (or don't) as a person who writes. Deborah Brandt signaled many years ago issues around the perceived unavailability of the identity label of *writer* when she stated that while being a *reader* is something most people feel able to claim as a part of their self-concept, the same is not the case for *writer*. Peter Elbow made a similar point in 1995, in "Being a Writer." More recently, Alexis delves into the reasons for this in a *Slate* article that posits the harmful effects of (fairly recent) trends to label only fiction and poetry "creative," thereby denying access to a positive identity association as a writer to those who write professionally in technical writing, as academics, and so forth (see also Alexis and Leake).

There is much WS can learn about how, when, and with what tools children and adults step into this identity role and begin to see themselves as a person who writes. How do writing materials mediate this process? What are parents' and teachers' roles in fostering this identity? At what points do people/students begin to reject this aspect of the self-concept? How does the label of writer interact with other intersectional dimensions of individuals' "global selves" (cf. Kleine et al., below)? These are questions that might be of particular interest to scholars researching writing from a lifespan perspective (cf. Bazerman et al.).

Although we do not have space here to detail the rich cross-disciplinary research on identity and possessions, we direct readers toward work in consumer research that for some decades has theorized what it means to have an identity that is developed, maintained, and even rejected through the use of possessions. This research, for example, has established that individuals have both a "global self" and particularized selves or "role" identities (musician, athlete) that they develop and maintain with "constellations" of possessions (Kleine, Kleine and Allen; Kleine, Kleine, and Kernan; Laverie et al.). As we've noted, this research could have potential for lifespan researchers looking into how and when students at a young age begin to envision themselves as writers and how they utilize spaces and tools to effect this role. But it also could help researchers think about the various pressures, circumstances, and experiences that impact how role identities wax and wane in intensity. When writers do not have access to necessary tools or they utilize specialized tools, for example, to aid with a disability, how does this impact role performance? How does having a cohort of like-minded students help writers to maintain the writer role? How does family identity impact self-identity as well as identity role development? Just how much significance do people invest in possessions they use everyday? These are questions that consumer researchers have studied with populations other than writers, leaving open terrain for WS scholars (Belk; Epp and Price, "Family Identity" and "Storied Life").

This scholarship dovetails with research in the sciences that tracks how and when students develop and reject an identity as a scientist. Aschbacher and coauthors find that "communities of practice" play a shaping role in "career and identity development" and underscore the need for students to receive positive feedback and encouragement in order to develop and maintain a STEM identity. They write that their findings "highlight how few adults at home or school enthusiastically invite students to learn about science or engineering, to value scientific ways of knowing, or to pursue an SEM degree or career." This insight parallels Brandt's findings that while reading is a skill and practice valued by parents and society (even valued in moralistic terms), writing is not similarly supported and—even more perniciously—is often devalued as both a practice and career by parents, teachers, and society ("Remembering Writing"). Her study participants could remember reading as a supported family activity, while writing was performed in private and was surrounded by feelings of secrecy and shame.

Research by other science-teaching scholars has looked at topics such as how students of color in science develop and maintain a science identity and persist in the field (Carlone and Johnson), how media influences children's perceptions of women in science and their possibilities of being scientists (Steinke et al.), and how media images of STEM professionals affect adolescent girls' STEM identities (Steinke). To cite one example, Carlone and Johnson developed a model of science identity to address how women of color persist and succeed in science, despite an exclusionary "culture characterized by white, masculine values and behavioral norms" (1187). Through interviews with fifteen successful women-of-color scientists, the authors document ways that these women pushed past this exclusionary culture in order to become successful despite the racism and sexism they encountered, sometimes ending up in academic science roles and sometimes taking alternative trajectories. Their model allows them to "pinpoint specific ways women of color get recognized, or fail to get recognized, as science people, highlighting the complex ways race, ethnicity, and gender complicate that recognition" (1211).

These identity research threads, read in tandem with work in MCS and parallel fields, open up endless possibilities for WS scholars. As WS and English departments, as well as writing centers, fight for their existence amidst dwindling resources and devaluation of the humanities in favor of STEM, the question of what it means to write, how accessible the identity of "writer" is for underrepresented students, how accessible the tools of writing and networks of writing support are, and how we might foster and encourage identity development around writing takes on extreme import.

The chapters in this section are each portals into specific manifestations of the ways that people come to understand themselves, and fight to be seen as writers, authors, and literate beings with and through material culture. Questions of access in relation to the availability of the role of writer and author pervade Desirée Henderson's chapter on ink and ink stains as gendered and racialized identity markers in nineteenth-century writing. She demonstrates how inks stains took on symbolic power in white women's writing, marking them as unmaternal and immoral, as women who abandoned traditional domesticity norms. While white women sought to undermine the idea that being authors reduced their womanhood, they did so with racially charged imagery of ink and ink stains that invoked miscegenation fears related to racial purity. Henderson demonstrates how in the same period, in enslaved and recently freed literacy narratives, ink evokes the systemic denial of access to literacy for the enslaved. She shows how African American authors invoked the associations between ink, paper, and skin color in order to interrogate racism, as well as how they ultimately resist racialized associations with writing objects and challenged impediments to access through creative improvisation.

While Henderson's chapter focuses on the social and racial significations of writing instruments broadly construed, the other three chapters in this section discuss particular writing artifacts in order to show how writers construct identities around writing (Alexis and Merrigan) and around being literate (Krichevsky). In Alexis's case, writers utilize the Moleskine notebook as a "facilitating artifact" that helps them to step into and maintain the role/identity of "writer." Alexis demonstrates how people absorb cultural narratives around particular artifacts such as the Moleskine and use them to craft themselves into and practice the writer role. Similarly, Jenny Krichevsky's chapter shows how deeply bound up people's sense of themselves as literate actors is with what she terms "discursive heirlooms," objects that move with transnational migrants across historical and geographical contexts. Like Alexis, she shows how powerful cultural narratives (in her case, around Soviet history and identity) shape how people invest heirlooms (textbooks, a bookcase, a piano) with meaning.

The last chapter in this section, Emilie Merrigan's, works from a Prownian methodology (cf. the introduction to this volume) to demonstrate the riches of one artifact, an early twentieth-century baby book owned by a mother named Jessie, in revealing how (writing) artifacts such as this one help mothers to understand, develop, and perform the identity of mother through writing. Baby books exhibit a tension between scientific discourse imprinted into the book upon purchase and the "singularization" efforts of mothers, who personalize these books with their own written memories and experiences. Jessie singularizes her baby book and develops her own identity as a mother, against the backdrop of a larger cultural narrative etched onto the book's pages about what it means to be a twentieth-century mother.

Taken together, the chapters in this section encourage more research into the ways that objects—either single or constellations—help writers to imagine, realize, perform, and practice identities as writers (and as literate people), both in personal ways and in concert with broader sociocultural narratives, norms, and material realities.

WORKS CITED

Alexis, Cydney. "Stop Using the Phrase *Creative Writing*." *Slate*, 6 Jan. 2017, https://slate.com/human-interest/2017/01/lets-banish-the-phrase-creative-writing.html.

Alexis, Cydney, and Eric Leake. "The Stylized Portrayal of the Writing Life in Spike Jonze's *Her*." *Style and the Future of Composition Studies*, edited by Star Vanguri, Brian Ray, and Paul Butler. Utah State UP, 2020.

Aschbacher, Pamela R., et al. "Is Science Me? High School Students' Identities, Participation and Aspirations in Science, Engineering, and Medicine." *Journal of Research in Science Teaching*, vol. 47, no. 5, 2010, pp. 564–582.

Bazerman, Charles, et al. "Taking the Long View on Writing Development." *Research in the Teaching of English*, vol. 51, no. 3, 2017, p. 351.

Belk, Russell W. "Extended Self in a Digital World." *The Journal of Consumer Research*, vol. 40, no. 3, 2013, pp. 477–500.

Belk, Russell W. "Possessions and the Extended Self." *The Journal of Consumer Research*, vol. 15, no. 2, 1988, pp. 139–168.

Brandt, Deborah. "Remembering Writing, Remembering Reading." *CCC*, vol. 45, no. 4, Dec. 1994, pp. 459–479.

Carlone, Heidi B., and Angela Johnson. "Understanding the Science Experiences of Successful Women of Color: Science Identity as an Analytic Lens." *Journal of Research in Science Teaching*, vol. 44, no. 8, 2007, pp. 1187–1218.

Committee on CCCC Language Statement. "Students' Right to Their Own Language." *College English*, vol. 36, no. 6, 1975, pp. 709–726.

Dolmage, Jay. *Disability Rhetoric*. New York: Syracuse UP, 2014.

Elbow, Peter. "Being a Writer vs. Being an Academic: A Conflict in Goals." *College Composition and Communication*, vol. 46, no. 1, 1995, pp. 72–83.

Epp, Amber M., and Linda L. Price. "Family Identity: A Framework of Identity Interplay in Consumption Practices." *The Journal of Consumer Research*, vol. 35, no. 1, 2008, pp. 50–70.

Epp, Amber M., and Linda L. Price. "The Storied Life of Singularized Objects: Forces of Agency and Network Transformation." *The Journal of Consumer Research*, vol. 36, no. 5, 2010, pp. 820–837.

Hyland, Ken. "Authority and Invisibility: Authorial Identity in Academic Writing." *Journal of Pragmatics*, vol. 34, no. 8, 2002, pp. 1091–1112.

Hyland, Ken, and Guinda Carmen Sancho. *Stance and Voice in Written Academic Genres*. Palgrave Macmillan UK, 2012.

Ivanič, Roz. *Writing and Identity: The Discoursal Construction of Identity in Academic Writing*. John Benjamins, 1998.

Kleine, Robert E., et al. "Mundane Consumption and the Self: A Social-Identity Perspective." *Journal of Consumer Psychology*, vol. 2, no. 3, 1993, pp. 209–235.

Kleine, Susan Schultz, et al. "How Is a Possession 'Me' or 'Not Me'? Characterizing Types and an Antecedent of Material Possession Attachment." *The Journal of Consumer Research*, vol. 22, no. 3, 1995, pp. 327–343.

Laverie, Debra A., et al. "Reexamination and Extension of Kleine, Kleine, and Kernan's Social Identity Model of Mundane Consumption: The Mediating Role of the Appraisal Process." *The Journal of Consumer Research*, vol. 28, no. 4, 2002, pp. 659–669.

Matsuda, Paul Kei. "Identity in Written Discourse." *Annual Review of Applied Linguistics*, vol. 35, 2015, pp. 140–159.

Matsuda, Paul Kei. "Voice in Japanese Written Discourse: Implications for Second Language Writing." *Journal of Second Language Writing*, vol. 10, no. 1–2, 2001, pp. 35–53.

Matsuda, Paul Kei, and Christine M. Tardy. "Voice in Academic Writing: The Rhetorical Construction of Author Identity in Blind Manuscript Review." *English for Specific Purposes*, vol. 26, no. 2, 2007, pp. 235–249.

Royster, Jacqueline Jones. "When the First Voice You Hear Is Not Your Own." *CCC*, vol. 47, no. 1, 1996, pp. 29–40.

Ruvio, Ayalla, and Russell W. Belk. *The Routledge Companion to Identity and Consumption*. Routledge, 2013.

Steinke, Jocelyn. "Adolescent Girls' STEM Identity Formation and Media Images of STEM Professionals: Considering the Influence of Contextual Cues." *Frontiers in Psychology*, vol. 8, 2017, https://doi.org/10.3389/fpsyg.2017.00716.

Steinke, Jocelyn, et al. "Assessing Media Influences on Middle School–Aged Children's Perceptions of Women in Science Using the Draw-A-Scientist Test (DAST)." *Science Communication*, vol. 29, no. 1, Sept. 2007, pp. 35–64.

Steinke, Jocelyn, et al. "Seeing Oneself as a Scientist: Media Influences and Adolescent Girls' Science Career-Possible Selves." *Journal of Women and Minorities in Science and Engineering*, vol. 15, no. 4, 2009, pp. 279–301.

Villanueva, Victor. *Bootstraps: From an American Academic of Color*. National Council of Teachers of English, 1993.

2
THE SYMBOLIC LIFE OF THE MOLESKINE NOTEBOOK
Material Goods as a Tableau for Writing Identity Performance

Cydney Alexis[1]

Writing is considered a sacred act and the writer a sacred cultural figure. People use objects when trying to access this desired identity. How a person approaches and uses an object is intimately connected to family, sense of self, writing history, relation to peers, media connections, social awareness, and life story. Hence, turning to objects is one way of uncovering the very complicated identities that perform the practice of writing and for understanding the writing process itself. In this essay, I turn to the Moleskine notebook, a popular writing object, to show how three writers develop, navigate, and maintain their writerly identities and writing practices through this seemingly simple object.

> We may impose our identities on possessions and possessions may impose their identities on us.
> —Russell W. Belk (1988)

During an interview, a writer tells me about a duffle bag the older kids carried around his high school campus. For him, this bag marked entry into a new stage of schooling; it helped him to imagine a future as a high school student. This is just one object of many that surfaced during my three-dozen "life story" (Atkinson) interviews[2] with people about the materiality of their writing environments, or "habitats," as I have described them elsewhere (Alexis, "The Writing Habitat"). Other participants mentioned the Trapper Keeper, a highly desired object that parents often would not purchase due to its cost and perceived superfluousness. The Trapper Keeper carries middle-class identity associations, and many students I spoke to could remember whether they did or did not have one and could cite the reason why.

Memories such as these, which tie objects together with identity and schooling, resonate with the way objects hang out in writing studies research, a field whose interest in material objects has been steadily mounting for the last decade. Objects are rarely the central focus of study in writing studies research, save some notable exceptions (Baron; Boyle and Barnett; Haas; Wyche; Wyche-Smith). Social scientists Mihalyi Csikszentmihalyi and Eugene Rochberg-Halton note that researchers in their fields of psychology and sociology, respectively, "tend to look for the understanding of human life in the internal psychic processes of the individual or in the patterns of relationship between people; rarely do they consider the role of material objects" (1). I find that this holds, as well, for writing studies. In writing studies, we see objects accompanying writers or writers using them as sets or props for desired purposes (Emig; Prior and Shipka), providing space or a stable frame or stage for literate activities (Brandt and Clinton; Gere; Heath) and greasing the wheels toward or hampering access to literacy (Bartlett; Brandt). Objects, in fact, are referenced all over the place in writing research. Yet it's safe to say that we do not know what objects are *doing* in writing studies. This is because writing studies scholars have not yet fully engaged with rich work by scholars of material culture studies and consumer culture research (referenced herein as consumer research, for brevity) who, for decades, have been theorizing and researching the relationship between humans and material goods and proving that even the smallest, seemingly insignificant object has a story to tell about the humans who use it (Arnould and Thompson; Belk; Csikszentmihalyi and Rochberg-Halton; Deetz; Epp and Price; Miller; Prown, "Mind" and "Style"; Schlereth).

We know from the possessions literature that rather than one single object, a "constellation" of relevant objects is necessary when an individual performs a particular *identity*[3] or practice (such as that of "athlete," for example) (Kleine III, Kleine, and Kernan; Reed II; Reed II et al.; Solomon). Individuals attach to particular possessions in intense ways, weaving them into self-concept as reflecting "me" (Belk; Csikszentmihalyi and Rochberg-Halton; Kleine, Kleine, and Allen). In other words, people use possessions to perform "purposive identity work" (Epp and Price) as well as to express a particular "social identity" (Reed II; Kleine III, Kleine, and Kernan).

Humans express their selves through possessions; they also rely on possessions to memorialize past events and identities (Belk; Csikszentmihalyi and Rochberg-Halton; Kleine III, Kleine, and Kernan) and attach intensively to possessions that reflect an identity that they have achieved (Kleine III, Kleine, and Kernan) or that they wish to embody (Reed II et al.; Solomon). Individuals who have the ability to imagine "possible selves," or future selves performing a particular task, identity, or trade, are more likely to complete tasks successfully themselves (Markus and Nurius; Oyserman et al., "Possible" and "Socially"). Considering the demonstrated power of objects in the process of becoming possible selves, and people's reliance on object constellations to perform identities and trades, we should be asking deeper questions about how objects assist, even shape, writers in learning, negotiating, and maintaining their writing practices and writing identities.

Elsewhere, I have remarked on the importance of material culture and possessions research to our field and explored how material writing environments impact writing practice (Alexis, "The Writing Habitat"). In this article, my goal is to take a deeper look at a particular object, the Moleskine notebook, which came up unprompted in one of my interviews and—it was impossible to miss—was exploding in popularity around me. Because of this, I solicited two more life story interviews with users of Moleskines to better understand this notebook phenomenon. I argue here that the Moleskine notebook, a seemingly simple object, is a "facilitating artifact" for the performance of the identity of "writer" (Kleine III, Kleine, and Kernan 229). Specifically, artifacts such as the Moleskine "stimulate reflexive self-evaluations leading to self-definitions" (Laverie et al.) The Moleskine also plays complex roles in the lives of those who incorporate it into their writing practice. Moleskine users often internalize the Moleskine parent company's branding of the object as a literati and artist notebook, which I demonstrate in the pages that follow.

In order to do this, I present a brief history of the Moleskine notebook and its emergence in popular culture. The Moleskine is a tableau onto which people project their hopes and fears about writing. In other words, it is interwoven with ideas about what it means to be a writer as well as people's lived experience of being writers. Not all writers attach to the objects they work with or incorporate objects into their self-concept. Those who do, do so to varying degrees. Here, I present the stories of three of the writers I interviewed whose narratives about writing with Moleskines reflect three different integrations of this object into their writing lives, writing identities, and writing practices. "Biographies" of objects, Kopytoff asserts, are useful because they reveal what might otherwise resist analysis; they can also help researchers to catalogue how objects are plucked out of the commodity realm to be used in novel ways by consumers (66–68). And yet these objects, as you will see, also shape the way writers approach their craft.

Figure 2.1. Manuela Hoffmann's image of a classic Moleskine.

BECOMING A WRITER, WITH POSSESSIONS

Fiona, a graduate student in English, remembers the time when she began to journal. She was in grade school, and she was causing trouble as a result of not being scholastically challenged. At nine years of age, a teacher recommended journaling. Around this time and through this practice, her writing identity emerged:

> At the time I started journaling, I would have been sharing a room with my younger sister, who wasn't engaged with reading or writing. . . . It was all a part of a process of claiming identities that were different from each other, and so by being the child who wrote, and by being the child with books and notebooks, I had an identity that was separate from the children on either side of me that hadn't identified with those things.

David, a writing program administrator, narrates a similar story. He was a freshman in college when he came across the Moleskine notebook (see fig. 2.1).

> At this time, he was trying to become a writer. He began reading writers' notebooks and writing in his own, and he began to attach to and fetishize this particular material object: "Fetishize is not too heavy a word. . . . I became so fixated on them. . . . At that time I was getting into writing. I was an English major. I was reading a lot. I was sort of discovering reading, really, for the first time. I was fantasizing about being a writer. . . . I started reading writer's notebooks. . . . I started reading the notebooks of Albert Camus."

I present these two stories in support of the idea that objects help writers to do the following:

- Imagine what it means to be a writer ("I was fantasizing about being a writer")
- Carve out identities for themselves ("By being the child who wrote," "I was getting into writing," "I was . . . discovering reading"), often in relation to important others ("It was all a part of a process of claiming identities that were different from each other," "I had an identity that was separate from the children on either side of me," "I was reading the notebooks of Albert Camus")
- Compel the desire to write by imitating the object use or practices of published writers ("I started reading writers' notebooks")
- Maintain writing identities over time

In consumer research terms, individuals have a self-identity (or identities) that is both personal and social. They draw from the social world cues that help them imagine and perform that self-identity. Goods, and the media surrounding them, trigger certain identity performances and also help individuals to maintain and perform identity (Kleine III, Kleine, and Kernan; Reed II; Reed II et al.). One who writes, then, will receive cues from the material world regarding an identity and the materials that might be used to perform it. David's narrative, for example, demonstrates how people utilize objects to imagine how to "think, feel, and be like" writers (Reed II et al. 315).

Fiona and David have personal identities as writers that developed around goods. They share something else in common: They both have had intense relationships with one particular notebook, the Moleskine, which, in Dorothy Holland and Jean Lave's terms, is a cultural symbol that helps them to understand and perform the work of a writer. And they are not alone.

THE MOLESKINE PHENOMENON

By now, you are likely familiar with the classic Moleskine pictured in figure 2.1. But unless you are a dedicated Moleskine user, and even if you are one, you may not be familiar with the expansiveness of the Moleskine phenomenon, which has progressed far beyond offering the one iconic type pictured above. It is not an exaggeration to say that users constitute a sort of cult. A simple search in newspaper archives yields hundreds of articles about the Moleskine. A Google search for "Moleskine" reveals hundreds of thousands of user photographs and blog entries and detailed images and accounts of writers' and artists' (often obsessive) uses of this object. A Moleskine user created a fan blog (*Moleskinerie.com*) that achieved such popularity that the company eventually assumed

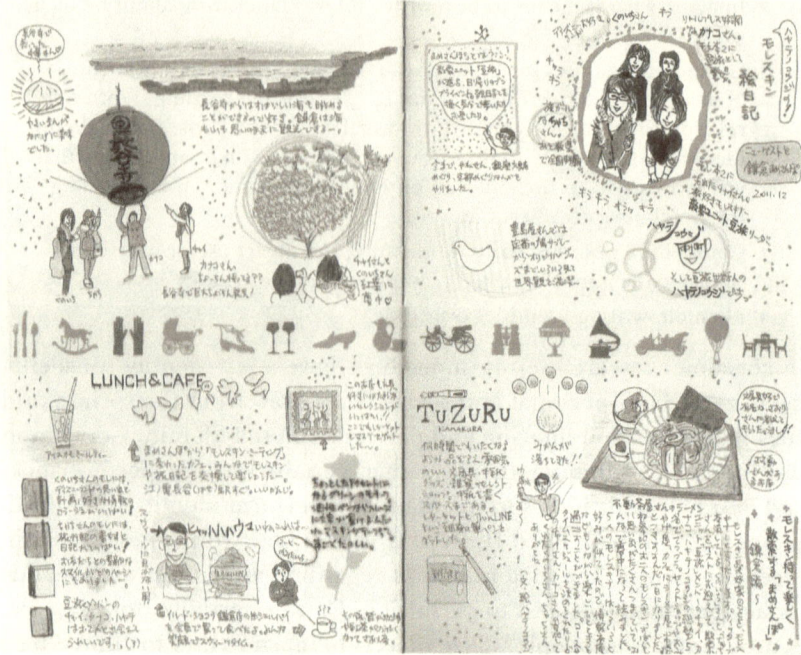

Figure 2.2. Kouji Hayateno's Moleskine.

control and now runs the blog. On Flickr and Instagram, users upload hundreds of thousands of images, such as the one pictured in figure 2.2.

The Moleskine company manages a Flickr group called "Moleskinerie" with more than 22,000 members and 116,000 uploaded photos. In 2014, Moleskine Spa reported 98.7 million euros in sales; Moleskine anticipates its market growing to 300 million people by 2020 ("Q4" 2014). More impressive than the numbers, however, is the company's awareness of its branding and its unmitigated success in marketing this object as an artist and literati companion. Each of the classic Moleskines are bound, covered in faux leather, held together symbolically and literally by a plastic band, and contain a pocket attached to the back cover into which is inserted a history of the notebook: "Moleskine is the legendary notebook, used by European artists and thinkers for the past two centuries, from Van Gogh to Picasso, from Ernest Hemingway to Bruce Chatwin." This history inscribes a promise to users: that they can tap into an exoticized literary and artistic heritage created by legendary writers and artists. The original Moleskine parent company Modo & Modo branded not only its creative past but also its aesthetic present:

A simple black rectangle with rounded corners, an elastic pageholder, and an internal expandable pocket: a nameless object with a spare perfection all its own, produced for over a century by a small French bookbinder that supplied the stationery shops of Paris, where the artistic and literary avant-gardes of the world browsed and bought them. A trusted and handy travel companion, the notebook held invaluable sketches, notes, stories, and ideas that would one day become famous paintings or the pages of beloved books ("Moleskine World").

The words *simple, nameless, spare,* and *small* are purposefully used to convey a classic aesthetic, one that foregoes the contemporary clutter of logos, overdesign, and corporate identity so that the brand might locate itself in the cultural longing for a perceived simpler, analog time. Moleskine personifies the notebook as a "companion" and suggests that by using it to write, one might someday become a Hemingway. Despite the company's expansiveness, it builds goodwill by conveying an image of a local artisan product.

Within this context, it is not difficult to understand why David, mentioned earlier, found the Moleskine compelling as an object that would help him to tap into the mindset and culture of being a writer. Moleskine now sees itself this way as well. In 2014, the company asserted that it is the "only brand that has successfully established itself as an identity marker starting from a notebook," although it did not describe itself in these terms when I first started researching the company in 2009 ("Q4"). Moleskine's identity-based branding is not unusual in today's market, as companies often "create or (re)position products and brands to embody a particular social identity oriented lifestyle" (Reed II 286). The company has been able to market not just a product, or a constellation of products, but also a community. The company now asserts, indeed, that it "sells much more than a notebook."[4]

What Moleskine is selling has been communicated well by journalists and bloggers who have prolifically published their thoughts on this object:

> In this digital age where everything is electronic and online . . . there is an unsurprising movement towards the simple pleasures of paper notebooks . . . the tactile nature of good-quality paper and the scratch of a pen as you write on it seems to enhance, even *sanctify,* the act of writing. (Shapshak 4, emphasis added)
>
> Writing in a Moleskine is different from writing on an ordinary piece of paper. There's a certain respect and reverence for your thoughts and ideas. It's not as transient as a scrap of paper, and there is nothing as disposable as a Word document. . . . It doesn't make what you're writing special, it makes that you're writing special. (Roderick, qtd. in Shapshak 4)

Moleskine has successfully connected its product with a simpler time, and the act of writing with an analog lifestyle. You can hear this in a bookstore manager's statement that "it's also nostalgic, to put your pen to paper.... It creates that sense of literature" (qtd. in Shapshak 4). This is ironic since the company markets digital products, such as a journal application available for both Mac and Windows platforms, and since its popularization has largely happened via the web.

Another irony casts a shadow over this whole business: the company's marketing narrative is largely spurious. "It's not even clear that Hemingway used a Moleskine at all," Joe Lavin writes. "He merely mentioned that in Paris he wrote part of a novel in a notebook that fit in his pocket." Indeed, small, anonymous, unnamed notebooks were produced by Parisian bookbinders until the 1980s. As the story goes, author Bruce Chatwin named this anonymous book the "Moleskine" upon discovering that the last family-run, artisanal bookbinder in Tours had gone out of business when its factory burned down ("Le Moleskine n'existe plus," Chatwin exclaimed in his novel *Songlines* [*Moleskinerie*]). Before this, Moleskine was a "Franglais generic term for stout waxed canvas: a waterproof cover that protected the contents of your pocket note-book from rain, spilt milk and bodily fluids" (Bywater 7). In 1997, a Milanese Italian design company, Modo & Modo, began producing the notebook we now know as the Moleskine, patented the name, and "began one of the most audacious branding exercises of recent decades" (Bywater 7).

Despite Moleskine's fabricated branding, this object has entered actual writers' lives, as David conveyed to me. After interviewing David, I conducted targeted interviews with other self-professed Moleskine users, two of whose stories I present here alongside his in order to understand how the branding played out in the lives of people who had integrated this notebook into their practices.

OBJECTS AS EXPRESSIONS OF SELF

Fiona discovered the Moleskine notebook once her journaling practice had developed and now, as an adult, she attaches quite strongly to this notebook for aesthetic and practical purposes. As a vast body of work has demonstrated, individuals cultivate, define, negotiate, and maintain their identities through attachment to goods (Belk; Csikszentmihalyi and Rochberg-Halton; Epp and Price; Kleine, Kleine, and Allen; Schultz et al.; Wallendorf and Arnould). Individuals generally attach to possessions over which they have a strong degree of control (Belk), that relate to parts of their selves that they value or that they admire in their social worlds (Kleine, Kleine, and Allen; Schultz et al.), toward which they hold a strong emotional charge or "cathexis" (Kleine, Kleine, and Allen 327), and that represent past associations or current ties (Csikszentmihalyi and Rochberg-Halton) as well as well-established parts of one's individual personality (Kleine, Kleine, and Allen) or family identity (Epp and Price). Attachments can tell a person's life story.

I learned a lot about Fiona's story—and personal relationships with writing objects—through her attachment to the Moleskine. Since grade school, when her teacher recommended she start journaling, she has used notebooks for uninhibited personal writing, for recording thoughts and feelings. Later, the Moleskine became so incorporated into her journaling practice that she stopped using other kinds of notebooks. She calls herself a "compulsive" writer in these notebooks. Their dominant use is not for writing projects, academic writing, or even lists; she uses them to record her thoughts in stream-of-consciousness format. She cites the Moleskine as a site of "unclogging" and contrasts the writing she does there with academic writing, which causes anxiety and blockage. In class, she sits with two notebooks. She takes academic notes in a generic notebook while she simultaneously uses the Moleskine to record her thoughts and emotions. The Moleskine, then, is a record of her mental life, thoughts, and emotions—aspects of her being.

Fiona always carries a Moleskine notebook fairly close to her body. She does not carry just any type; she prefers the small navy-blue version pictured in figure 2.3, the inside of which is comprised of graph paper.

Fiona has been using this type of Moleskine for years; what you see pictured is only a fraction of the total collection. She buys purses that have Moleskine-sized pockets, so that she can keep one near, if her clothing does not accommodate carrying the notebook. Others have recognized her use of this object, frequently giving her Moleskine gifts. She told me this makes her feel badly because she will not use any type except the blue graph paper style, so she ends up giving away the gifted Moleskines.

Fiona's investment in this artifact, which is attached to her person at most times, is an example of what Belk calls "self-extension" (139). Possessions come to be revered as part of the self and in some cases literally extend the self, as is the case with some prosthetic devices. But a large component of this phenomenon is metaphoric. Belk argues that "a key to understanding what possessions mean is recognizing that, knowingly or unknowingly, intentionally or unintentionally, we regard our possessions as parts of ourselves" (139). Indeed, after the brain and face, humans will rate possessions as much as, and sometimes more,

Figure 2.3. Fiona's Moleskines.

a part of their self-concept than body parts. In short, "the feeling of identity invested in material objects can be extraordinarily high" (144). It is this investment that leads Fiona to characterize her relationship to the Moleskines as "stewardship"; she feels responsible not necessarily for the writing contained in them but for the value they have as objects. Fiona has associated objects with identity work since she was young. She cultivated the identity of writer to distinguish herself from her four siblings. In my interview with her, she quickly expressed the idea that because her family was large, "self-definition was related to having and owning things. . . . [I]t was really just a way of saying, 'I am an individual person.'" She described back-to-school shopping trips as "chaotic," her family as "territorial," and the home governed by an "economy of theft and exchange." If something was left in a common area, it disappeared. At holidays, gifts of different colors were given to each child. This is an example of objects being pulled out of the commodity realm and "singularized" as they are used in the expression and maintenance of identity (Epp and Price 821).

"Singularization" is an individuated experience of making meaning from a thing and decommodifying it by integrating it into one's life (Epp and Price 821). For Fiona, this takes the form of selecting particular Moleskines that reflect her identity and purpose. For other Moleskine users, singularization takes on even more dramatic forms. Figure 2.4, for example, shows a trend called a "hack": user-designed customizations of objects.

Figure 2.4. "The Geekster Moleskine," by Sebastian Delmont.

All one has to do is type "Moleskine hack" into Google to access a vast resource for individuating one's Moleskine (a more recent example of this phenomenon can be observed by searching with the hashtag #bulletjournal on Instagram). Figure 2.5 depicts a user's hacked, hand-crafted Moleskine; she details the process of hacking a Moleskine planner on her blog, which also contains gorgeous and elaborate Moleskine notebook artwork (Cole).

The elaborate tabbing and hacking systems discussed above can help a writer to transform and ritualize what might otherwise be seen as mundane work (such as keeping a calendar) or to organize what is perceived as already singular and as a representation of selfhood: one's writing.

Hacking and cutting up Moleskines appears to contradict a dominant thread in the discourse around this object, which is that due to their cost,[5] aesthetics, and cultural resonance, they have a "sacred" status that prevents them, at times, from being used. As Belk and coauthors note, "In an increasingly secular world, consumption has become a sacred act"; through consumption, people "sacralize experience" and objects are treated as "set apart, extraordinary, or sacred" (1, 2, 9–12). "I have tons of Moleskine," one person writes, "all empty. . . . It's terrifying to aim anything that resembles a writing implement at it. I've gone back to those sordid, crass pedestrian notebooks" (Dalisay). However, it is also possible that hacking the notebooks makes them more sacred, not less.

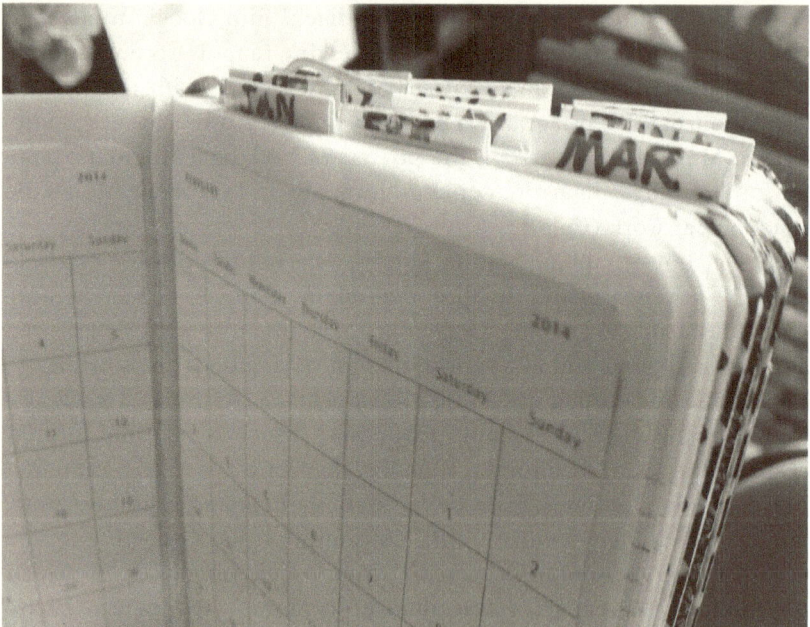

Figure 2.5. "Hacked Moleskine Planner," by Joyce Harbin Cole.

OBJECTS AND AFFILIATION

Fiona's story represents the ways that objects are used as self-expression in service of building an identity around writing. Her use of the Moleskine is also fairly uncomplicated. She performs only one type of writing in her Moleskines and avoids using them for more stressful genres. She does not appear to use her notebooks for many of the oft-cited reasons in popular discourse: to counter the digital, to achieve writerly status, or to bring gravitas to her ideas. Rather, her story exemplifies how the "strongest attachments form with things that mark a realized identity development path," in this case, as a person who journals (Kleine, Kleine, and Allen 341).

David's story raises other points: first, what happens when our narrative around an object consumes our ability to use it; second, how objects reflect our affiliations with important others, such as peers, family, and friends; and, third, how our identities (around writing) intersect with and get bound to objects in ways that make their study an important component of understanding writing practice.

Throughout my interview with David, he narrated relationships with material goods that had a sacred tone. He told me a story about a poem ("Ezekiel's Wheel" by Geoffrey Hill) that he carried around in his wallet; he did not understand the poem and this lack, for him, represented an identity conflict. In his words, "it was an object that I was carrying around as a kind of way of dealing with a larger problem, which was that I was not a poet." He folded the poem up with the desire to continue carrying it around until he could understand it. The folded-up poem became even more weighted when one day he was working at a potter's wheel in a ceramic studio and the man who normally occupied that wheel entered the shop; the man's name, he realized, was Ezekiel. And he was sitting at Ezekiel's wheel. He shared this story as a means of explaining the series of coincidences and religious intersections that occurred during this time period, as he was trying to understand and forge his identity as both a person and writer. That day, he was uncomfortable because he was a novice ceramicist sitting at an expert potter's wheel. The folded-up poem was one object onto which he had projected ideas about himself.

This tension of wanting to become something that he is not, yet witnessing it in others and trying to access it, is observable in his childhood and in what I read as the emergence of his identity as a writer, which developed with and against his siblings and peers. David grew up in a family of three and shared a room with his brother, against whom he defined his identity. His brother was a musician whose part of the room was occupied by musical equipment. David asked his parents to buy him a desk at a young age. He was trying to claim space in a room he shared with his brother, demarcate territory, and signal his developing writerly persona (Alexis, "The Writing Habitat" 86). This resonates with Fiona's use of private, material space to claim an identity tied to writing. Possessions were not only tied to self-definition but Fiona also successfully argued for her own room because she needed space and time to write, and she was the only child of five siblings who won this private space (86). In both cases, the material (object or space) is used for self-definition, for oneself internally and against others.

David grew up close to two male friends with and against whom he defined his identity. Speaking about who influenced his writing most, he says:

> The people I think of as influential were the people I was competing with more than anything. I remember two friends . . . every year or every semester there would be an award for language arts, an award for social studies, a little medal, in grade school. And the three of us always won it. . . . But it was somewhat uncomfortable because one of them was a real reader, a pathological reader and he was extremely imaginative and my mother sometimes used him as a—to try and get me to read. She'd say, "Nate reads all the time." And I'd say, "I don't want to do that." You know, it would really bug me . . .

What struck me throughout David's interview is his perception of himself in relation to others who are practicing similar activities or, put another way, the deep influence that close others have on our developing literate identities and sense of self when young. This tension between self and others ricochets throughout my interview with him, as he describes his developing persona as one who writes. His awareness of others continues in college, where David meets the woman who would later become his wife. He describes trying to doodle in his notebooks to make them interesting to her. He says, "I would spend hours a day just writing in these notebooks. I'm not an artist at all, so I was fiddling around with visual design stuff, but not effectively." Yet as he describes his fascination with his wife's artistry, he also narrates a tension with how he perceives his own use of Moleskines. Whereas he felt that his notebooks were not to be "sullied with class notes," her notebooks reflected another orientation: "That's something that kind of both upset me and fascinated me about her notebooks when I first started flipping through them. She would just write on anything and everything. She'll be writing, you know, a poem or a story and there'll be some information about a doctor's appointment and then class notes from a history class."

David's interview displays the degree to which he is conscious of how identities and orientations manifest in material goods. He narrates a story about giving a Moleskine to a cousin who was embarking on a long vacation:

> Since that time he's become this compulsive journaler in these notebooks. Recently he picked up one of mine and flipped through it and said, "This is just a list. It's lists of stuff to do, like to-do lists, and mine's a story." And I said, "Yes. I don't have time to do that." I felt kind of sad to hear that. And he was just observing something, saying, "We do this really differently." So yes, I still use these notebooks. I have tons of them, but they're more of just information than anything else.

David feels angst that he is not a "real" writer, by which he means a writer of fiction and poetry; he sees himself as just writing down plain "information." He worries that he is profaning the sacred space of the Moleskine. Part of the Moleskine's sacrosanct quality for David is its design. As he says,

> I have a sentimental attachment to [the Moleskine]. I like the way it looks. But I don't know the first thing about design. I wish I could look at a building or a painting and discern the language of design. . . . And I envy people who can do that. And I feel that rather than being literate in that way, I'm pretty much at the mercy of that kind of visual rhetoric or design rhetoric.

The awe he feels for the Moleskine, then, is bound up with conflict over his own identity as a writer and his relation to others who write. Although he earned high honors in his discipline and is a successful writer and administrator, he laments, "I wish I were a better writer than I am. I wish I were a scholar, but I am not. I am a writing teacher." The Moleskine seems to lodge, or at least help us to unravel, anxieties about what it means to be a creative and productive writer. There is some "identity conflict" (Reed et al. 311) between his desire to be a writer and what he "principally understands himself to be" (Schatzki 54).

The Moleskine is an object that is bound to and reveals identity negotiation. In a sense, David uses this object to understand who he is. His relationship with the Moleskine demonstrates how the triad of self, other, and possessions intertwine with identity work. It supports Kleine, Kleine, and Allen's conclusion that identity research focused only on "the self as me," and not the self in "relations with others," is incomplete (341). As they write, "Self-identifying possessions reflect who I am as a unique individual, and/or who I am as I am connected to others" (341).

At a critical moment in his development as a writer, David, like Fiona, found the Moleskine and identified in it something valuable to his self-narrative. Through this object, he tries to understand and define his writing identity and his relation to others. At the same time, it is undeniable that the Moleskine also reveals more troubled feelings David holds about writing and his relationship to others who write. It is possible that David's sacred connection with the Moleskine has affected his ability to use the object freely. Housed in it is a tension between the writer he imagined, continues to imagine, and perceives himself to be.

INTEGRATED OBJECT USE

If Fiona's story communicates the idea of objects reflecting "who I am as a unique individual" and David's "who I am as I am connected to others," Lily, also a graduate student at the time of our interview, provides another perspective. Like Fiona and David, she could narrate the history of the Moleskine notebook, though initially she did not know or remember that the narrative is inserted in the back of the book. Unlike Fiona and David, however, Lily resists the Moleskine's narrative and is even a bit hostile to the company's association of writing with masculinity, through its references to the classic male literary canon via mentions of Picasso and Hemingway and through its use of stark black leather design motifs. She bought her first oversized bound Moleskine because she could not find another that she liked better and that had large enough pages to house her work.

What fascinated me about Lily's use of the Moleskine was, on the one hand, her lack of attachment to the object, and on the other, that her use of it was the most integrated and broad of those whom I interviewed. As you can see in figure 2.6, Lily uses the Moleskine for all types of writing: taking class notes, mapping paper ideas, and sketching PowerPoint presentations.

Lily is fond of drawing in Moleskines, as opposed to drawing on loose paper, because this keeps her drawings "contained." For her, invention, space, and the Moleskine are linked; of the Moleskine's large dimensions, she said, "I like the ideas to come out; I like that space." This example illustrates how, in purchasing products, writers link aesthetic concerns to utilitarian or process-related ones. Lily chose this design because it was big enough that her hand could rest on the page while she writes, because of its narrow rule ("wide rule is a waste of space"), its binding ("the ring on spiral-bound notebooks always gets caught on my backpack"), and its black cover, though she also dislikes that the cover is "boring" and "gendered masculine." Lily switched to the Moleskine in graduate school. Because they are bound, she states, they "have a kind of permanence that other notebooks don't." She feels her writing is being

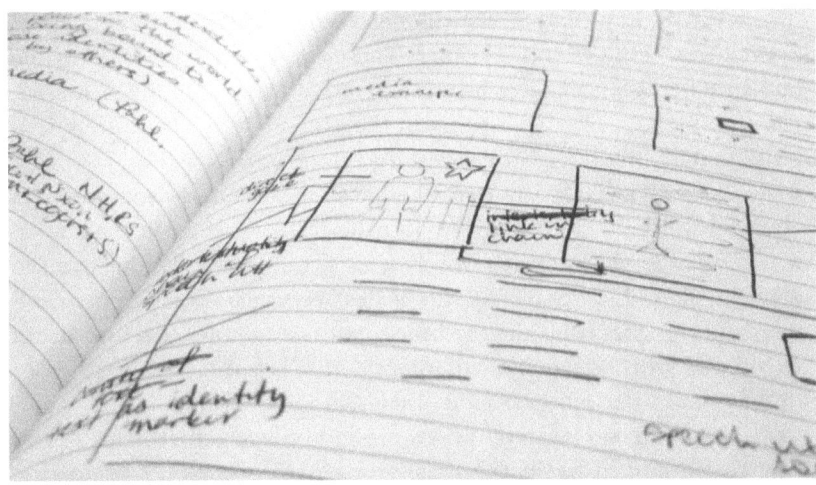

Figure 2.6. Lily's Moleskines.

"preserved." Although she seems fairly unattached to the Moleskine, she did speak about writing in strong positive tones: "I have an emotional attachment to the act of writing and keeping my life ordered or keeping the ideas going or the creativity that can be engendered through the act of writing in this book. . . . I am emotionally attached to thinking through ideas in this way." Her reference to "attachment" highlights how one can be invested not in an object but in the practice that accompanies it. Understanding how and why writers rely on objects, even if, as in David's case, they might have a negative impact on practice, is important for our field.

Surprisingly, Lily told me that she hates writing but likes every stage of the process where she is the primary audience. When I asked her if the Moleskine helps her manage her displeasure with writing, she answered, "Yes, absolutely. . . . I enjoy writing in the Moleskine . . . because there's no risk to it . . . this stage is what gets me out of writer's block. . . . In fact, I sometimes will just take this to the coffee shop and not my computer . . . because it will help me to get over just the fear of having to actually do the writing of it." This accords with Fiona's view of the Moleskine as a site of "unclogging." Lily often keeps the Moleskine side-by-side with her computer, and she goes back and forth between taking notes and working at the computer, in the same way that Fiona utilizes two Moleskines side by side, with one reserved for stream of consciousness writing.

For Lily, then, the Moleskine is a tool and a space that helps her to produce writing, to begin the creative part of the practice of writing that she loves. It is a stress reliever when she is working on less pleasurable tasks like the academic writing that is so central to her career. But it is not an object of obsession, affection, or attachment. In fact, Lily noted that if and when she finds another notebook that offers what the Moleskine does, she will switch. The Moleskine has not been integrated into her self-concept. This could possibly be because, unlike David and Fiona, Lily found the Moleskine at a much older age, once her identity as a writer and understanding of her writing-practice needs were already cemented. In addition, the notebook's branding conflicts strongly with her sense of self, as it is connected to the male canon through the Hemingway myth.

Of the writers with whom I spoke, Lily has the most untroubled history with and most integrated use of the Moleskine. Whereas Fiona has attached the Moleskine to a segmented part of her writing practice, Lily's lack of attachment allows her to use it in complex, integrated ways. Her use of the Moleskine asks us to consider whether it might be the case that writers use objects in the least segmented or restrictive ways, and for the most broad purposes, when intense and positive attachments are not present.

CONCLUSION

In this essay, I have attempted to understand the significance of one material object in writers' lives as a means of portraying the complexity of the relationship between writers, writing goods, and the practices and rituals that support literate performance. Rather than suggesting that all writers who use this object use it in the same way, I hope instead to point to similar types of work performed by material objects as writers attach to them for a variety of reasons.

Fiona, David, and Lily have different relationships to the Moleskine. Fiona has found a consistent use of this notebook; as a result, her practice is compelled, not thwarted, by this object. In contrast, the Moleskine appears to be a vexed object for David, one that initially signaled possibility and now reflects his feeling that he has not embodied the identity he wished to achieve. I am careful to say "his feeling" because experience suggests that many who write on a daily basis for their work (and I'd include many academics in this category, including the majority of those whom I interviewed) do not see themselves as *writers* per se. David's internal sense of what *writing* means is a problem for writing studies, as only certain types of writing are marked off as "creative" and hence valuable, which I believe has led to the devaluing of the majority of writing performed by those who do it for their profession (for more information, see Alexis, "Stop Using"). Through the Moleskine, David will likely continue to work through his anxieties regarding his writing identity, anxieties that manifested during our various discussions of what this tiny object means in his and his family members' writing lives. David retains this object in his writing life because it was instrumental in helping him to envision a possible self as a writer, an identity that he still attempts to embody. At the same time, his competing and more easily inhabitable identity as an administrator troubles his relationship with the Moleskine since he does not see administrative writing as appropriate for this particular symbolic material possession. David's identities are in tension and motion, a liminal state that the Moleskine reveals. Yet a commonality binds David's and Fiona's narratives: The Moleskine is performing identity work, inviting an attachment, providing an entry into a desired identity or practice, and spurring internal reflection. In this way, the material object presses its own identity on writers, dictating certain types of disciplinary performance. Lily actively resists the identity components of the notebook; they do not reflect her "me." Her case compels consideration of whether attachment increases or hinders complex, broad, untroubled use of a possession.

The Moleskine notebook is just one facilitating artifact through which writers perform critical identity work that is an instrumental component in the development of a writing practice. Becoming a writer is composed of many instances in which one both imagines what writers do and performs similar acts. A chief way that this imagining occurs at a young age is through goods. Writers lean on chosen objects such as desks, pens, knick-knacks, and notebooks to begin to occupy a desired self and to practice it alone and, perhaps more importantly, for and with others. A practice of writing, then, cannot be understood without considering the various tools and settings with and within the habitats in which writers work—beginning with the kitchen in childhood, the bedroom in adolescence, and numerous other sites, both public and private, as adults. Writers practice their craft with a strong awareness of their relation to those around them, whether it is the identities of siblings and peers or of authors in a literary canon.

Siblings, peers, family members, and others who surround us as we are developing and articulating a writing self play important roles. Hence, rather than study writers in isolation (Emig; Flower and Hayes; Prior and Shipka), we need to study them in relation to the others they write with, against, and around. Besides the institutional and structural "sponsors" who support writing work is the vast network of what one of my students termed lowercase "s" sponsors who enable and disable our access to literate resources (Brandt).[6] These sponsors are at the very least a tableau against which we project desired selves. Writing is considered a sacred act and the writer a sacred cultural figure. People trying to access this desired identity use objects. How a person approaches and uses an object is intimately connected to that person's family, sense of self, writing history, relation to peers, media connections, social awareness, and life story. Turning to objects, and to facilitating artifacts, is one way of uncovering the very complicated identities that perform the practice we call "writing."

NOTES

1. This chapter first appeared in *Composition Studies* 45.2 (2017): 32–54.
2. For this project, I conducted twenty-eight interviews with people who currently or formerly wrote regularly for school or work. The majority of my participants, at the time, were undergraduate and graduate students. However, a little over a third were not. Schoolteachers made up nearly 20 percent of my study participants. I am interested in this population because teachers not only use objects in their own practices but also design writing environments for students. I also interviewed three generations of one family (two of these individuals were retired), and four individuals who identify as fiction and poetry writers or writers who work in business and administration.
3. A brief sketch of what I mean by *identity* is useful here, since writing studies has yet to treat in depth the subject of *writing identity* as a distinct type of identity with associated practices and object constellations. Cross-disciplinary research on identity has established that there is indeed a self that has some degree of control over one's own actions (Erikson; James; Sartre), that develops in stages and emerges from some form of group belonging (Erikson), and that gets shaped over time, both due to personal interests and associations and historical and social forces that impact the individual (Holland and Lave; Holland et al.). I find compelling Holland et al.'s articulation of

identity as "a central means by which selves, and the sets of actions they organize, form and re-form over personal lifetimes and in the histories of social collectivities" (270). Holland and Lave refer to these as "personal identities" and note that they can be evoked "via cultural symbols" that help one to learn expectations for behavior in a particular realm. Additionally, Reissman notes that when constructing identities, individuals often perform identity to a desired end, often "involv[ing] their audience in 'doing' their identities" (5). A succinct definition of identity has been forwarded by consumer researchers Reed II et al. as "any category label to which a consumer self-associates either by choice or endowment" (312). Building on the above, I define identity as any category label or positionality to which a person self-associates either by choice or by endowment, due to identification with that label or because the performance of it will lead to some desired end. Identity is not a stable category and is not singular; hence, individuals may self-associate with more than one identity category and these identifications may shift over time.

4. Moleskine's commentary on its own success is fascinating. About its customer base, Moleskine writes, "They are global, they share a number of basic cultural elements, they want tools to help them bridge analog and digital, they are relatively less price sensitive. And, most importantly, they live on the move, and need brands that can help them convey their identity" ("Q4"). Moleskine explains its appeal as providing "distinctive aspirational values, supported by a strong reason to believe, a unique cultural heritage, which we maintain relevance [sic] by constantly engaging with expressions of contemporary culture."

5. Moleskine's Wikipedia page indicates that there is some fan controversy over the Moleskine's high cost in light of its production in China, a notoriously cheap labor market.

6. I am indebted to Rowan University graduate Lauren Buck for this point, which she raised in my fall 2014 section of Evaluating Writing.

WORKS CITED

Alexis, Cydney. "Stop Using the Phrase *Creative Writing*." *Slate*, 6 Jan. 2017, https://slate.com/human-interest/2017/01/lets-banish-the-phrase-creative-writing.html. Rpt. in *Bad Ideas About Writing*. "Creative Writing Is Unique Category." Edited by Drew Loewe and Cheryl Ball. Morgantown: Digital Publishing Institute, 2017.

Alexis, Cydney. "The Writing Habitat: Objects, Environment, Practice." *Rhetoric, through Everyday Things*, edited by Scot Barnett and Casey Boyle. U of Alabama P, 2016, pp. 83–95.

Arnould, Eric J., and Craig J. Thompson. "Consumer Culture Theory (CCT): Twenty Years of Research." *Journal of Consumer Research*, vol. 31, no. 4, 2005, pp. 868–882.

Atkinson, Robert. *The Life Story Interview*. Sage Publications, 1998.

Barnett, Scot, and Casey Boyle, eds. *Rhetoric, through Everyday Things*. U of Alabama P, 2016.

Baron, Dennis. "From Pencils to Pixels: The Stages of Literacy Technology." *Passions, Pedagogies, and 21st Century Technologies*, edited by Gail E. Hawisher and Cynthia L. Selfe, Utah State UP, 1999, pp. 15–33.

Bartlett, Lesley. "To Seem and to Feel: Situated Identities and Literacy Practices." *The Teachers College Record*, vol. 109, no. 1, 2007, pp. 51–69.

Belk, Russell W. "Possessions and the Extended Self." *Journal of Consumer Research*, vol. 15, no. 2, 1988, pp. 139–168.

Belk, Russell W., Melanie Wallendorf, and John F. Sherry Jr. "The Sacred and the Profane in Consumer Behavior: Theodicy on the Odyssey." *Journal of Consumer Research*, vol. 16, no. 1, 1989, pp. 1–38.

Brandt, Deborah. *Literacy in American Lives*. Cambridge UP, 2001.

Brandt, Deborah, and Katie Clinton. "Limits of the Local: Expanding Perspectives on Literacy as a Social Practice." *Journal of Literacy Research*, vol. 34, no. 3, 2002, pp. 337–356.

Bywater, Michael. "The Touch of Genius: This Notebook Will Help You Paint Like Van Gogh, Sketch Like Picasso and Write Like Hemingway—or at Least That's What Its Makers Would Have You Believe." *Independent*, 3 Aug. 2003, Features 7. Accessed 26 Aug. 2016.

Cole, Joyce Harbin. "Hacking a Moleskine Planner." *Draw Daily*, 27 Dec. 2013.

Csikszentmihalyi, Mihaly, and Eugene Rochberg-Halton. *The Meaning of Things: Domestic Symbols and the Self*. Cambridge UP, 1981.

Dalisay, Jose. "In Praise of Moleskine." Comment by Raymond Arzadon on Jose Dalisay's blog entry. http://homepage.mac.com/jdalisay/blog/PenmanSep107.htm. Accessed 23 Oct. 2011.

Deetz, James. *In Small Things Forgotten: The Archaeology of Early American Life*. Anchor-Doubleday, 1977.

Emig, Janet A. *The Composing Processes of Twelfth Graders*. NCTE, 1971.

Epp, Amber, and Linda Price. "The Storied Life of Singularized Objects: Forces of Agency and Network Transformation." *Journal of Consumer Research*, vol. 36, no. 5, 2010, pp. 820–838.

Erikson, Erik H. *Identity and the Life Cycle*. Norton, 1980.

Farry, Oliver. "G2 Etcetera: Why I Love Moleskines." *Guardian* [Manchester], 20 Apr. 2004, final ed., p. 23. Accessed 18 Aug. 2016.

Gere, Ann Ruggles. "Kitchen Tables and Rented Rooms: The Extracurriculum of Composition." *CCC*, vol. 45, no. 1, 1994, pp. 75–92.

gtdfreak. "infobook-after-50." 6 Jan. 2007. Online image. *Flickr*, https://www.flickr.com/photos/gtdfrk/347593171/in/pool-51462541@N00. Accessed 28 Apr. 2017.

Haas, Christina. *Writing Technology: Studies on the Materiality of Literacy*. Lawrence Erlbaum Associates, 1996.

Hayateno, Kouji. Untitled photograph. Facebook message. Permission to use granted via email 14 Feb. 2013.

Heath, Shirley Brice. *Ways with Words: Language, Life, and Work in Communities and Classrooms*. Cambridge UP, 1983.

Hill, Geoffrey. *Canaan*. Penguin, 1996.

Holland, Dorothy, and Jean Lave. "Social Practice Theory and the Historical Production of Persons." *Actio: An International Journal of Human Activity Theory*, vol. 2, 2009, pp. 1–15.

Holland, Dorothy, et al. *Identity and Agency in Cultural Worlds*. Harvard UP, 1998.

James, William. *The Principles of Psychology, Volume 1*. Henry Holt, 1890.

Kleine, Robert E., III, Susan Schultz Kleine, and Jerome B. Kernan. "Mundane Consumption and the Self: A Social-Identity Perspective." *Journal of Consumer Psychology*, vol. 2, no. 3, 1993, pp. 209–235.

Kleine, Susan Shultz, Robert E. Kleine III, and Chris T. Allen. "How Is a Possession 'Me' or 'Not Me'? Characterizing Types and an Antecedent of Material Possession Attachment." *Journal of Consumer Research*, vol. 22, no. 3, 1995, pp. 327–343.

Kopytoff, Igor. "The Cultural Biography of Things: Commoditization as Process." *The Social Life of Things: Commodities in Cultural Perspective*, edited by Arjun Appadurai, Cambridge UP, 1986, pp. 64–94.

Latour, Bruno. "On Interobjectivity." *Mind, Culture, and Activity*, vol. 3, no. 4, 1996, pp. 228–245.

Laverie, Debra A., Robert E. Kleine III, and Susan Schultz Kleine. "Reexamination and Extension of Kleine III, Kleine, and Kernan's Social Identity Model of Mundane Consumption: The Mediating Role of the Appraisal Process." *Journal of Consumer Research*, vol. 28, no. 4, 2002, pp. 659–669.

Lavin, Joe. "Novel Going Nowhere? Must Be Your Notebook: Pricey, Leather-Bound Moleskine Journals Have 'Wannabe Writer' Written All Over Them." *Gazette* [Montreal], 26 Sept. 2005, final ed., p. D4. Accessed 26 Aug. 2016.

Markus, Hazel, and Paula Nurius. "Possible Selves." *American Psychologist*, vol. 41, no. 9, 1986, pp. 954–969.

Miller, Daniel. "Why Some Things Matter." *Material Cultures: Why Some Things Matter*, edited by Daniel Miller, University College London Press, 1998, pp. 3–24.

"Moleskine Store." *The Official Moleskine Website*, Moleskine SpA, 14 Nov. 2010, http://www.moleskine.com/us/. Accessed 18 Aug. 2016.

"Moleskine World." *MOLESKINE®*. http://www.moleskine.com/us/moleskineworld. Accessed 7 Apr. 2017.

"Moleskinerie: Legends and Stories." *Moleskine*, Moleskine SpA, http://www.moleskinerie.com. Accessed 18 Aug. 2016.

Oyserman, Daphna, Deborah Bybee, and Kathy Terry. "Possible Selves and Academic Outcomes: How and When Possible Selves Impel Action." *Journal of Personality and Social Psychology*, vol. 91, no. 1, 2006, pp. 188–204.

Oyserman, Daphna, Larry Gant, and Joel Ager. "A Socially Contextualized Model of African American Identity: Possible Selves and School Persistence." *Journal of Personality and Social Psychology*, vol. 69, no. 6, 1995, pp. 1216–1232.

Popov, Dimitri. "Moleskine Travel Kit." 1 Sept. 2006. Online image. *Flickr*. Accessed 28 Apr. 2017.

Prior, Paul, and Jody Shipka. "Chronotopic Lamination: Tracing the Contours of Literate Activity." *Writing Selves, Writing Societies: Research from Activity Perspectives*, edited by Charles Bazerman and David R. Russell, WAC Clearinghouse, 2003, n. pag., http://wac.colostate.edu/books/selves_societies/prior/. Accessed 18 Aug. 2016.

Prown, Jules David. "Mind in Matter: An Introduction to Material Culture Theory and Method." *Winterthur Portfolio*, vol. 17, no. 1, 1982, pp. 1–19.

Prown, Jules David. "Style as Evidence." *Winterthur Portfolio*, vol. 15, no. 3, 1980, pp. 197–210.

"Q4 2014 Moleskine SpA Earnings Call-Final." *Fair Disclosure Wire*, 11 Mar. 2015. Accessed 18 Aug. 2016.

Reed, Americus, II. "Activating the Self-Importance of Consumer Selves: Exploring Identity Salience Effects on Judgments." *Journal of Consumer Research*, vol. 31, no. 2, 2004, pp. 286–295.

Reed, Americus, II, Mark R. Forehand, Stefano Puntoni, and Luk Warlop, "Identity-Based Consumer Behavior." *International Journal of Research in Marketing*, vol. 29, no. 4, 2012, pp. 310–321.

Reissman, Catherine Kohler. "Narrative Analysis." *Narrative, Memory, and Everyday Life*. University of Huddersfield, 2005.

Rodriguez, Juan. "Following the Paper Trail: In a City with No Shortage of Writers, Both Legendary and Aspiring, the Right Canvas Can Make All—Okay, Some—of the Difference." *Gazette* [Montreal], 16 Aug. 2007, final ed., p. D8.

Sartre, Jean-Paul. *Being and Nothingness: A Phenomenological Essay on Ontology*. Philosophical Library, 1943.

Schatzki, Theodore R. *The Site of the Social: A Philosophical Account of the Constitution of Social Life and Change*. Pennsylvania State UP, 2002.

Schlereth, Thomas J. *Material Culture Studies in America*. American Association for State and Local History, 1982.

Schultz, Susan E., Robert E. Kleine III, and Jerome B. Kernan. " 'These Are a Few of My Favorite Things': Toward an Explication of Attachment as a Human Behavior Construct." *Advances in Consumer Research*, vol. 16, no. 1, 1989, pp. 359–366.

Shapshak, Toby. "A Moleskine Love Affair." *Business Day* [South Africa], 28 Apr. 2007, weekend rev. ed., p. 4.

Solomon, Michael R. "The Role of Products as Social Stimuli: A Symbolic Interactionism Perspective." *Journal of Consumer Research*, vol. 10, no. 3, 1983, pp. 319–329.

Wallendorf, Melanie, and Eric J. Arnould. "'My Favorite Things': A Cross-Cultural Inquiry into Object Attachment, Possessiveness, and Social Linkage." *Journal of Consumer Research*, vol. 14, no. 4, 1988, pp. 31–47.

Wyche, Susan. "Time, Tools, and Talismans." *The Subject Is Writing: Essays by Teachers and Students*, edited by Wendy Bishop, 1st ed., Boynton/Cook, 1993, pp. 111–123.

Wyche-Smith, Susan Lee. *The Magic Circle: Writers and Ritual.* 1988. University of Washington, dissertation.

3

BLACK INK, WHITE BODIES
Gender, Race, and Writing Instruments

Desirée Henderson

What do the material objects that enable writing mean to writers? There are many different ways of approaching this question including researching corporate records regarding the production or marketing of writing instruments, exploring consumer practices regarding the purchase or use of writing instruments, and talking directly to writers about their preferences and passions—invaluable approaches which can be found in many of the essays in this volume (see Alexis; Krichevsky; Merrigan, this volume). An additional resource for investigating the material culture of writing takes the form of literary texts, including works of fiction in which the concrete objects, spaces, and behaviors associated with writing are transformed into powerful symbols of larger social concerns. Although the turn toward fictional sources may appear to be a turn away from materiality, in fact, stories document, imagine, and mediate the material nature of writing and, for this reason, a study of such stories compliments historical, anthropological, and autobiographical accounts of writing. Fictional texts may not necessarily tell us how writing instruments were "really" used but the portrayal of writing can give us insight into what writing instruments meant—what cultural messages, values, or biases were expressed by or were believed to be inherent within writing instruments. It is in this way that literary studies can assist in bridging the disciplinary gap between writing studies and material culture studies by showing the extent to which people's beliefs about and experiences with writing are shaped by the stories that are told about the objects that make writing possible.

    Literature is a particularly valuable resource for identifying the meaning of writing in historical periods for which records regarding the production or use of writing instruments are not easily accessible, or for which direct interviews with writers are not possible. One way in which we can attempt to learn what the material objects of writing meant to people in the past is to examine how writers represented writing in literature from the past. This essay takes such an approach to nineteenth-century America by examining how and why authors during this time prominently featured writing instruments within their narratives. I focus on a selection of stories that were written in response to a pivotal moment in American literary history when the rising popularity of women's writing sparked the idea that authorship might be a viable career path for educated white women.[1] This phenomenon created a corresponding cultural backlash as critics sought to squash women's authorial ambitions by condemning women writers as unfeminine, unmaternal, and immoral. The debate for and against women's authorship played out in part through the depiction of writing instruments, as some writers sought to show that pen, ink, and paper could be harmoniously integrated into women's domestic lives, while others argued that the possession and use of writing instruments were fundamentally incompatible with traditional gender roles.

Within this debate, ink and ink stains took on a particular symbolic power. Although a practical problem that confronted all writers of the era, ink stains were invoked in many nineteenth-century literary texts as an affliction specific to writing women. According to the logic of this iconography, ink spilled on hands, clothes, or domestic interiors served as evidence of women's inability to combine authorship with housekeeping responsibilities or with protocols of feminine self-presentation. Whereas women who successfully prevented or cleaned up after ink stains could lay claim to the qualities of cleanliness, purity, and discipline valued in women's deportment and character. As these contrasting sets of images indicate, the divergent views regarding whether women could combine authorship and femininity were frequently couched in racialized terms. In this essay, I introduce readers to a series of recurring scenes in nineteenth-century fiction portraying white women's skin stained with dark ink. My analysis of these scenes shows how the colors associated with writing and print materials (black ink, white paper) were called upon to echo and substantiate a Black/white racial binary. These color associations were then used in the debate over white women's authorship in order to stoke racist fears about Blackness and miscegenation. Ink and ink stains appear in these stories to evoke the threat of racial indeterminacy or racial mixing, sensationalizing the loss of status that faced white women who defied conventional gender roles. Ultimately the analogy established in these stories between writing instruments and skin color fostered racial division by turning the visual dimensions and color contrasts inherent to the material objects of writing into an argument for racial purity.

In this chapter, I begin by discussing the history of writing instruments in the nineteenth century and how they became associated with these gendered and racialized ideologies. I then analyze the representation of writing instruments in literature by and about white women writers in order to explore how white femininity was imagined as constituted through the use and misuse of writing ink. I conclude by addressing how African American writers take up these themes, particularly the satirical reappropriation of ink by the author Charles Chesnutt in his condemnation of the persistence of anti-Black racism in postslavery United States. As this portion of my argument demonstrates, while the debate over women's authorship was specific to educated white women—and presented as an issue with specific gender and racial stakes for white women—the color imagery central to these stories was not limited to literature by and about white women. African American authors also invoked the associations between ink, paper, and skin color in order to interrogate the racial binary and white supremacy. Within these counternarratives, the racialized tropes associated with writing instruments were reimagined for the purpose of overturning the legal and cultural prohibitions on African Americans' access to literacy.

THE MATERIAL POLITICS OF WHITE WOMEN'S WRITING

In the nineteenth century, writing required a significant number of tools. To borrow language from Konstantine Dierks's study of early American letters, writing "involved a complex array of one-time investments in writing equipment as well as regular purchases of certain stationery supplies" (178). The one-time investments might include a desk or writing table, inkstand, inkwell, pounce pot or blotter, and penknife. In addition, a writer would need a number of goods that would have to be constantly replenished: ink, paper, quills, nibs, pounce or blotting paper, pencil and eraser, and so forth. In a memorable scene in Susan Warner's sentimental novel, *The Wide, Wide World* (1850), the heroine shops for writing instruments at a fashionable stationer's shop and purchases over twenty items, depicted as the bare essentials for a young white woman venturing out on her own.[2] Possession of these objects was, however, only the start of the writing process, which required a host of repetitive acts before writing could occur. Ink was bottled in the United States as early as the 1820s and could be purchased in large jars from ink sellers or stationer's shops, from which it would be decanted into smaller inkpots for daily use. Many writers would, however, have elected to make their own ink from ink powder or from other ingredients; as we will see, instructions for making ink were common in magazines and newspapers of the time. Steel and gold nibs were developed in the 1830s, but some writers would still have cut and trimmed their own quills. Fountain pens or refillable reservoir pens became available in the 1850s, but the ink reservoir had to be filled manually and was notoriously leaky, requiring the use of pen wipes or other cleaning materials. While paper was increasingly sold in pre-cut sizes, appropriate for its different uses, some writers would have cut paper for their own needs and some paper still had to be treated with pounce (a fine powder) or sand before writing; the paper would then be treated with pounce again or blotted with a blotter or blotting paper after writing to assist in the drying and fixing of the ink on the page. As this cursory overview suggests, writing in the nineteenth century was an act that involved the tactile manipulation of multiple objects that served very specialized purposes. Access to these objects was determined by class status and could also become evidence of one's status, as possession of high quality or decorative writing instruments was a popular way of displaying wealth and education.[3]

The proliferation of writing instruments as consumer goods throughout the eighteenth and nineteenth century, as well as rising literacy rates among women, resulted in the development of specialized writing instruments for women. Dierks writes, "Whenever genteel versions of increasingly common household objects were introduced to the consumer market, whether pocketbooks or writing desks, gender distinctions became salient" (95). Writing on the parallel phenomenon in France, Dena Goodman states that the "invention, promotion, and development" of female writing instruments was a "market response to the participation of the new and expanding group of literate women" (161). Writing desks display these gender differences in their size and function: they tended to be smaller than men's desks and many were designed to be portable or moveable. Nan Johnson identifies the "separate-desks motif" as a recurring "cultural trope" in letter-writing manuals of the time; men and women were shown employing two different kinds of desks—a flat-surface office desk for men, a slanted lap desk or parlor desk for women (84). The portability of the female writing desk was linked to the idea that women would complete their writing within the semipublic space of the parlor, rather than a discrete writing space.[4] Moreover, as Goodman writes, "The small writing desk was associated with ladies, not because it was used exclusively by them, but because it supported the kind of writing they were encouraged and expected to do" (229). The material form of women's desks was predicated upon gendered ideas about writing itself, mirroring the different value ascribed to men's and women's writing.

Women's writing instruments and their uneasy status within the home were popular subjects in nineteenth-century American fiction, particularly in stories about white women writers. Responding to the ongoing cultural debate about whether or not it was appropriate for women to pursue careers as published authors, these stories portray male scrutiny of a woman's writing instruments as a prelude to judgment regarding her compliance with gender norms. A story like Fanny Fern's "A Practical Bluestocking" (published in *Olive Branch* in 1852) exemplifies the overarching characteristics of these stories. In the story, the male narrator confidently predicts what he will find when he goes to visit a friend, recently wed to a renowned bluestocking: "a disorderly house, smoky puddings, and dirty-faced children," proof that any wife who "spends her time dabbling in ink" is incapable of maintaining a clean and organized home (122).[5] However, the narrator's expectations are quickly and humorously overturned. Left alone in the parlor, he observes that it is "neat and tasteful," making particular note of "a little light-stand or Chinese table [that] stood in the corner, with pen, ink, and papers scattered over it" (123). Rather than indicating the woman's neglect, the narrator's surveillance proves the opposite and, as the story progresses, additional achievements are presented for his inspection, including her cooking and her newborn. The product of her pen (her writing) remains off-stage, replaced by an examination of her tools of writing, domestic space, body, clothes, and deportment. In this story, Fern's rebuttal of the stereotypical image of the woman writer who shirks her familial responsibilities and, by extension, her feminine identity swings emphatically in the opposite direction by presenting a paragon of domestic virtues—the perfect wife, mother, housekeeper, and cook—who is also a successful published author. Her writing instruments fit seamlessly in the home; even their slight disorder serves only as evidence of a creative mind at work.

As Fern's story intimates, ink was one of the tools of writing that was open to scrutiny in fictional depictions of women's writing. Female authorship was frequently depicted as placing women in close physical proximity to ink; as was stated of one woman writer: "She breathes, lives, moves, and has her being in ink" (Elma 336). This blurring of material boundaries was expressed most concretely in the dreaded ink stain upon a woman's hand or finger. "Any stain for woman's pretty fingers but the stain of ink!" exclaimed an anonymous essayist in 1869 ("Clever" 44). Describing the stereotypical appearance of literary women, novelist and educator Caroline Kirkland wrote, "It is inky fingers—corrugated brow—unkempt locks—unrighteous stockings—towering talk—distain of dinner—aspirations after garments symbolical of authority" (92). While the ink-stained finger tops Kirkland's list, it is linked with shoddy personal appearance, poor social skills, and an aspiration for masculine gender roles in an ever-widening series of negative associations. Nineteenth-century women writers were well aware of the meaning attached to the ink stain and frequently expressed their fear that ink on their persons would expose them to public censure or ridicule. More than one story depicts a woman scrubbing away the ink on her hands or presenting her ink-free hands for inspection. For example, a fictional female character who has given up writing to return her attention to her domestic duties describes herself as "wash[ing] the ink-spot [on my finger] away with a lemon (it was a very deep stain)" (Wallace 234). The anxieties surrounding the ink-stained female body carried over into the space of the home, through the specter of the dirty house, wherein furniture, rugs, or clothes might have become soiled by their proximity to writing instruments or neglected by the mistress of the home who is too busy writing to fulfill her domestic duties.[6]

Concerns about ink stains were not limited to the fictional realm but also appear within nineteenth-century advice literature directed toward female homemakers. Technological developments over the course of the century, including the shift from the use of quill pens to steel nib pens and eventually to fountain or reservoir pens, meant that writers were often learning to use new tools of writing or working with unreliable writing instruments in the early stages of development—increasing the likelihood of leaks, blots, or stains. While faulty pens meant that many writers contended with the annoyance of ink stains, the proper management of ink was associated with other housekeeping duties as the particular responsibility of women. For example, although ink was available in bottled form, women's periodicals like *Godey's Lady's Book* and *Harper's Bazaar* are replete with instructions for concocting or mixing ink, including multi-step "recipes" that underscore the relationship between ink making and cooking.[7] Because ink was understood to be the potential source of mess, women's periodicals also presented a host of strategies for containing ink and cleaning up after its use or misuse. Instructions for ink stain removal were a common feature within domestic advice columns, including stains on skin, clothes, carpets, and furniture.[8] "Take courage, poor child," exhorted Mrs. Henry Ward Beecher, before providing a series of "short and well-tried directions" for cleaning ink stains, which promised to "enable [the young housekeeper] to keep her pretty furniture and fondly prized treasures fresh and attractive" (218). At the same time, women's periodicals provided lavishly illustrated instructions for projects that transformed writing instruments into objects of design and decoration. This impulse towards ornamentation corresponds to the elaborate aesthetic of the Victorian age, in which few interior surfaces were left untouched by paint, embroidery, or other embellishment. The paraphernalia associated with the use and storage of ink are identified as inviting additional adornment, such as a penwipe in the shape of a leaf with gold beaded trim or a writing stand adorned with a border of beads and silk.[9] Publications like these indicate how making, storing, decorating, and cleaning up after ink could become a means of managing women's access to writing instruments, perhaps designed to replace the act of writing itself. Together, these short stories and periodical advice literature sought to address the concern that writing would distract women from their domestic responsibilities by imagining ways in which the acts and objects of writing could be feminized and therefore rendered ordinary, harmless, and even decorative elements within the home.

WRITING IN BLACK AND WHITE

Race enters into this constellation of practices, images, and fictions in a number of ways and with important consequences for the construction of an idealized white femininity. The racialization of writing instruments originates in a simplistic association between the color of ink and paper and skin color. Both print and manuscript texts rely upon the contrast between dark ink and lighter-colored background for legibility, but this functional color system has often been conflated with and seen to reinforce racial binaries. The common idiomatic phrases "black as ink" and "white as a sheet" were coined as early as the sixteenth century, evidence of the longevity of the conflation of skin color and writing instruments.[10] But these associations gain particular potency in the nineteenth century; as literary critic Jonathan Senchyne argues, "In the antebellum period where black ink and white paper were racially coded, the black/white dualism underwriting print legibility further naturalized black/white racial dualism" (143). It is important to note that ink was not always black in the nineteenth century; stationers offered an array of ink colors including green, violet, and pink, and the hand mixing of ink meant that the darkness or lightness of ink was highly variable. Likewise, Senchyne shows that the whiteness of paper could range widely across the color spectrum (146). Despite these realities, black ink and white paper were often represented as distinct and reliably differentiated objects. Nineteenth-century advertisements for writing instruments and other consumer goods reinforced these color distinctions, particularly those that featured Black bodies as evidence of color durability, bearing slogans like "Remains black" or "De Color won't come off by wettin."[11] The use of black ink to write or print was similarly invested with a sense of permanence; the phrase "get it in black and white" is still used to convey legitimacy and legal authority. Yet, at the same time, the close proximity of black and white in written and print texts raised the prospect of intermingling and interdependence, the blurring of the racial binary enacted by ink seeping into and becoming an indelible component of the fibers of a sheet of paper.

The possibility that ink would mark not the sheet of paper but the hand of the writer appears in nineteenth-century fiction in order to reference or provoke specific anxieties around white womanhood. The image of ink-stained skin draws upon an influential religious and moral vocabulary: to be stained is to be sinful, unpure, unvirginal, and so forth. It likewise draws upon nineteenth-century ideas about blood and racial purity; the "one drop" rule infamously characterized Black heritage as a taint or stain of the blood (Salvant 49). Reasserting the whiteness of paper and corollary whiteness of the author's hand depends upon the presence of Blackness, both as figure and as embodied fact. As Toni Morrison has powerfully written, the Africanist other is "used to limn out and enforce the invention and implications of whiteness"; in particular "it is made possible to explore and penetrate one's own body in the guise of the sexuality, vulnerability, and anarchy of the other—and to control projections of anarchy with the disciplinary apparatus of punishment and largess" (52, 53).[12]

Short stories about white women's authorship that employ the image of ink-stained skin are important documents for explaining how writing instruments could be invested with racial significance and symbolism. For example, M. T. Caldor's story "The Authoress's Wife" (published in *Ballou's* in 1860) registers concerns about how women's writing introduces anarchy into domestic spaces and family relations through emblematic references to whiteness, Blackness, and their intermixture.[13] The story focuses on Fredric, a man who possesses a "horror of literary women" (515). When he discovers his new wife, Helen, composing a poem, his reaction is swift and dogmatic: he affirms as fact that women's writing is always "at the expense of domestic happiness. No good wife can be an authoress" (516). When Fredric imagines a life with an authoress for a wife, he pictures "the house littered from one end to the other, with scraps of paper, rolls of manuscript, and everything, from the table-linen to Helen's rosy fingers, bespattered with stains of ink" (516) and demands that she immediately give up writing.

Helen promises she will, telling Fredric, "Rest assured you shall never be disturbed by any further literary attempts by your wife," but secretly she vows to change his mind (516). While Frederic believes she is complying with his will, she reveals her continued writing to a confidante by displaying her "dainty fore-finger, on whose fairness rested a tiny black stain." The ink stain is the "guilty proof" of her disobedience, which Helen compares to Mrs. Bluebeard's "fatal key," though her words display more pride than shame. Helen's reasons for feeling proud of her accomplishments are revealed in the end, as two other life-changing events coincide: Fredric's financial ruin and the birth of their first child. From her bed after the difficult delivery, Helen interrogates Fredric about whether she has ever failed to fulfill her wifely duties and, when the answer is no, reveals that she has written and published a successful book. She presents Fredric the account books for her profits, declaring, "I have dabbled with pen and ink . . . [but] it has not been . . . at the expense of home comfort or affection" (519). Caldor uses repeated references to whiteness in the final paragraph of the story to affirm Helen's purity and nobility, including the paleness of her skin and the white color of the bedclothes. The only contrasting image in the scene is the "dark, downy little head" of the newborn beside her; indeed, Helen's two products—the printed book and the dark-haired baby—are symbolically linked as if the ink stain had been externalized through her procreative acts (517). Yet, precisely at the moment of Helen's triumph, when she succeeds in teaching her husband a lesson about women's intellectual capacity, she dies. This surprising climax puts a question mark to the story's purported proauthorship message by appearing to suggest that the effort of creating both book and baby were too much for Helen. The murky moral leaves the reader to wonder whether Fredric's injunctions against the writing wife were justified and whether the ink stain was, indeed, a fundamental corruption of Helen's mind and body. Moreover, the dark-haired baby hints at racial mixing, conflating writing and miscegenation in a subtle but meaningful way; did Helen have nonwhite ancestry or a nonwhite lover? The question hovers, unanswered, on the margins of the story but leaves open the possibility that Helen's "darkness" was either the cause or consequence of her nonnormative acts of authorship.

Another short story from this time period, Auber Forestier's "In Waters of a Literary Hue" (published in *Godey's* in 1873), takes the ink stain theme to an extreme, turning the symbolic drop into a whole body ordeal.[14] This story makes the use and misuse of ink its centerpiece, providing one of the longest and most explicit explorations of the gendering and racialization of writing instruments. The story opens by informing us that the main character, Alma Winters, is "infected with the scribbling mania" but "she is fully determined that it shall not wholly swallow up [her] purely feminine characteristics" (512). That authorship and femininity are competing attributes is an idea that is seconded by Alma's fiancé, Charlie, who fears that "his darling may grow too 'blue' some day" (512). The emblem of blueness references bluestockings but is also linked to the ink that Alma uses in her writing; Alma greets Charlie by providing her finger for his inspection and is gratified when he can find no ink stain. As this moment demonstrates, Alma's efforts to moderate her authorial ambitions are materialized through her body and through her writing instruments. She has recently relocated her writing instruments to a new room, with a renewed dedication to keeping it clean and organized. Alma specifically identifies ink as a substance that threatens this newfound order and, as a result, takes incredible care with it: "Ink shall flow abundantly from the pen, but no traces of it shall otherwise appear. Upon this Alma is determined" (512). Yet, despite her resolutions, the chaos threatened by Alma's writing is already in evidence through her wastepaper basket, which overflows with discarded drafts. Like the dreaded ink stain, the overflow of the wastepaper basket indicates the ways in which Alma's writing threatens through uncontrolled excess.

These tensions come to a head one evening after Alma has spent the day writing. Forestier states that Alma "was in haste to finish a story for a prominent magazine" and that she remained preoccupied by the fictional world she had created (513). As Alma and her future sister-in-law, Sallie, dress for a party in white muslin dresses, Sallie notes Alma's paleness (implicitly caused by the strain of her authorial labor) and recommends that she bathe her face in cologne. However, Alma's distracted state causes her to take up not a bottle of cologne but a bottle of ink, which she vigorously rubs all over her face and neck. At this moment, the ink-stained finger is replaced by the exaggerated spectacle of Alma doused in ink.

Alma's white face covered by black ink simultaneously materializes sexual and racial fears in order to convey the potential dangers of women's writing. Alma's association with whiteness is affirmed through the paleness of her skin, the color of her dress, and her last name, Winters; even her first name, which translates as "soul" or "spirit," conveys clarity and purity. On the one hand, these tropes serve as standard references to innocence and virtue; to be stained with ink thus indicates that Alma's virginal purity has been sullied through her use of writing instruments.

On the other, Alma's correlation with whiteness maximizes the impact of the scene through the provocative image of white skin transformed into black. The ink is explicitly identified as black in color; Alma discovers her mistake by realizing that the ink-soaked sponge she had been applying to her face is "as black as her shoe" (513). Alma is also described as wearing a "sable-striped mask," a phrase that correlates Blackness with both animality and deceptiveness (514). Through such layered imagery the story makes a shift from blueness, which is the explicitly identified anxiety of the text, to Blackness, which emerges as a parallel threat. As Jennifer Putzi attests, bodies that are already marked as other because nonwhite or female are frequently reinscribed in their subjugated positions through the addition of exterior marks, including tattoos, scars, and ink stains.[15] In this way, the spectacle of Alma's blackened skin taps into white fears about the mutability of racial identity in order to reinforce the story's critical portrayal of female authorship.

These extreme implications remain, however, the subtext of the story. On the surface, Alma's dowsing is represented as a source of humor. Sallie is the first to realize Alma's mistake and she "convulsed with laughter," while Alma "joined in her friend's merriment and laughed until the tears rained down her cheeks" (513). Their uproarious reactions affirm the harmlessness of Alma's experience, but the narrative waits on Charlie's response as the ultimate arbiter of meaning. Forewarned about Charlie's fears regarding Alma's potential corruption by the "fatal stain" of ink, the reader may anticipate his horror or rejection. Instead, he responds with an even more dramatic expression of humor: "he made the walls ring with his peals of unrestrained merriment" (514). The narrative approaches a condemnation of female authorship in the image of Alma's ink-stained face but retreats from this stance through the deployment of humor. The oscillation between the two tones of the story—anxiety about Alma's altered state, hilarity over her silly accident—becomes legible when read within the context of the cultural tradition the scene appears to reference: blackface minstrelsy. Alma's inked face resembles the blackened face of the minstrelsy performer, which achieved its entertainment value from the collapse of seeming opposites. As Eric Lott has written of the forms of "racist pleasure" cultivated by minstrelsy, "the white subject could transform fantasies of racial assault and subversion into riotous pleasure, turn insurrection and intermixture into harmless fun" (147).[16] In a similar way, the laughter generated by Alma's black face displays the transgressive pleasure derived from witnessing a genteel white woman take on a non-normative and prohibited identity. On its surface, of course, the violation of norms hinges on the hilarious/terrifying image of Blackness, but my reading suggests that this invocation of race is primarily intended to police Alma's violation of approved roles in her pursuit of authorship.

Against such destabilizing forces, the story insists that Alma's whiteness is quickly reinstated. Forestier writes that Alma "restored [her] face to its original white loveliness" with water and that "a powerful acid had removed the few stains from the purity of her robe" (514). Once cleaned, Alma is presented to Charlie, who inspects, approves, and reclaims her. Yet, the experience provokes Alma to articulate to Charlie her struggle to guard against the "literary eccentricities" that they both associate with female authorship. Alma's tearful confession leads to Charlie's affirmation that "he had no fear of her allowing any interest, however absorbing, to interfere with the most trivial duty of everyday life" (514). This exchange reveals the stakes behind the humorous portrayal of ink. For Alma, authorship is not easily reconciled with feminine norms and her efforts to do so are largely played out in the material realm through her use and care of her writing instruments. Charlie's statement of encouragement is intended to mark him as the epitome of male love and commitment, but simultaneously manages to minimize both Alma's writing and her domestic responsibilities. He states that her writing will not interfere with her "trivial dut[ies]"—by implication, all of her duties are trivial. Authorship may have profound effects upon the female wielder of the pen, but it does not rise to a sufficient level of importance to upset patriarchal authority, which maintains its power in part through a lighthearted denigration of all things feminine and nonwhite. In the end, both Caldor's and Forestier's stories promote the moral that authorship may be reconcilable with femininity but only if femininity's correlation to whiteness and subservience to patriarchy remain intact.

WRITING, RACE, AND RIGHTS

Although this chapter focuses centrally on stories written by and about white women writers, it is worthwhile to explore how the visual and symbolic associations between writing instruments and race were also taken up in works of African American literature. Nineteenth- and early-twentieth-century African American authors were concerned with a different set of writing-related issues than those addressed above.

Authorship was an appealing professional path for many African Americans of the period—and a successful one for writers such as William Wells Brown and Frances Watkins Harper—but the question of the status of authorship as a viable profession that preoccupied white women writers was generally eclipsed in African American literature by other issues. These include the prohibitions on reading and writing under slavery, the extension of those prohibitions through Jim Crow and segregationist laws in the antebellum period, and the many other forms of violence employed to literally and figuratively preserve the idea that literacy was the unique domain of white Americans. Yet, African American writers often represented such concerns through the same material objects of writing, including pen, ink, and paper, and through the colors or ideas about color associated with these objects. In the subsequent pages, I bracket the theme of gender that was prominent in my previous analysis in order to highlight some instances in which African American authors employed ink and ink stains to imaginatively overcome or to outright condemn the racist ideologies that transformed writing instruments into emblems of white supremacy.

Numerous slave narratives portray the struggle of enslaved or recently freed people to gain access to the tools of reading and writing as a prerequisite to laying claim to the immaterial benefits of literacy, a theme perhaps most famously detailed in Frederick Douglass's *Narrative of the Life* (1845), in which he describes how he cobbled together impromptu writing instruments, stating "my copy-book was the board fence, brick wall, and pavement; my pen and ink was a lump of chalk" (35).[17] While Douglass emphasizes possession and use of writing instruments irrespective of their color, other slave narratives invoke the binary color imagery that I described above. For instance, the 1888 biography of a formerly enslaved man named Bartley Townsley includes a lengthy "as told to" literacy narrative that unsettles even as it references the racialized associations of writing instruments. Townsley's account presents his story of learning to read and write despite the dangers he faced as an enslaved person in the form of a fantastical allegory.

> One night, when he had gone to bed and had fallen asleep, he dreamed that he was in a white room, and its walls were the whitest he ever saw. He dreamed that some one came in and wrote the alphabet on the wall in large printed letters, and began to teach him every letter, and when he awoke he had learned every letter. . . . One night very late, when he had come from his coal-kiln, he gathered his books as usual and began to try to spell but it was not long before he came to a word that he could not pronounce. . . . [R]emembering an old man who as on the farm . . . who could read a little, he thought he would go and ask him what the word spelt. The word was i-n-k . . . [He called to the man:] Uncle Jesse!. . . . I want to know what i-n-k spells! The old man hallooed out, ink! He then returned to his cabin saying ink, ink, ink. After that night he never had

any more trouble with ink. In 1852 he began to learn how to write well enough to write his own passes [to steal away]. (qtd. in Conquergood 153)

In his analysis of this narrative, Dwight Conquergood argues that the whiteness of the dream room grants Townsley only the bare semblance of literacy; it is only when he hears the letters "i-n-k" translated by Uncle Jesse's Black voice that Townsley is truly able to claim ownership over the tools of writing and, therefore, over himself (152). For Conquergood, what is significant is the role of voice and orality in this transformative moment but equally significant is the way in which Townsley's story adapts the color analogies between writing instruments and racial identity we've seen in previous stories. While literacy is symbolically associated with whiteness, Townsley imagines the white room as a space of learning and inclusion rather than prohibition and scarcity. While ink is associated with darkness, an association reinforced by Townsley's nighttime journey in search of enlightenment, ink is not something to be avoided, controlled, or contained but instead something to be sought out and used. The concluding phrase "he never had any more trouble with ink" (153) echoes the material or somatic "trouble" that ink posed to white female characters in the stories discussed above. But obviously for Townsley the trouble with ink is not one of body management, cleanliness, or domestic order; the trouble that he confronts and overcomes is the structural denial of education and literacy under the institution of slavery. In Townsley's story, the possession of an understanding of the word "ink" makes possible his implementation of pen, ink, and paper to write the pass that secures his freedom, exemplifying the role of writing instruments within many early works of African American literature as icons of individual liberation.

Autobiographical narratives like Douglass's and Townsley's place writing instruments in Black hands in order to valorize literacy as a form of empowerment. Postbellum authors complicate these themes by documenting the persistence of white racism against free and literate Blacks in the Reconstruction Era. For example, in Charles Chesnutt's novel, *The Marrow of Tradition* (1901), writing instruments, literacy, and print culture offer no protection from legalized discrimination and racially motived mob violence. The novel recounts the events that preceded the race riots that occurred in Wilmington, North Carolina, in 1898, centering on the fictional Carteret family—a white family headed by Major Carteret, the editor of a local newspaper and a vocal white supremacist. In the novel a white woman is murdered, and her death foments anti-Black violence, almost resulting in the lynching of the Black man who is suspected in her death. The actual murderer is a white man who wore blackface when he committed the murder. Although the lynching is initially prevented, the novel concludes with the race riot, which unleashes death and violence across the community.

The Marrow of Tradition is a long and densely plotted novel through which Chesnutt explores many aspects of postbellum American culture. My interest is in one scene in which Chesnutt revisits the symbolic associations between writing instruments and racial identity. The scene portrays a meeting between Major Carteret and other white civic leaders regarding how to use the popular press to drive out the Black inhabitants of the city. The meeting is interrupted by the appearance of Carteret's Black servant, Jerry Letlow, and Carteret's bewildered observation that Jerry's face is "splotched with brown and yellow patches" (673). Carteret discovers that Jerry has been inspired by advertisements in the local Black-owned newspaper to try a treatment that promised "dark skins lightened two shades; mulattoes turned perfectly white." Carteret is offended by this attempt to disrupt what he sees as the immutable differences between Black and white people. Jerry tries to soothe Carteret's ire by reblackening his skin with printer's ink but "the retouching left the spots as much too dark as they had been formerly too light" (675). This exchange encapsulates Chesnutt's argument throughout the novel that the racial binary of Black and white is fluid and unreliable, a point he makes at length through his exploration of the uncertain social status of mixed race characters. It also reinforces the idea that racial identity is performative, not innate, a perspective that Chesnutt also demonstrates through the plot line about the white murderer who is mistaken for Black when he wears blackface—even causing the Black man he is imitating to wonder if he saw his own ghost. Yet by locating this exchange between Jerry and Carteret in a newspaper office and having Jerry reblacken his skin with printer's ink, Chesnutt extends his critique to print culture and literacy more generally. The white newspaper is an explicit tool for provoking anti-Black violence but Chesnutt's satire encompasses even the Black press, which reinforces colorism by peddling skin-lightening treatments, and its readers (including Jerry), who internalize these views. Jerry's susceptibility to this message shows that the ability to read is not synonymous with liberation from white supremacist ideology. And while Jerry is never shown writing, his act of blackening his skin with ink transforms this literary motif into a visual shorthand for the ways in which access to and employment of writing instruments does not inevitability lead to personal empowerment or social justice. Chesnutt takes up the imagery that associated black ink with Black racial identity and that generated such anxiety about white womanhood in the stories outlined above, but he does so in order to pose the question of whether ink, or the writing it symbolizes, can ever be delinked from its role in the disenfranchisement of Black people.

In this scene, Chesnutt speaks back to the literary motif of spilled or misused ink, which was so often designed to galvanize white fears about the instability of racial categories. As he reimagines it, black ink on Black skin proves the fallacy of the racial binary, even as it offers a bleak assessment of the role that writing plays in upholding that binary. Chesnutt recognizes that in postslavery United States, control of both the material use and metaphorical value of writing instruments—and print culture more generally—was designed to consolidate and preserve the ideology of white supremacy. While his critique is particularly vehement, Chesnutt is not alone in using the material tools and spaces of writing as literary devices for addressing the status of writing and authorship within African American communities. The fictional representation of writing instruments as a means to expose racial injustice remains common in twentieth- and twenty-first-century African American literature, evident in novels from Toni Morrison's *The Bluest Eye* (1970) to Jesmyn Ward's *Where the Line Bleeds* (2018). The ongoing battles by African Americans and other communities of color for equal rights, equal education, and access to public platforms mean that although writing instruments have evolved from pen and ink to keyboard and screen, they continue to be sites of contestation rather than positive symbols of autonomy.

CONCLUSION

In this chapter, I have shown that in the nineteenth century, white women writers and their critics were preoccupied with the question of whether or not professional authorship was compatible with traditional gender roles. This debate was represented in part through the tools of writing, as writing instruments appeared in their visual and material form to reference both the promise of female self-expression and the threats it was thought to present to conventional domesticity. Yet, this debate took place against the backdrop of a larger cultural and political debate regarding racial equity. The association between black/white color contrasts in print and written texts and the Black/white racial binary that structured the system of slavery and Black disenfranchisement informs a host of popular materials regarding white women's writing, including many that use the instability of the racial boundary to express ambivalence about female authorship. These stories use the specter of ink-stained skin to advance a version of white femininity that was considered compatible with heteropatriarchy. When African American writers take up similar imagery they do so for a variety of reasons—to lay claim to literacy as a mode of personal liberation and social advancement or to challenge the idea that reading and writing are skills sufficient to protect Black people from white supremacist violence. Ultimately, the persistent image of ink-stained skin in American fiction invites us to examine the role that writing instruments have played within the divisive practice of pitting white women against people of color in a competition for supposedly limited resources, as if access to and use of pen, ink, and paper were privileges to be fought over, instead of the means by which the myths of gender and race will be deconstructed.

That the humble ink pot and the fluid it contains have figured so memorably within American literary history reveals how much meaning is invested in the objects that facilitate the act of writing. Literary representations of writing instruments like pen and ink provide a point of entrance into this history of meaning, values, and beliefs. Stories about writing instruments flesh out our understanding of what writing meant to people in the past and give us new ways of perceiving what writing continues to mean today, especially to communities for whom the act of writing and the aspiration toward professional authorship remain contested. Although they exist only within the imaginations of writers and readers, these fictional objects of writing are invaluable resources for documenting the social and cultural impact of writing's material forms.

NOTES

1. The question of when authorship became a possible career path available to white women is one that continues to intrigue literary critics. Many cite Susanna Rowson as an eighteenth-century forerunner but most agree that it is in the mid-nineteenth century, and thanks to popular women-focused periodicals like *Godey's* and to the unprecedented best-selling status of novels like Harriet Beecher Stowe's *Uncle Tom's Cabin*, that white women writers achieved professional status. See Homestead and Williams.
2. The objects Ellen Montgomery purchases are: a writing desk, large and small letter paper, envelopes, note paper, an inkstand, ink-powder, lights, steel-point pens, quills, a pen knife, wax and seal, wafers, an ivory leaf-cutter, a paper-folder, a pounce-box, a ruler, a silver pencil and drawing pencils, an India-rubber eraser, and sheets of drawing paper (Warner 32–36).
3. For an overview of the history of writing instruments, see Finlay, Nickell, and Whalley. The materiality of the eighteenth-century writing process is particularly detailed in Goodman and Stabile.
4. For more on the parlor as a site of writing, particularly as it contrasted to the masculine study, see Grier and Shamir.

5. Fanny Fern was the pseudonym of Sarah Payson Willis, one of the most popular and successful women writers of the nineteenth century, well known for satirizing gender roles.
6. The bluestocking's filthy house as an object of male horror can be seen in Harland. For a humorous rebuttal see Cleary.
7. Some examples include: "Marking Ink" (1854), "Ink" (1861), and "Preparation of Black Ink" (1880).
8. See, for example, "Removing Stains" (1865) and "The Eradication of Stains" (1876). At least one contemporaneous work of fiction features techniques for removing ink stains from carpet as the plot climax; see Branch.
9. See "Leaf Penwiper" (1864) and "Embroidered Writing Stand" (1874).
10. The "sheet" in "white as a sheet" is commonly thought to originate as a reference to a bedsheet, but the multiple meanings of the word "sheet" make "sheet of paper" an equally viable candidate. A less common but relevant phrase is "white as the page." See Ammer.
11. These slogans appear on advertisements for John Bond's Crystal Palace Marking Ink and for J. &. P. Coats' Thread. The latter features the Topsy character from Stowe's *Uncle Tom's Cabin*; see "Come in Topsy." Other writing instrument advertisements that employ Black bodies include Carter's Inky Racer (For Removing Ink Spots) and Solidhed Thumb Tacks; all advertisements can be viewed through a Google Image search. Pilgrim also reproduces a 1916 advertisement featuring a Black baby drinking from a bottle of black ink.
12. I am necessarily abbreviating several complex issues here drawn from critical race theory, color history, and language history. In addition to the sources cited in the text, my claims are informed by Babb, Dyer, Heneghan, Hill, Pastoureau, and Watson.
13. M. T. Caldor published extensively in American literary magazines but I have been unable to locate additional information about her biography. The possessive apostrophe "s" in the title of this story appears to be a typo, because the authoress is the same character as the wife.
14. Auber Forestier was the pseudonym of Aubertine Woodward Moore, a prominent translator of Norwegian fiction.
15. "[W]hite women's textuality, or their ability to be marked . . . demonstrated a blurring of the cultural boundaries between race and gender" (Putzi 9).
16. Within the story, Forestier references not blackface but a German novel, Friedrich Spielhagen's *Through Night to Light* (published in English in 1870), comparing Alma to the story's main character, a high-strung poetess who inadvertently pours ink over her manuscript and dress. My analysis, however, emphasizes minstrelsy as the more salient literary parallel.
17. Douglass also conveys the ambivalent relationship he has with his own literacy when he writes, "My feet have been so cracked with the frost, that the pen with which I am writing might be laid in the gashes," using a pen as the measure of his deprivation (26).

WORKS CITED

Ammer, Christine. *Seeing Red or Tickled Pink: A Rainbow of Colorful Terms*. Plume, 1993.
Babb, Valerie. *Whiteness Visible: The Meaning of Whiteness in American Literature and Culture*. New York UP, 1998.
Beecher, Mrs. Henry Ward. "The Household: Simple Directions for the Inexperienced." *Christian Union*, 7 Mar. 1877, p. 218. American Periodical Series.

Boyd, Anne E., ed. *Wielding the Pen: Writings on Authorship by American Women of the Nineteenth Century.* Johns Hopkins UP, 2009.
Branch, Mary L. B. "The Purple Jar," *Christian Union*, 12 July 1876, p. 36. American Periodical Series.
Caldor, M. T. "The Authoress's Wife." *Ballou's Dollar Monthly Magazine*, June 1860, pp. 515–519. American Periodical Series.
Chesnutt, Charles. *The Marrow of Tradition. Three Classic African-American Novels*, edited by Henry Louis Gates. Vintage Classics, 1990.
Cleary, Kate M. "The New Man" (1895). *Wielding the Pen: Writings on Authorship by American Women of the Nineteenth Century*, edited by Anne E. Boyd, Johns Hopkins UP, 2009, pp. 403–404.
"Clever Women." *The Eclectic Magazine of Foreign Literature*, Jan. 1869, pp. 40–55. American Periodical Series.
"Come in Topsy" [caption]. J. &. P. Coats' Thread advertisement, c. 1900. *Uncle Tom's Cabin and American Culture*, edited by Stephen Railton, 1998–2012, http://utc.iath.virginia.edu/tomituds/toadsf.html.
Conquergood, Dwight. "Rethinking Elocution: The Trope of the Talking Book and Other Figures of Speech," *Opening Acts: Performance in/as Communication and Cultural Studies*, edited by Judith Hamera, Sage Publications, 2006, pp. 141–162.
Dierks, Konstantine. *In My Power: Letter Writing and Communications in Early America.* U of Pennsylvania P, 2009.
Douglass, Frederick. *Narrative of the Life*, edited by William L. Andrews and William S. McFeely, Norton, 1996.
Dyer, Richard. *White.* Routledge, 1997.
Elma. "A Woman's Book." *Godey's Lady's Book and Magazine*, Apr. 1862, pp. 336–341. American Periodical Series.
"Embroidered Writing Stand." *Harper's Bazaar*, 17 Oct. 1874, p. 668. American Periodical Series.
"The Eradication of Stains." *Harper's Bazaar*, 23 Dec. 1876, p. 823. American Periodical Series.
Fern, Fanny. "A Practical Blue-Stocking" (1852). *Wielding the Pen: Writings on Authorship by American Women of the Nineteenth Century*, edited by Anne E. Boyd, Johns Hopkins UP, 2009, pp. 122–124.
Finlay, Michael. *Western Writing Implements in the Age of the Quill Pen.* Plains, 1990.
Forestier, Auber. "In Waters of Literary Hue." *Godey's Lady's Book*, June 1873, pp. 512–514. American Periodical Series.
Goodman, Dena. *Becoming a Woman in the Age of Letters.* Cornell UP, 2009.
Grier, Katherine. *Culture and Comfort: Parlor Making and Middle-Class Identity, 1850–1930.* Smithsonian Institution Press, 1988.
Harland, Marion. "Bred in the Bone." *Godey's Lady's Book and Magazine*, Oct. 1872, pp. 309–316. American Periodical Series.
Heneghan, Bridget T. *Whitewashing America: Material Culture and Race in the Antebellum Imagination.* U of Mississippi P, 2003.
Hill, Lena. *Visualizing Blackness and the Creation of the African American Literary Tradition.* Cambridge UP, 2014.
Homestead, Melissa. *American Women Authors and Literary Property, 1822–1869.* Cambridge, 2005.
"Ink." *Friend's Review*, Nov. 1861, pp. 156–157. American Periodical Series.
Johnson, Nan. *Gender and Rhetorical Space in American Life, 1866–1910.* Southern Illinois UP, 2002.
Kirkland, Caroline. "Literary Women" (1850). *Wielding the Pen: Writings on Authorship by American Women of the Nineteenth Century*, edited by Anne E. Boyd, Johns Hopkins UP, 2009, pp. 91–97.

"Leaf Penwiper." *Godey's Lady's Book and Magazine*, Nov. 1864, p. 435. American Periodical Series.

Lott, Eric. *Love and Theft: Blackface Minstrelsy and the American Working Class*. Oxford UP, 1995.

"Marking Ink." *Godey's Lady's Book and Magazine*, Dec. 1854, pp. 564–565. American Periodical Series.

Morrison, Toni. *Playing in the Dark: Whiteness and the Literary Imagination*. Vintage, 1992.

Nickell, Joseph. *Pen, Ink, and Evidence: A Study of Writing Material for the Penman, Collector, and Document Detective*. Oak Knoll Press, 2000.

Pastoureau, Michel. *Black: The History of a Color*. Princeton UP, 2009.

Pilgrim, David. *Understanding Jim Crow: Using Racist Memorabilia to Teach Tolerance and Promote Social Justice*. PM Press, 2015.

"Preparation of Black Ink." *Harper's Bazaar*, 21 Feb. 1880, pp. 1–2. American Periodical Series.

Putzi, Jennifer. *Identifying Marks: Race, Gender, and the Marked Body in Nineteenth-Century America*. Georgia UP, 2006.

"Removing Stains." *Godey's Lady's Book and Magazine*, Mar. 1865, p. 276. American Periodical Series.

Salvant, Shawn. *Blood Work: Imagining Race in American Literature, 1890–1940*. Louisiana State P, 2015.

Shamir, Milette. *Inexpressible Privacy: The Interior Life of Antebellum American Literature*. U of Pennsylvania P, 2006.

Stabile, Susan. *Memory's Daughters: The Material Culture of Remembrance in Eighteenth-Century America*. Cornell UP, 2004.

Wallace, Susan Elston. "Another Weak-Minded Woman" (1867). *Wielding the Pen: Writings on Authorship by American Women of the Nineteenth Century*, edited by Anne E. Boyd, Johns Hopkins UP, 2009, pp. 231–238.

Warner, Susan. *The Wide, Wide World*. Feminist Press, 1987.

Watson, Veronica. *The Souls of White Folk: African American Writers Theorize Whiteness*. U of Mississippi P, 2015.

Whalley, Joyce Irene. *Writing Instruments and Accessories: From the Roman Stylus to the Typewriter*. Gale Research Co., 1975.

Williams, Susan S. *Reclaiming Authorship: Literary Women in America, 1850–1900*. U of Pennsylvania P, 2006.

4

INDEXICAL HEIRLOOMS IN IMMIGRANT LITERACY HISTORY NARRATIVES

Jenny Krichevsky

"You know, there was a Soviet habit in schools back then, that if some leader was removed, we had to go into the textbooks and cross them out, as if they fired him or something." Vera, a retired chemical engineer, recounted this memory during our interview as she sat across from me at the Pearl, a community center for Russian-speaking elder immigrants in the Boston area. She had been only a few years old during the Second World War, so her school years were spent in the postwar decade of the late 1940s and 1950s of the former Union of the Soviet Socialist Republics (USSR), a period replete in tensions between economic and territorial expansion, intermittent optimism, and centralized government control. Vera remembered that some of her postwar years in school were spent doctoring textbooks to fit the political rhetorical landscape of the day: "We would spend time crossing out the pictures, because they had already decided to take [the former leader] out. . . . [W]e glued it over, painted over it. No books were ever changed. Where was the money to change textbooks? They fought with everything they labeled 'anti-Soviet.'" The practice of having students scratch out and glue over government-issued textbooks is a historically documented phenomenon, and similar practices also extended to portraits and statues of leaders (Yurchak 37). Through the memory of the textbook in its material form, which was malleable but also discursively timeless, Vera communicates the complexity of the school literacy conditions that surrounded her. The particular materiality of the textbook can be juxtaposed with the materiality of other books that populated her schooling and homelife. Novels and volumes of poetry were less guarded by the school than the textbooks, which were protected for their scarcity and ideological discourse, and Vera reported often taking home the fiction and poetry and memorizing their contents to "keep them with [her]," and thus possessing them in the way the glued-over textbooks never could be.

Now, nearly eighty years later, Vera and other immigrants like her in my study pull on these objects to create literacy history narratives. These narratives emphasize what New Literacies Studies scholars have contended since the 1980s: literacy values and practices emerge out of particular historical and social conditions. However, the study of literacies that are spatially and temporally mobile has continued to prove methodologically and conceptually challenging (Lorimer Leonard, "Traveling," 14). In Vera's narrative, for instance, a textbook's power is inculcated in more than the discursive content of its pages. Rather, the materiality of the textbook in a literacy landscape like Vera's represents a way of relating to language and literacy. That is, the very thing-ness of amended textbooks—years of layered glue, ink, graphite, and paper—indicate not only changing Soviet figureheads but shifting policies that had tremendous impact on how people composed as well as related to knowledge production. Moreover, these textbooks stand out as significant memories in her literacy history, in her explications of how she understands all academic discourse objects, as well as her sense of purpose around reading and writing in school. Using Vera's narrative and the narratives of four other Russian-speaking immigrants to the United States, this chapter investigates the relationship between objects and writers, particularly writers who have experienced multiple transnational migrations and historical upheavals.

The data in this chapter is derived from a larger ethnographically informed study, which uses life history interviews conducted with seventeen participants in total, five of whom are members of three generations in one family. Specifically, my research questions centered on how immigrant families pass literacy practices across generations and national contexts. All the participants were recruited through snowball sampling within the Pearl. Demographically, fourteen of the seventeen participants are women. Further, most of the participants are ethnically Jewish and have varying degrees of cultural identification with this category. The interviews, with two exceptions, were conducted in Russian and translated into English before the first round of coding. The findings of this analysis were informed by a grounded theory approach (Charmaz), and after four rounds of substantive coding (Holton), the data pointed to practices of intergenerational literacy-passing as a form of adaptation and survival. The narratives featured highlight the significant ways in which the material presence or absence of objects shapes their literacy, but it is important to note that these heirlooms appear in nearly all the interview data in this study.

I refer to the objects explored here as *discursive heirlooms*: this term creates a useful theoretical lens that bridges the participants' literacy practices, which emerge from their multiple discursive contexts and the passable materiality of the objects themselves. I focus on three main types of discursive heirlooms that had repeatedly come up in my qualitative analysis: *heirlooms of cultural literacy values*, such as beloved books of literature and the bookcases that hold them; *heirlooms of familial endurance*, such as an inherited encyclopedia set and a piano; and *heirlooms of national belonging and alienation*, such as lost passports, books, and military medals. I show how literacy heirlooms (1) *index* the conditions of elders' literacy and language development, and the circumstances they have had to adapt to; and (2) *impact* how the elders access their literacy repertoires.[1]

I chose to describe these objects as heirlooms, rather than possessions as consumer culture theory researchers do, or as "cultural artefacts" as Lesley Bartlett does (3), because "heirlooms" underscore how the objects' familiality and passability function in their literacy narratives, in addition to the identity formation that they retain. Objects are frequently, according to consumer research scholars Epp and Price, "active, or mobilized as part of a network and nested in a set of practices that may be intentional or embedded in the habitus of everyday life" (823). Further, these objects, which act as important identity nodes within families, persist across time and space, as research in heirlooms has shown (823). The ways in which elders indicate "attachment" (Csikszentmihaly and Rochberg-Halton; Belk) to, possession, and "disposition" (Curasi et al; Lastovicka and Fernandez) of these objects can tell literacy scholars a great deal about how objects function in not only identity work and ineffable or affective ways but also within material and observable literacy practices. I also rely on the way in which Curasi and coauthors have conceptualized the indexing properties of belongings that "provide a physical (evidentiary) association with a time, place, or person" (609–10).

Moreover, I wish to invoke traditionally Marxist meanings around position and disposition, which indicate the processes by which subjects lose access to life, land, labor, or resources through endemic conditions of inequality. While this use is related to disposition as the capitalist condition of *disposability*, as often explored in material culture studies literature (Lucas), the participants' Communist context adds important value to the notions of possession and loss of possession. In consumer research, the decommodification of a replicable and often mass-produced object—the phenomenon of singularization—has been tied to significant identity work in both families' and individuals' lives (Kopytoff). Processes of singularization, as Epp and Price argue, depend on the physicality of the object in its durability, how long a person has related to it, and "the overarching value system" of the group that the object is embedded in (823). In this volume, for instance, Emilie Merrigan describes the singularization of early twentieth-century baby books, arguing that women were able to claim and reclaim particular identities around motherhood by interacting with, as well as eschewing, the baby books they owned. Singularization, as Merrigan describes, can open possibilities for subverting oppressive or dominant frameworks that individuals may have to navigate.

However, given that the research around singularization has been focused on decommodification of objects through personalization in capitalist contexts, it is also necessary to ask how this phenomenon may function for immigrants from the Soviet Union, wherein commodified objects had wholly different histories and trajectories within their non-capitalist contexts. Despite living in the USSR, characterized by sociologists Ekaterina Gerasimova and Sof'ia Chuikina as a "repair society," participants in my study were still dispossessed of particular objects, which were significant both to their identity formation (Bartlett) and the development of their literacy repertoires. Sociologist Ol'ga Gurova's study of the life span of underwear in the USSR shows how longevity and use value of objects shifts significantly in a different sociocultural context and economic structure. Objects singularized through processes of bespoke refitting necessitated the possessor of the object to develop craftsmanship skills like sewing, building, and designing. For instance, a "real woman" in Soviet society was meant to know how to read and use a design pattern as well as sew or refashion any item of clothing. While this articulation around a "handiwork" literacy may seem solely a representation of internalized patriarchal values, Gurova argues that, more than anything, it was an adaptation to "shortages and the idiosyncrasies of the material environment in Soviet society" (50). Further, Gurova shows that keeping items and handing them down was a widespread practice in the USSR, giving everyday objects like a bookcase, and even the memory of a bookcase as we will see below, the status of heirlooms. I wish to highlight this distinctly Soviet process of relating to material objects because it plays significantly into the ways in which objects become indexical for participants in my study. Curasi and coauthors make a particular point of the "corporeal" aspect of indexicality, which enforces the argument that objects are more than just reminders or metaphorical references to literacy events or memories, but in fact materially impact the way people practice literacy. That is, whether objects were to be created from scratch or refitted, and whether the participants in the study have retained physical possession of these objects, the material manipulation of objects indexes the significance the objects have made in the participants' literacy development.

Additionally, literacy studies researchers have explored the ways in which high-profile objects like migration bureaucracy documents facilitate access to powerful institutions like education and citizenship (Wan; Vieira; Lagman). More literacy research has recently used letter-writing as a lens for exploring mobile literacy in migrants' writing (Lorimer Leonard, "Correspondence"). Literacy scholarship that draws on material culture studies in particular has extended these ideas around textual objects to give attention to the connection between a *possession* of and *attachment* to a particular object, textual or not, and the writing practices that emerge. For instance, Cydney Alexis's examination of the Moleskine notebook posits that beyond performing an ineffable kind of identity for writers, wherein through its use they gain only symbolic access to an "exoticized literary and artistic heritage," this object actually acts as a "facilitating artifact," deeply impacting the writers' composition process (34). Similarly, Jamie White-Farnham has examined commonplace household writing texts like recipes and grocery lists to trace how these "rhetorical heirlooms" carry "'intellectual inheritance' generally and writing practices in particular" within families (208). To that end, looking at a wide spectrum of significant objects that live in writers' literacy landscapes, and subsequent literacy narratives, can tell literacy scholars a great deal about identity work in the communicative repertoires of writers across their lifetimes (Mehta and Belk; Alexis). This spectrum could include traditional textual objects, like letters and books, or writing technologies themselves, but also ought to extend to more "evocative" and "symbolic" objects, like a table or a picture (Turkle), or as this chapter will show, a handmade bookcase or a piano.

HEIRLOOMS OF CULTURAL LITERACY VALUES

For the majority of the participants in my study, the value of reading, and more so, the condition of being "literate," held inherent, obvious value. To possess certain objects, and pass them on through various methods, to younger generations, was very important. This value was expressed by participants who were members of the Soviet "intelligentsia" class—white collar professionals like doctors, teachers, and engineers—as well as those who would be classed as trades people.[2]

Being "cultured" was strongly tied to literacy—how comfortable one was with reading and writing—but even more concretely to one's facility with Russian literature (Rivkin-Fish). Home libraries and books in general, as many of the elders described, were discursive heirlooms of high value in their material forms, since they represented a connection to a broader "culturedness." Moreover, the availability of material book copies was often variable, not only due to scarcity—the scarcity of raw materials for printing books, as well as slow production bureaucracy—but also to the year-to-year variability in what the government saw as appropriate for publication. Thus, specific books in home libraries became particularly valuable, sometimes priceless, because of their possible irreproducibility. Vera, with whom we began this chapter, had a "sacred relationship" with the books in her collection (Alexis 43), and this sanctity translated to the ways she writes, reads, and passes what she reads not only to her family but to her community at the Pearl senior center.

Vera was certainly one of the most conversationally effusive participants in this study, and in the course of our interview, she told me not only about her literacy experiences but her observations on the American education system, Abraham Lincoln, anti-Semitism, and Russian literature, to name only a few things. She characterized herself as widely read and endlessly curious. Despite being a chemical engineer her whole career in the Soviet Union, she described being interested in everything that "there is left to know." When she moved to the United States and started to attend the senior community center, she would give afternoon lectures on American history, literary theory, and philosophy, sometimes even reading from her favorite Russian books. In fact, Vera attributed much of what motivates her to read and share knowledge with the Pearl community now to what she called her "literary" birthplace. She was born in the late 1930s in Oryol, a city about two hundred miles south of Moscow, known for being the hometown of famous Russian poets and writers like Mikhail Bakhtin, Ivan Turgenev, Sergei Yesenin, and Ivan Bunin.

What Vera felt was most important for her children was to have a similar relationship to books and writing. "A bookstore was opened in Harvard [Square], far away from us," she recounted. In this bookstore, her son had found a book by Aleksandr Kuprin, a pre-Revolutionary Russian novelist, that they used to own in Russia. "He calls me and says: 'This is *our* Kuprin in the same blue binding, seven whole volumes worth!' So I say: 'Yes, just buy it and go.'" This collection of novels, the exact edition as the old copy Vera's family had before they left the Soviet Union, jumped out at her son, so much so that he called her to let her know that this collection, *their* collection, was right there in a

Russian bookstore in Cambridge, Massachusetts, even though the specific physical copy had, of course, been left continents away. "We all had such libraries," Vera remembered proudly. "It was just so expensive to ship books out, it was impossible." Vera's children had all bought a great deal of Russian literature since their immigration and "invested a lot" in their books, which was, according to Vera, all from *her* "efforts." These efforts were tied not only to the physical connection to the books that surrounded them before immigration but also to the affective connection to the literature that meant so much to her: "How could I live in a way that they did not know at all who Kuprin was, and that such a great literature exists?" The physical book her son found in Cambridge, as well as the other heirloom facsimiles in her children's homes, simultaneously represent and shape the literacy values Vera has worked to foster in her family through reading and writing in Russian. Vera's attachment to these books underscores that "indexical or iconic associations persist" even when the objects themselves are substituted (Epp and Price 823). It was the presence of the Kuprin books in Vera's home that reinstated her and her children's access to this desired literacy of culturedness.

However, it is not only the book object itself that indexes this kind of literacy: an abundant home library entails the possession of sufficient shelf space. The procurement of shelves and bookcases in the Soviet Union, as multiple participants in my study reported, was sometimes as tricky as the books themselves. Bookshelves in the literacy history narrative of Elina, a retired design engineer born in 1926, highlight even more strongly both how discursive heirlooms represented the complicated political context she learned to read and write within and how these heirlooms inflected her literacy practice. To start, bookcases may seem like a commonplace object to a reader unaware of the "idiosyncrasies of Soviet shopping" (Gerasimova and Chuikina 66); however, the ability of most citizens to walk into, say, a furniture store, and buy a needful item like a bookcase at any given moment was complicated due to the endemic shortages of material goods (Boym; Ledeneva; Shleifer and Vishny). As Gurova deftly explains, the economy of the Soviet Union was constituted by a deep division between "the field occupied by the producers of items and that occupied by the consumers of items," and this rift manifested in a "divergence between the quantity and quality of goods produced and the needs, preferences, and tastes of Soviet people . . . [keeping] the quantity of things in Soviet culture lower than it needed to be, [and] making objects rare and insufficiently accessible" (49). Thus, when one was unable to buy a much-needed object, or barter something for it from a person in their social network, an individual had to make the object.

When Elina's father bought her and her sister books—"we had few toys but many, many more books"—she remembered proudly how he had to make more bookcases "with his own hands" to store them all. As a worker at a tool factory in St. Petersburg, he was much better socially connected than her mother's family, because he worked with key revolutionary figures like Nadezhda Krupskaya (Lenin's wife) in the very nascent years of the USSR. Whereas before 1917, Elina's father's proletariat background made it more difficult for him and his family to survive and go to school, in the context of the new government, his lack of intelligentsia connections was a badge of honor that strengthened his publicly perceived commitment to workers' rights and Marxist ideology, garnering him not only social and economic capital but enabling him to survive at a time when class origin-based population purging was happening all around the USSR (Dunstan xv). While the Communist Revolution had temporarily interrupted his formal education, he used his new connections to get back into school and spent much of Elina's childhood making up his education through supplemental professional school. Elina remembered both parents attending a professional academy where she and her sister spent much time on the grounds. Reading was what Deborah Brandt calls a "salutary" given in Elina's family: "Dad read a lot. Actually, we would even work on school stuff together: I did my homework while he did his [night school] assignments." She describes herself as being one of those "annoying honors students" who would read the textbooks ahead of time, before the school year even started. Sitting around the same big table, she would read through all the materials while her father read his own homework from night school and they would ask each other questions.

Thus, Elina enmeshed smoothly the ubiquity of books in her home and the values assigned to reading, alongside the casual mention of her father building a bookcase for all their books. This enmeshing is telling because it indicates the equivalency Elina draws between literacy and carpentry as mechanisms of adaptation to an environment of ever-scarce and unpredictable resources. Her father literally built the literacy framework around her from scratch; Elina received this bookcase heirloom in its material form, which enabled her to inhabit the identity of a studious and hardworking person. As significant, however, is the way in which Elina internalized this crafting literacy. In her literacy history narrative, she time and again overlaid descriptions of artistic or crafting practices with her adept use of literature and other literacies of culturedness. Elina spent much of her childhood sick and thus absent from school, which made it difficult for her to participate in mandatory Soviet youth collectives like the Young Pioneers and the Komsomol, organizations central to social and academic success (Kirschenbaum 128). It was Elina's dual passion for crafting and literature, however, that eased her back into these circles, as she would make up for her absences in school by making props and decorations for school plays. Using her knowledge of Russian fairy tales and literary canon, she would craft half-masks from clay for the younger students to wear and help them remember and recite lines backstage, quickly becoming the social focal point in these school settings. Indeed, she remembers that for most of her later schooling, she became the "star" of her class academically and socially, eventually becoming a Komsomol leader. This is an adaptive practice that she would rely on for the rest of her life. Remembering the wartime evacuation, for example, Elina recalled entertaining the wounded soldiers at the hospital by drawing cartoons that were enlarged and displayed in the hospital windows, as well as narrating any screened movies for vision-impaired patients. Even though her father's bookcase was not present in all these moments, the material conditions that necessitated its creation persisted throughout Elina's life in the USSR, and she resorted to the same practice as her father of conjuring discursive heirlooms not only to adapt and "make do" but to thrive and survive.

In their study of one singularized object, a kitchen table, Epp and Price show how this family heirloom is not just a manifestation of one family's values and practices but is actually central in facilitating the family members' "web of interlocking identity practices" (828). Their research traces how the family tried to incorporate the table into their lives over and over despite changing spatial and logistical constrictions, pointing to the significance of the table's resurfacing at particular identity- and practice-enacting junctures in the family's life. However, their findings show that when the table is absent, the family practice of crafting is otherwise displaced (831). Unlike the family in the study, however, the discursive heirlooms in Vera and Elina's narratives, the Kuprin collection that Vera's son finds by chance and the bookshelves built by Elina's father, index the specific literacy circumstances they lived through, but moreover, their materiality shapes their practices and connects them to certain ways of being like "culturedness" as well as skillful know-how, such as craftsmanship and herblore. Vera and Elina use these discursive heirlooms to express ways of being, and they see them as valuable and important enough to share with both their family members. However, the heirlooms that suffuse the literacy narratives of other elders, as we will see below, do not always act in such elevating or clear-cut ways. The next section touches on how, in addition to the literacy conditions, values, and practices they represent, discursive heirlooms can index the survival and even subversion—a family's ability to endure—within unpredictable and sometimes dangerous literacy contexts.

HEIRLOOMS OF FAMILIAL ENDURANCE

"Come in, come in, don't worry about your shoes," Sabina told me as she ushered me into her apartment where we held our interview. "I just cleared all the books out so the rug isn't clean anyway." Clearing out the books she referred to so casually, it turned out, was no small feat since there were three full collections of different encyclopedias she and her family had shipped during their late 1970s emigration out of Soviet Moldova. First they shipped the encyclopedias to Israel—the first of their emigration stop points—then Austria, where they awaited their US refugee visas, then finally the United States—Memphis, then Boston. Sabina's bookshelves included a set of the Encyclopedia Britannica in English, which she gave away to her building supervisor. She also had a forty-volume set of Russian military medical encyclopedias that belonged to her husband, "heavy, brown books" from the 1960s, and some bibles and prayer books in Hebrew, "more bibles than in a synagogue." When asked why her family shipped those tomes across such distance, Sabina shrugged: "I don't know . . . in Russia, books were . . . it seemed to me that everyone had books, because I remember my mother collecting books after the war, when there was nothing. I remember some rickety bookshelf, and there were books on it. I can see this shelf even now." As with Vera and Elina, Sabina communicates a kind of preciousness around the book objects that she and her family were able to collect in the Soviet Union. The ability to obtain physical books, especially after surviving the Second World War, where people like Sabina's parents were constantly trying to overcome deep scarcity—not just of cultural artifacts, but basic survival resources like food and fuel—signified comfort and survival. "I couldn't understand [then,]" Sabina said, "how anyone could throw away books."

In contrast to those participants, however, Sabina described a detachment to this book collection that happened in the last ten years, especially the medical encyclopedias. The transference of the collection was so labor-intensive and cost-prohibitive that the family had to leave them in Israel for some years while they acclimated to their new American context. There is an observable tension between the felt social and cultural capital of the books, and the very practical physical transportation of the books. Thus, I would argue that Sabina and her husband's decision to hold onto the cumbersome collection lay in more than holding onto a "literate" identity or a state of "culturedness," as, for instance, Vera had. The books were a way of retaining a professional identity, a claim to Sabina's husband's training and expertise. However, the family of four—Sabina, her husband, and her two sons not yet in high school—experienced a difficult adjustment period in the United States, but it was her late husband in particular, a doctor back in the USSR, who had a "very difficult adaptation." The professional adjustment had proven particularly difficult, since his medical credentials and training held little value in the United States; the medical encyclopedias, which linked him to his work in the USSR, offered a material representation of his knowledge and experience, and a way of surviving in quite inhospitable immigration conditions. To use Herng-Dar Bih's framework terms, in addition to being an "extension of memory," the book set worked as a "manifestation of achievement," or in the case of Sabina's husband, frustration at achievement, and a degree of disillusionment with immigrant life (Bih 138). It was not until he passed that Sabina decided to shed the books: "I went out, found cardboard boxes, packed them up, then put them on the dolly on these wheels and carried everything down [to the street]." The desire to have the books removed quickly was clear, as she described removing the books in one day by herself using a cart. While her sons had taken some of the books, most of the encyclopedias had ultimately gone to people outside the family, including unknown strangers on the street, who had, according to Sabina, cleared everything out "that same day." The family's possession, and later disposition, of these heirlooms represents a complicated process of adjusting, or "adapting," to immigrant life, as Sabina herself calls it. The books represent the loss of Sabina's husband's professional agency, and their weight, physical and emotional, hung heavily on the shelves. The encyclopedias inherently dictated, through their content and their affective history, the space they were in and the space they were possibly going to end up within, since one of Sabina's sons, a doctor like his father, ended up inheriting part of the collection.

Whereas Sabina's family retains and sheds book objects to survive in conditions that delimit or cut off their professional identity, sometimes objects that are no longer present in their material form aggregate significance in a family's narrative of survival. In the literacy history of another participant, Asya, the *memories* of some objects, and their properties of survival and subversion, render them discursive heirlooms. When I asked Asya about memories of reading and writing in her childhood, she began doing the math of when she started reading by remembering her eighth birthday, which came four days after the German troops invaded Ukraine. Her mother had given her a piano that day:

> When the Great Patriotic War began in 1941, I turned eight years old, and my parents wanted to make me happy so they bought me a piano. On the 22nd [of June], the War began, and my Birthday is on the 26th. And on Sunday, they delivered the piano—but I was already reading at that point, I think. That would be to the credit of my mother and father, because my mother taught me.... Somewhere, probably, four years before then I already started reading.

I quote this moment in our interview because it showcases the ways in which Asya tried to recall a more factual detail—when and how she learned to read and write—by remembering the gift of the piano and the start of the Second World War. The piano was left behind when the family evacuated out of Kiev, but despite that, the gift became an index in her narrative, similarly to Vera and Elina, for the literacy conditions and practices that she recalled. It indexes both the start of the War and the subsequent interruption of her formal education, as well as the methods in which her mother taught her to read, to write, and to count before the War. Asya uses the piano to remember her mother practicing Socratic knowledge-building with her, not just with alphabetic literacy, but also in acquiring math skills, when she and her sister would practice division with beans in saucers, their mother wondering aloud to them about how much more should go in this or that saucer.

Nevertheless, I would argue that unlike Vera's Kuprin volumes, which can retain indexicality through substitution, and Elina's bookcases, which can retain their indexicality through recreation, Asya's piano acts as an additional index of survival. The piano anchors her literacy development in a timeline that is deeply wrapped up in physical danger—the family's need to abandon this object lest they perish. In that way, it is an irreplaceable possession, to use Kent Grayson and David Shulman's term, because another piano would simply not be able to sustain the same meaning as the piano they left behind in Kiev. Building on Peirce's definition of indexicality, where an index emerges when the object has a "factual connection" with what it represents, Grayson and Shulman argue that objects that retain an irreplaceability become indices "because they have a factual, spatial connection with the special events and people they represent" (19). Perhaps even more significantly for the piano heirloom, Grayson and Shulman argue that the indexicality of irreplaceable possessions "allows them to serve a factual or evidentiary function for their owners" (19).[3] The piano, then, is a witness to the life they had before the War, as well as what was inevitably lost.

The long quote above also demonstrates how tightly wound the memories of familial kinship are around the memories of literacy: the piano is a birthday gift from the parents, who desire to pass written and musical literacy to their daughter. When asked what kinds of literacy Asya would like to pass onto her granddaughter Bella, Asya answered that Bella needed to know the family's history more than anything else. Asya, who was a second parent to her, spent time not only on Russian reading and writing with Bella but also telling her tales from her own grandfather and mother's childhoods, as well as Asya's own early years: "[Bella] knows about her great-grandfather, she knows about her great-great-grandfather, she knows about her grandmothers." Asya could not pass on the piano to her granddaughter, nor could she pass on many textual objects like books and letters. When citizens would emigrate out of the Soviet Union through official channels, as Asya had, all the belongings they would pack or ship would be thoroughly examined, registered, and stamped[4]—this would be doubly true for texts that had come in contact with important government officials. Still, Asya would tell the story around significant objects, like the piano, to show her granddaughter "what kind of people were in her family."

A discursive heirloom representing this connection to family history in Asya's narrative is showcased poignantly through the story around one letter Asya's aunt Roza wrote in the 1950s. Roza was a well-known and respected actress in the Riga State Yiddish Theater, working during the Doctors' Plot,[5] which was, as she said, "a very hard time for Jewish people." During this period, many of the State Yiddish Theaters, which employed mostly Jewish citizens, were closed down by the government. Asya's Aunt Roza ("clever woman, may she rest in peace!"), wrote a letter to Kliment Voroshilov, a member of the Central Committee, outlining "seventy-five questions and answers on what to do with Jewish culture, and so on, and so on." Roza's letter, like Roza herself, became legendary in Asya's family when the Central Committee, rather than arresting her, wrote back with an offer for Roza to read Yiddish texts on the state radio once a month in the middle of the night. "And read for whom?" Asya asked me coyly. "For people who are asleep. In order for the Voice of America to believe that Jewish culture was supported. . . . You understand? That's all! And how they didn't take her away, only God knows!" Asya's oblique explanation alluded to the way in which the Soviet government desired to control the image they garnered outside the USSR as a state that actively oppressed Jewish people. Voroshilov asked Roza to read in Yiddish during a time of day that few Soviet citizens would be hearing, but potential Western radio signals might pick up on, and infer, through this Jewish cultural broadcast, that Jewish people were not oppressed after all. The significant aspect of this letter, of course, is how brazen Asya found it of Roza to write in opposition to Soviet policy, in 1952, of all years, and send the letter to the highest powers in the Soviet government in order to advocate for herself and her community.

It would have been impossible for the family to obtain or keep any physical copies of Roza's correspondence with the highest governing body in the USSR. The letter, in its physical form, was rendered irreplaceable. It indexed, however, the survival and subversion that Asya, then her daughter, and finally her granddaughter, honored. The family's disposition of the piano and the letter do not threaten the highly indexical ways in which these heirlooms are passed within the family and add to the family's identity formation, especially within the broader sociohistorical contexts in which they lived. Both Sabina and Asya's literacy narratives showcase their respective family's endurance in unpredictable, even dangerous, circumstances despite the disposition of the discursive heirlooms they bring up. One participant in my study, however, describes the adverse ways that discursive heirloom disposition has impacted him.

HEIRLOOMS OF NATIONAL BELONGING AND ALIENATION

"I served [in the Soviet Army] from February 1944 to January 1950, just about, give or take a few weeks—6 years," Borya told me, nodding proudly to the far wall of the common room of the Pearl community center where, in celebration of the May 9 holiday, Victory in Europe Day, the center had hung up posters of members who had served. "You can see all my military activities there. Just go there and read it." He pointed. I could see, even from afar, Borya's young face in black and white, wearing his navy uniform, including his formal army hat and medals. Next to the picture was a written blurb outlining his service. While the Second World War was ubiquitous in most of my participants' interviews, Borya's memories of the war, particularly his time in the military, loomed especially large. The two discursive heirlooms that surface in Borya's narrative, a passport and a set of military medals, are suffused with the danger and loss he experienced as both a child and soldier of the war. More importantly, they clearly show the ways in which the disposition of these objects determined not only how Borya practiced literacy after the war, but also how his identity, and his family's identity as Jewish citizens in the Soviet Union, were inflected during their subsequent immigration to the United States.

Borya told me about the multiple evacuations he experienced, being forced to travel by train cars from Ukraine to the Northern Caucasus Mountains then to the Ural Mountains, as the German army advanced the front eastward. All of the family members' identifying documents, including Borya's passport, birth certificate, and any records of public schooling—burned up in the house they fled during the evacuation. The only remaining record of his and his siblings' existence remained in his mother's own passport, which she had tucked into her brassiere when they fled. He remembered first working at the local Kolkhoz[6] with all the people in the area who had not been drafted. The number of adults who could read, write, or count had been diminished, and when the head council member of the Kolkhoz discovered Borya had seven years of schooling, he took him off the field and made him keep the accounting books of the butter-making division. At fourteen years old, Borya was running numbers for the dairy plant with an abacus. During the second evacuation Borya lived through, officials made similar use of his reading and number literacy by putting him in a locksmith workshop at a makeshift nickel factory. At a very young age, Borya found himself receiving the beginnings of what was to become the future of his professional training, first by apprenticing at the locksmith workshop, then working as a repairman of the nickel ore transport cars. He spent the last year of the war enlisting in the military and continuing to serve for another five years afterward until his early twenties.

After his service, Borya tried to pick up his interrupted high school education, like many returning young veterans. Yet, it proved quite difficult for Borya to register, since not only had he completed just seven of the ten official grades in Soviet schooling but there was no official record of his grades or education. Despite his engineering and military experience, which he began at an early age during the evacuation, he had to seek out formal schooling through informal social networks. Borya managed to get into a night school through a friend of a friend, another young veteran who had taught there. Borya remembered that despite "lagging a little behind" in Russian grammar, literature, chemistry, "and maybe everything," the teacher "accepted [him] without any documents, just on [his] words." This vote of confidence remained meaningful to Borya, and he remembered not only how hard he studied in those years, at the expense of his health, but also the teachers who tutored him for free, because, as he said, "They saw that I was so stubborn.... So that's how I finished high school." While this experience may not have been unique to Borya, as, indeed, many people leaving the SSRs went through similar things, his literacy history narrative hones in on a particular tenuity in material possessions. Thus, I refer to his mother's passport as a discursive heirloom for several reasons. First, the passport acts as a familial node of connection, as it is the only remaining textual link between Borya's mother and her children. In a way, she is able to protect her children through this document by retaining a bureaucratically legible kinship and circumventing separation during evacuation and staying together as a family unit—children were frequently separated from their parents during train evacuations. Second, Soviet passports held information not only about one's name, place of origin, and birth, but also ethnicity. For a Jewish family that was fleeing encroaching Nazi forces, this is a significant and multifarious document in terms of survival. Lastly, this discursive heirloom clearly demonstrates the consequence of disposition, since it took Borya significant effort compensate for the loss of his own passport in order to continue his education.

The gravity of disposition is similarly evident through another discursive heirloom, Borya's army medals. When Perestroika began, Borya and his wife decided to apply for exit visas that would reunite them with his father, who had already left for the States. Borya was told, however, that the only way he could receive a visa was to denounce his father as an "enemy of the State" on the radio. Borya had refused, and his visa status was delayed for nearly another decade. Their eventual emigration, bargained for dearly, was a bitterly mixed experience. "Everything was in the suitcases," Borya said. "All my documents were lost—that is, all my award documents, military orders, medals—two gold medals were lost: one was mine, the other was my son's, all including the permits, special permits for transportation—everything was lost!" The suitcases, Borya suspected, were confiscated by the government. Even during this more lax time of Perestroika, to leave the Soviet state, even with permission, made emigrants "enemies of the state"; when people left the USSR, they were frequently stripped of objects with high social capital, objects that linked them favorably to the state (Gitelman 49). Building on Csikszentmihalyi and Rochberg-Halton's large-scale study of contemplative objects, Mehta and Belk show in their research on the possessions of Indian immigrants living in the United States how "older people tend to be strongly attached to contemplative possessions that help them survey their pasts" (399). This is evidently true for Borya, who keenly felt continuous disposition due to forced mobility and migration. Throughout his interview, Borya described his experiences as a veteran extensively, underscoring the significance that his army service held for him, especially as a Jewish person with the Holocaust in the fore. He also described with proud detail the various ways his career as an electrical engineer shaped audiotechnology in the USSR, all despite the moments of ubiquitous anti-Semitic interactions he recalled offhand. The status of a respected veteran and citizen that was conferred onto individuals by the government—the social, economic, and political capital this status garnered—was highly contingent on the physical possession of documents and medals, a possession that can be difficult to maintain during war and migration.

Borya's war medals indexed the time and life force he had given the State. The *loss* of the medals made Borya keenly aware of how he, as a Jewish Soviet citizen, was frequently alienated from feelings of fully belonging to the Soviet nation, and more importantly, stripped him of the ability to pass those objects down to his grandsons, which he regretted. His grandsons, with whom he is close, were less invested in the stories he had about the war and more intrigued by their last name, which came down from Borya—an heirloom of its own. While Borya could not pass down his medals, he did sit down with one of his grandsons to sketch out a family tree, all in Russian. "And our tree is very very big," Borya told me. "Just as an example, before the war, our family was big-big, 238 people there were. That's a lot of family. After the war? 32." In the absence of medals and documents, Borya has had to share the experiences of loss through other forms of writing. Thus objects, but also memories of objects, loom powerfully within literacy narratives of immigrants from the former Soviet Union like Borya, but more than that, these discursive heirlooms shape the literacy and language practices that individuals use and also then desire to pass to members of their families.

CONCLUSION

The three discursive heirloom clusters presented in this chapter knit tightly into one another: cultural literacy, for instance, is intimately tied to the familial intergenerational connection that happens across and within generations, as well as during the traversal of transnational spaces. Similarly, experiences of belonging and alienation are inflected by emergent construction of cultural literacy values, and how these values are passed around within families. However, as material culture scholarship urges, these objects act as more than just markers of experience. Alexis considers the "demonstrated power of objects in the process of becoming possible selves," as well as writers' "reliance" on objects and object constellations to "perform identities and trades," to ask how objects *actively shape* the writing lives of individuals beyond just becoming symbolic meaning containers (33, my own emphasis). In addition to passing alphabetic literacy skills—particular reading/writing practices, traditions, and languages—to their children and grandchildren, elders also communicated passing, or hoping to pass, more ineffable "ways of looking at the world" and "knowing how to do something." Those ways of being and doing are part of how literacy repertoires figure in individuals' adaptation to immigration and cannot be unlinked from more conservative understandings of written literacy. As their literacy practices change in response to fluctuating or contingent circumstances, the study participants used, and continue to use, discursive heirlooms to adapt to those conditions. The boon of studying literacy objects as material culture, then, seems to lie in the traceability of these heirlooms through otherwise messy and turbulent circumstances. In the case of my participants, the heirlooms they highlight and attend to in the larger tableaus of their literacies are indicative of adaptive discursive repertoires, which not only include the often "unstable" practices that can frequently show up within multilingual writing (Lorimer Leonard, "Writing Across") but also elders' strategies of adaptation to linguistic, social, and political contingency. Whether objects are carefully preserved and carried through evacuations and immigration, whether they are destroyed or lost through war or transnational movement, or whether they are passed down as stories, these discursive heirlooms do not only act as indices of familial identity and history but fundamentally impact literacy practitioners' trajectories of reading, writing, and communication.

NOTES

1. I use Rebecca Lorimer Leonard's definition of literacy repertoires as "the complex cluster of reading, writing, listening, and speaking strategies and experiences that multilingual writers call on to write" (*Writing* 7). Lorimer Leonard's use of the term builds on Blommaert and Backus's "repertoires" by suggesting that rather than carrying around a static toolbox, or container, of literacy skills, multilingual writers develop "dynamic sets" of strategies, experiences, and memories of reading, writing, speaking, and listening in order to communicate (*Writing* 7). Moreover, sometimes these repertoires, which may appear to be "incomplete" (Blommaert and Backus), are actually "in process before, during, and after migration" (*Writing* 10).
2. Of the fourteen elders in the study, only two or three people were considered "working class" in Soviet bureaucracy and discourse. Class was tied to occupation, rather than economic status (Rivkin-Fish).
3. It is also important to note Grayson and Shulman's additional claim that a *reproduction* of a possession "cannot claim an indexical (real, factual, and spatial) association with the context and/or people that are represented by the object," even when it looks like the object that was replaced (19).
4. All the paintings and sculptures my own family was able to bring over from the Soviet Union in 1990, for instance, have blue inspection stamps on them.

5. In 1952–1953, the year preceding Joseph Stalin's death, a group of predominantly Jewish doctors from Moscow was accused by the government of an attempt on Stalin and other Soviet leaders' lives. This incident spurred an extended period of anti-semitic discourse and anti-Jewish policies that included closure of Jewish cultural centers and the arrests of Jewish citizens in particular professions (Ro'i).
6. A collective farm run by the state (from the Russian *kolektivnoye khozaystvo*).

WORKS CITED

Alexis, Cydney. "The Material Culture of Writing: Objects, Habitats, and Identities in Practice." *Rhetoric, through Everyday Things*, edited by Scot Barnett and Casey Andrew Boyle, U of Alabama P, 2016, pp. 83–95.

Alexis, Cydney. "The Symbolic Life of the Moleskine Notebook: Material Goods as a Tableau for Writing Identity Performance." *Composition Studies*, vol. 45, no. 2, Fall 2017, pp. 32–54.

Bartlett, Lesley. "Identity Work and Cultural Artefacts in Literacy Learning and Use: A Sociocultural Analysis." *Language and Education: An International Journal*, vol. 19, no. 1, Jan. 2005, pp. 1–9.

Belk, Russell W. "Possessions and the Extended Self." *Journal of Consumer Research*, vol. 15, no. 2, Sept. 1988, pp. 139–168.

Berry, J. W. "Immigration, Acculturation, and Adaptation." *Applied Psychology—An International Review*, vol. 46, no. 1, 1997, pp. 5–34.

Bih, Herng-dar. "The Meaning of Objects in Environmental Transitions: Experiences of Chinese Students in the United States." *Journal of Environmental Psychology*, vol. 12, no. 2, June 1992, pp. 135–147.

Blommaert, Jan, and Ad Backus. "Superdiverse Repertoires and the Individual." *Multilingualism and Multimodality*, edited by Ingrid de Saint-Georges and Jean-Jacques Weber. Leiden, The Netherlands: Brill, 2013, pp. 9–32.

Boym, Svetlana. *Common Places: Mythologies of Everyday Life in Russia*. Harvard UP, 1994.

Brandt, Deborah. "Remembering Writing, Remembering Reading." *College Composition and Communication*, vol. 45, no. 4, Dec. 1994, pp. 459–479.

Charmaz, Kathy. *Constructing Grounded Theory*. Sage, 2014.

Csikszentmihalyi, Mihaly, and Eugene Rochberg-Halton. *The Meaning of Things: Domestic Symbols and the Self*. Cambridge UP, 1981.

Curasi Folkman, Carolyn, Linda L. Price, and Eric J. Arnould. "How Individuals' Cherished Possessions Become Families' Inalienable Wealth." *Journal of Consumer Research*, vol. 31, no. 3, 2004, p. 609.

Dunstan, John. *Soviet Schooling in the Second World War*. Macmillan Press/St. Martin's Press, 1997.

Epp, Amber M., and Linda L. Price. "The Storied Life of Singularized Objects: Forces of Agency and Network Transformation." *Journal of Consumer Research*, vol. 36, no. 5, 2010, p. 820. Web.

Gerasimova, Ekaterina, and Sof'ia Chuikina. "The Repair Society." *Russian Studies in History*, vol. 48, no. 1, summer 2009, pp. 58–74.

Gitelman, Zvi. "Exiting from the Soviet Union: Emigrés or Refugees?" *Michigan Yearbook of International Legal Studies*, 1982, pp. 43–61. Web.

Grayson, Kent, and David Shulman. "Indexicality and the Verification Function of Irreplaceable Possessions: A Semiotic Analysis." *Journal of Consumer Research*, vol. 27, no. 1, 2000, p. 17.

Gurova, Ol'ga. "The Life Span of Things in Soviet Society." *Russian Studies in History*, vol. 48, no. 1, summer 2009, pp. 46–57.

Holton, Judith A. "The Coding Process and Its Challenges." *Grounded Theory Review*, vol. 9, no. 1, Mar. 2010, pp. 21–40.

Kesler Rumsey, Suzanne. "Holding on to Literacies: Older Adult Narratives of Literacy and Agency." *Literacy in Composition Studies*, vol. 6, no. 1, 2018, pp. 81–104.

Kirschenbaum, Lisa A. *Small Comrades: Revolutionizing Childhood in Soviet Russia, 1917–1932*. Routledge Falmer, 2001.

Kopytoff, Igor. "The Cultural Biography of Things: Commoditization as Process." *The Social Life of Things: Commodities in Cultural Perspective*, edited by Arjun Appadurai, Cambridge UP, 1986, pp. 64–91.

Lagman, Eileen. "Moving Labor: Transnational Migrant Workers and Affective Literacies." *Literacy in Composition Studies*, vol. 3, no. 3, 2015, pp. 1–24.

Lastovicka, John L., and Karen V. Fernandez. "Three Paths to Disposition: The Movement of Meaningful Possessions to Strangers." *Journal of Consumer Research*, vol. 31, no. 4, 2005, p. 813.

Ledeneva, Alena V. *Russia's Economy of Favours: Blat, Networking, and Informal Exchange*. Cambridge UP, 1998.

Lorimer Leonard, Rebecca. "Writing across Languages: Developing Rhetorical Attunement by Negotiating Difference." *Literacy as Translingual Practice: Between Communities and Classrooms*, edited by A. Suresh Canagarajah, Routledge, 2013, pp. 162–169.

Lorimer Leonard, Rebecca. *Writing on the Move: Migrant Women and the Value of Literacy*. U of Pittsburgh P, 2017.

Lorimer Leonard, Rebecca. "Writing through Bureaucracy: Migrant Correspondence and Managed Mobility." *Written Communication*, vol. 32, no. 1, 1 Jan. 2015, pp. 87–113.

Lucas, Gavin. "Disposability and Dispossession in the Twentieth Century." *Journal of Material Culture*, vol. 7, no. 1, Mar. 2002, p. 5.

Mehta, Raj, and Russell W. Belk. "Artifacts, Identity, and Transition: Favorite Possessions of Indians and Indian Immigrants to the United States." *Journal of Consumer Research*, no. 4, 1991, p. 398.

Rivkin-Fish, Michele. "Tracing Landscapes of the Past in Class Subjectivity: Practices of Memory and Distinction in Marketizing Russia." *American Ethnologist*, vol. 36, no. 1, pp. 79–95.

Ro'i, Yaacov. *Jews and Jewish Life in Russia and the Soviet Union*. Cass, 1995.

Shleifer, Andrei, and Robert Vishny. "Pervasive Shortages under Socialism." *The RAND Journal of Economics*, vol. 23, no. 2, 1992, p. 237.

Turkle, Sherry. *Evocative Objects: Things We Think With*. MIT Press, 2007.

Vieira, Kate. *American by Paper: How Documents Matter in Immigrant Literacy*. U of Minnesota P, 2016.

Wan, Amy J. *Producing Good Citizens: Literacy Training in Anxious Times*. Pittsburgh Series in Composition, Literacy, and Culture. U of Pittsburgh P, 2014.

White-Farnham, Jamie. "Revising the Menu to Fit the Budget: Grocery Lists and Other Rhetorical Heirlooms." *College English*, no. 3, 2014, p. 208.

Yurchak, Alexei. *Everything Was Forever, Until It Was No More: The Last Soviet Generation*. Princeton UP, 2006.

5

MATERIAL MOTHERHOOD
The Disconnect of Science and Consumerism from Nostalgia in Baby Books

Emilie Merrigan

As I removed the small baby book from its mailing package, I was surprised by the softness of the brown leather cover, the intricately embossed images and text. I opened the only slightly marred pages, expecting them to be dull or colorless, and was presented instead with vibrant illustrations. When posted on eBay, the seller had provided only a handful of preview images, allowing me to discover each element of the nearly ninety-year-old item in my own way. My goal was to find an object of writing and analyze its materiality—its physical and visual attributes rather than textual content—and I was, in fact, more immediately entranced by the material aspects of the book than its 60-some pages of content. A quick glance showed that the first half of the book is dedicated to recording memories and facts about a baby, while the last half contains childrearing advice—two related yet very different purposes coexisting in one small book. Despite the clearly prescriptive intentions of the book for mothers to complete the themed pages in the first half and follow the advice in the second half, I found myself holding a combination of illustrations, mother's handwriting, pictures, and pages that communicate a disconnect between this book's content and its materiality.

In writing studies and many other disciplines, we concern ourselves with words, written and spoken. However, to better understand writing and writers, many in writing studies are looking beyond words to consider the objects and artifacts—material culture—related to writing studies. Material culture refers to objects or artifacts that are part (or product) of and therefore provide evidence about the events, beliefs, and values of a culture (Csikszentmihalyi and Rochberg-Halton; Deetz; Glassie; "The Truth"). With roots in anthropology, history, art, and consumer research, material culture studies can add to our understanding of any aspect of culture by revealing the (conscious or subconscious) identity and intentions of the person(s) involved (Alexis; Glassie; Prown; "The Truth"). From the lens of material culture studies, value can come from inspecting the content of documents and "uninscribed artifacts" to learn about history and culture (Belk; Deetz). We can take a topic of interest in writing studies (text, practice, group, etc.) and add considerations of related material artifacts to address not just the content but the objects, processes, and people related to that content.

A growing number of writing studies researchers have incorporated material culture studies; however, I find that their roots in writing studies result in an overwhelming focus on individuals such as students, teachers, and writers, and the objects and situations related to those more traditionally recognized writing roles (Alexis; Bartlett; Emig; Wyche). As material culture studies pushes us to explore the ordinary, I sought to delve deeper into a cultural identity less commonly associated with writing, the mother. Having studied rhetorics of motherhood from twentieth-century America[1] in writing and communication studies, I was curious to see what a material culture lens could add to this research and selected the above-detailed baby book, a 1915 publication of *The Book of Baby Mine* (see fig. 5.1 for the cover of the singularized copy centered in my analysis; throughout, I include illustrative images of single pages from this copy.)

"Baby book" is a term broadly applied to books containing both medically based childcare advice as well as blank pages for notes or photographs and preprinted template pages to record infant health and social milestones, of which *The Book of Baby Mine* contains both (Apple; Golden and Weiner). It and many other baby books contain a rhetoric of motherhood known as "scientific motherhood," used widely in America since the early twentieth century. Sometimes called medicalized or psychologized motherhood, scientific motherhood refers to the attempted influence of the male-dominated medical community on all aspects of motherhood and childrearing (Apple; Grant; Klausner; Vandenberg-Daves). This influence began with in-person medical care and continued with various literature (pamphlets, books, etc.) given to mothers for use in the home. While scientific motherhood in America was not outwardly challenged until about the 1960s, "mothers had been quietly shifting cultural and social patterns" around motherhood for decades, in part by pushing back against scientific motherhood (Vandenberg-Daves). I argue that baby books are one material example of the quiet yet unmistakable ways in which mothers worked to form

Figure 5.1. Cover of a 1931 copy of The Book of Baby Mine *from Hamilton, Ohio. Photo Credit: Emilie Merrigan.*

their own identity, thus contributing to the larger cultural identity of motherhood.

While the content of these books helps illuminate the cultural effects of scientific motherhood, we can glean even more through analysis of this artifact that was brought into the home. Baby books have been regarded as "a rich historical source" (Golden and Weiner 669), yet Pascali was inspired to study over five hundred baby books because she argued they had been largely ignored by researchers and archivists for their seemingly personal and ordinary nature rather than cultural and historical value (4–5). Like Pascali, my analysis falls back on the grounds of material culture studies that argues it is precisely the personal and ordinary nature of things that lend insight into culture and history. My goal was to explore how this text along with its physical and visual attributes informs our understanding of the very common cultural role and identity of mother as it faced the overbearing influence of scientific motherhood. I argue that motherhood was less likely to adhere to the pragmatic, rigid recommendations of scientific motherhood, but instead through means such as baby books, mothers could create an identity and experience that was romantic, nostalgic, idealized toward their personal wants and needs. To be sure, mothers benefited from scientific advances but needed space to decide how those and other cultural changes could or should be incorporated into their identities and relationships.

Materiality adds a layer of cultural significance and meaning to a text, in part through the identity of its writer and/or owner. With scientific motherhood attempting to infiltrate and control the identity of motherhood, material objects provide evidence of some of the ways in which mothers worked to navigate and define this identity for themselves. Possessions become "extensions" of ourselves, part of our identity, as we exert energy directly into them, or work to earn money to purchase them (Belk; Csikszentmihalyi and Rochberg-Halton; "The Truth"). To be clear, this "identity" can be "both personal and social," but even to inform a cultural identity, many material culture scholars tout the importance of analyzing individual objects (Alexis 35). Objects transcend their status as mere commodities when they are "singularized" and "given personal meanings" (Epp and Price 820; Kopytoff 74). While Pascali discovered various patterns in her review of hundreds of baby books, I chose to analyze one singularized copy of *The Book of Baby Mine* owned by Mary Louise Grabel, born 1931 to Jessie Grabel, from Hamilton, Ohio. Through analysis of a singularized sample, I can look more closely at the identity work Jessie performed through this material object, which supported by the history of scientific motherhood also contributes to the formation of a larger cultural identity of mother.

First, I will provide a brief background of scientific motherhood, followed by an overview of baby books as a cultural material artifact of "memory" and "genre of self" (Katriel and Farrell). The research I offer on baby books includes that by Golden and Weiner, who examine the influences of medicine and marketing on the content of baby books. Then I will provide an analysis of Jessie's/Mary's singularized *Book of Baby Mine*. My analysis follows the Prownian method in which one performs an exhaustive examination and description of the desired artifact(s) in order to experience history through the senses rather than words (Prown and Haltman, "Style as Evidence" 65). I will also refer to my material object as an artifact, which Prown uses to mean both fact (events) and art (skill and intention) in order to highlight an artifact's "historical facts" and "artistic fictions" ("The Truth" 2–3; 5–6). This focus on the "art" (again, not mainstream "aestheticized" art as we primarily think, but created with skill and intention) informs my understanding of the baby book, as it is the skill and care in the original illustrations and materials, as well as the intentions included by its singularizer, Jessie, that communicate the value of a romantic, personally idealized motherhood through this artifact. While some existing research on baby books focus on their value to the child's identity (Katriel and Farrell; Pascali), my analysis provides insight into the personal and cultural identity of the mother, highlighting the influences of scientific motherhood and the textual and material strength of Jessie's romanticized, nostalgic experience of motherhood.

BACKGROUND AND CONTEXT

Around the start of the twentieth century, perceptions of childhood and the culture of parenthood (specifically motherhood) shifted in America. Scientific advances—namely a sharp decrease in infant and child mortality—meant that families could form bonds with children at earlier ages with less fear of losing those children (*"Anxious Parents"* 3). Industrialization also contributed to changing family and parenting dynamics through increases in urban populations and working mothers who required different knowledge and tools for accessible and time-efficient care and feeding of infants (Aysan and Thompson; Klausner; Vandenberg-Daves; Wolf). The rise in prenatal care, hospital births, and the pediatric branch of medicine in the early twentieth century greatly increased the presence of medical professionals in women's lives. Women also faced the nationalist pressure and scrutiny to raise healthy children post–World War I (Golden and Weiner). While higher life expectancy and quality of life for children (and mothers) presented the opportunity for a more romanticized family experience, societal advances and challenges presented mothers with scientific motherhood, the input and influence of the male-dominated medical profession on motherhood.

Medical professionals positioned themselves as indispensable authorities on motherhood. Scientific motherhood was founded in scientific advances and supported by traditional gender roles (Apple; Klausner). The medical and scientific communities professed that proper childrearing advice came exclusively from qualified professionals, rather than family, friends, or even a parent's instinct (Apple; Klausner). Yet despite the attempted controls of scientific motherhood, any missteps in infant health and well-being were often ultimately attributed to mothers (Wolf). Women taking advantage of medical services were then more often removed from family and friends, whose advice was not welcome or valued by the medical community. Science was a "mixed blessing" as it both inarguably improved the health and lives of infants but also "belittled maternal knowledge" (Vandenberg-Daves). The instructional relationship between mother and doctor began in the doctor's office or hospital, but the attempts to influence motherhood went beyond those in-person interactions as women, especially soon-to-be mothers, were provided with medically-based literature to guide their childrearing practices at home.

Scientific motherhood was a strong catalyst for the production and distribution of baby books. Some baby books were purchased or given as gifts, while others were given by hospitals, doctors, and local organizations as more "doctors and social welfare organizations entered the baby book business;" books were also distributed by local merchants who placed advertisements in the books (Golden and Weiner 671, 675–76). Baby books had the potential to be a useful resource for mothers working to fulfill their societally expected role of raising healthy children (Grant; Wolf). Books like the widely circulated *Book of Baby Mine* contained pages for mothers to record milestones and memories. Golden and Weiner describe baby books as "situated between biographies—with their accounts of lives lived within particular historical contexts—and scrapbooks—with their displays of accumulated materials deliberately arrayed for presentation" (667). The prescriptive page titles and childcare information, including recommended growth charts for comparison, begs the question of whether these books pressured mothers into documenting their adherence to and success in approved childrearing or provided them space to document their own chosen experience of motherhood.

While I don't contest the presence of scientific motherhood in these books, the freedom for a mother to have any creative control over this narrative of herself and her child indicates the strength of a more romantic outlook on motherhood.

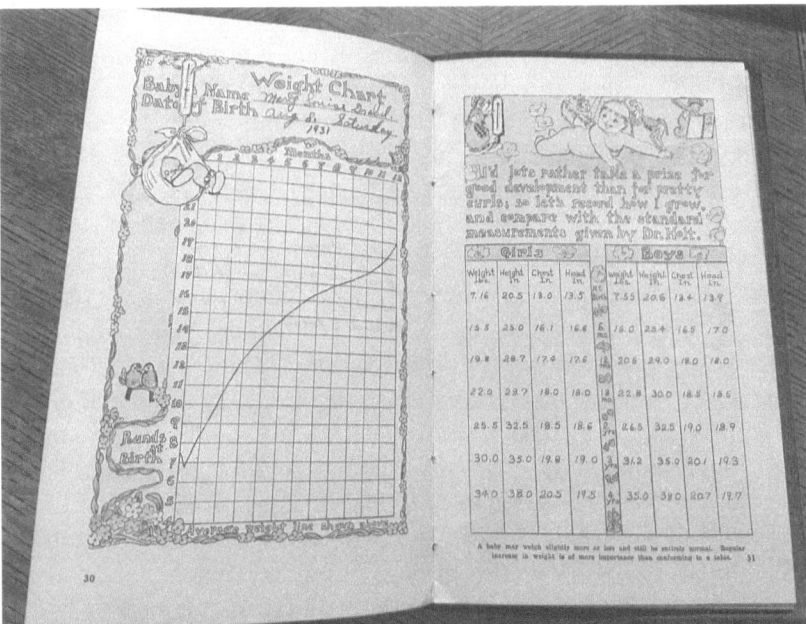

Figure 5.2. "Weight Chart" (page 30) provides a location for mother to document baby's weight progress. The smooth nature of the curve of the child's documented weight indicates a less precise estimated documentation rather than specific plot points. This page is also far less detailed or personal than numerous other pages containing nostalgic notes and photographs. "Infant Growth Chart" (page 31) indicates suggested appropriate infant weight ranges at respective ages for perceived comparison to a specific infant's progress documented on the opposite page's "Weight Chart." Photo Credit: Emilie Merrigan.

Research on baby books has included not just the rhetoric of scientific motherhood but also their function in culture as a material artifact. Baby books can be classified as a "genre of self" whose purpose is "self-narration" and "life review" (Katriel and Farrell 2). In "Scrapbooks as Cultural Texts: An American Art of Memory," Katriel and Farrell point to baby books as "predecessors" of children's "self-made scrapbooks" because although not created *by* adults like baby books, scrapbooks were "heavily influenced by adult prompting" (3). Where we typically think of biographies as texts, Pascali refers to baby books as "material biographies," thereby drawing attention to their similarities to both written biographical records and object-laden scrapbooks (5–6). Baby books leave room to include both text and small objects such as photographs or locks of hair, bridging the genres of biography and scrapbook memorabilia.

The subject of a baby book is the child, and yet baby books are completed—singularized—mostly by mothers. Recording the history of infants has proved difficult as they are "inarticulate," dependent on adults to record their history, often leading to more focus on the adult's point of view and experience with a child ("Challenges in the History of Childhood" 35–36). Although babies were the intended subjects of baby books, the inclusion of scientific motherhood as well as advertisements indicates that these artifacts were purposed at first for mothers, which informs our understanding of mothers as singularizers of the books. Furthermore, research on baby books dictates that mothers as singularizers often display an overwhelmingly positive rhetoric that demonstrates preference for culturally valued positivity and personal success over rigid scientific adherence (Katriel and Farrell). The nostalgic rhetorical purpose of baby books is evident in the expression of the cultural value of positivity and contentedness. Both memorabilia and text "immediately suggests that [baby books] represent not just a possible or potential life, but also a sense of life as *perfected*, as 'well-lived'" (Katriel and Farrell 5). Although this authorship limits the agency of the primary intended subject, it also leads to mothers singularizing baby books as much for themselves as for their children.

OBJECT ANALYSIS

In order to examine the influence of scientific motherhood and experience of nostalgic motherhood through both rhetoric and material culture, I analyzed a widely circulated baby book, *The Book of Baby Mine*. Even prior to singularization, the materiality of this book demonstrates a disconnect between scientific and nostalgic motherhood. Written and illustrated by Melcena Burns Denny and published by the Simplicity Company (later to become the Baby Mine Company) of Grand Rapids, Michigan, *The Book of Baby Mine* was first published in 1915, with new editions published every decade from 1938–1981 (Hollenbeck 41; Golden and Weiner 674).[2] The reach and longevity of *The Book of Baby Mine* were expansive; the books were sent to a wide variety of locations and demographics around the country (41). These 6.5 by 5.5-inch leatherbound books contained ninety-two pages. The first thirty-seven pages are devoted to recording baby and family information. Page thirty-eight begins "The A, B, C, of Baby's Health," scientific-based parenting instructions, printed on the left pages, with three to nine of the right pages printed with advertisements for local merchants targeting new parents, and the additional pages to the right remained blank for more infant records and/or photographs.[3]

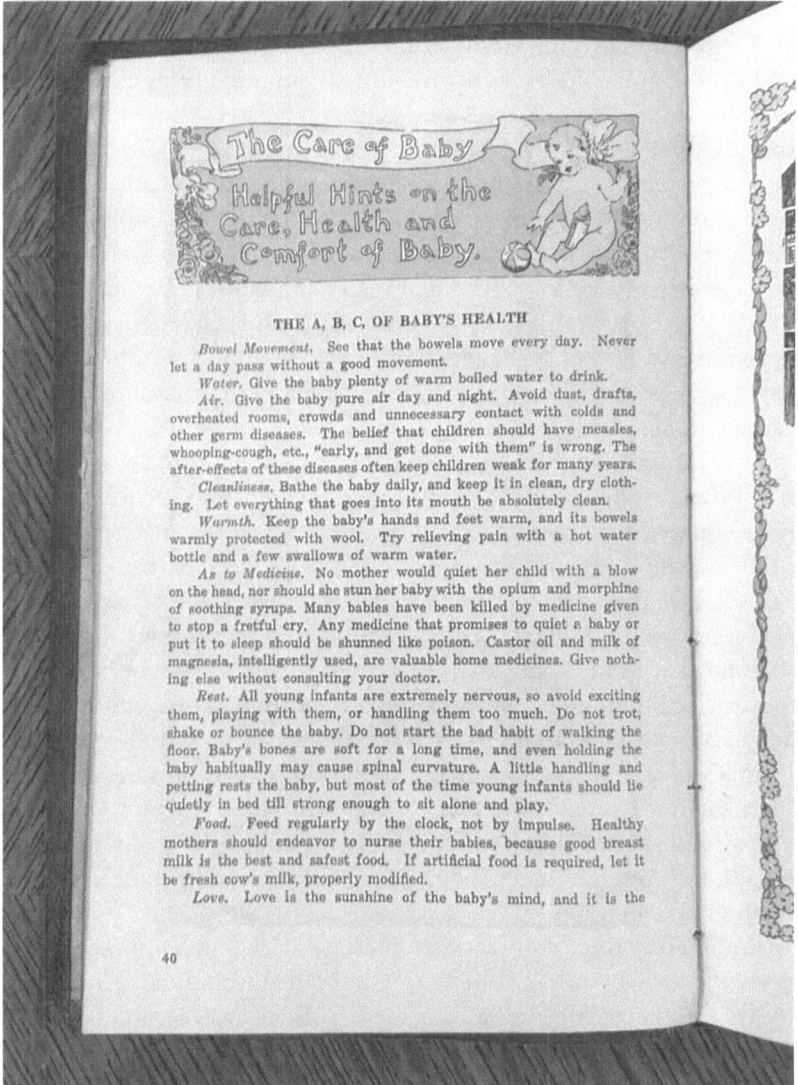

Figure 5.3. "The A, B, C of Baby's Health" detailing "hints" or guidelines for infant care; page 40 of The Book of Baby Mine. *Photo Credit: Emilie Merrigan.*

My analysis of this book as a material artifact shows that despite the dual influence of parenting advice from medical experts coupled with advice-related, local advertisements, the book's physical attributes help to distinguish a more nostalgic aspect of motherhood that in these books is mostly disconnected from the influence of science and medicine reflected in the last half of the book.

Baby books show the attempted influence of science on motherhood, but *The Book of Baby Mine* shows a preference toward nostalgic motherhood over scientific in the structure and organization of its content. We can only speculate as to how closely mothers followed doctors' orders as explicitly as recommended, but material analysis of baby books shows that there are aspects of motherhood and childrearing in the early twentieth century that were disconnected from scientific-based parenting advice. While the influence of scientific motherhood meant more space in baby books devoted to medical advice and records, "many mothers continued to fill in only the most traditional (and observable) milestones, such as first words and first steps" (Golden and Weiner 675). The baby's record section of these books was completed to varying degrees but for the purpose of nostalgia rather than for medical reference. In *The Book of Baby Mine*, twenty-four pages in the back half of the book contain advice for care of the baby, but the first thirty-seven pages of baby's records include only six pages that remotely suggest scientific influence encroaching on the nostalgic section of the book. In a study detailed in "The Most Cherished Objects in the Home," Csikszentmihalyi and Rochberg-Halton detail numerous household items that families in their study found "special," and they found various books to hold personal value because they serve as "a cultural model around which one can organize one's actions and goals" and "embody ideals" (70–71). This baby book embodies both the ideals of scientific and nostalgic motherhood and provides mothers with a guide for organizing their actions and goals surrounding their motherhood role and identity. We can't know this book's true value to its owner, but through its materiality we can gather its value to us in understanding this cultural role.

Even considering the varying amounts of scientific motherhood inserted into baby books, this book's uneven distribution of scientific influence in the advice section compared to the records section begins to distinguish the records section as more nostalgic than for medical reference, and also demonstrates the disconnect between these two aspects of motherhood that the book's creators attempted to literally join. While the back half contains detailed instructions for caring for an infant, the front half contains only a few pages in which to record evidence of adhering to the book's guidelines. The only trace of intended scientific motherhood in the first half includes pages to record initial and growing height and weight, and pages to record gifts, which might include items recommended by doctors such as clothing or grooming items. Instead, the records section that comprises the first half of the book is intended to be nostalgic by recording momentous events and information. Arguably

Figure 5.4. Title page for The Book of Baby Mine *noting author Melcena Burns Denny and this edition's copyright 1915. Photo Credit: Emilie Merrigan.*

there is enough blank space throughout the book for an owner to focus on and highlight aspects of scientific motherhood, but the disconnect from scientific motherhood is present before singularization of the book.

The overall aesthetic of *The Book of Baby Mine* presents the disconnect from scientific motherhood. Despite the difference in content of the two halves of the book, the colors and images are consistent throughout, evoking a more nostalgic, sentimental portrayal of infancy and motherhood.

Infants are drawn plump, smiling, or with eyes coyly askew. The cartoon infants sit or play, which is not only more casual than the tone of scientific motherhood but also defies many pieces of advice from medical professionals, even within this book, that explains the importance of infants lying rather than sitting or being held, and not playing due to fear of over-stimulation (Denny 40). Decorative drawings include small fairies and flowers with greenery. The colors are bright and childlike: pink, blue, yellow, and green. The subtle floral border around pages in the advice section of the book also seem to contradict the formal tone and intent of the inclusion of parenting and childcare advice, making its plain font visually overshadowed by the colors and lively drawings introducing and surrounding that information. Certain elements of the book such as the appearance of average-sized babies, and their placement outdoors reflecting suggestions of fresh air, adhere to medical advice. But as with other elements of this book, the lasting effect of these images is one of nostalgia rather than for medical record.

Advertising in *The Book of Baby Mine* posed an opportunity to enhance scientific motherhood's effective infiltration into the culture of American motherhood. Various publications of *The Book of Baby Mine* served as "concerted efforts to turn baby books into advertisements" due to the blank pages intended to be filled with advertisements, as the books were eventually "bought en masse by local merchants who filled the back pages with advertisements before sending them to new mothers in their community" (Hollenbeck 41). Many of these targeted advertisements in baby books, such as food and life insurance, can be linked to advances in science and medicine. The range of topics listed in the records and advice sections of these books provided advertisers many opportunities to connect to the content and reach audiences of mothers. *The Book of Baby Mine's* "longevity spoke to its value to advertisers and its widespread use indicated its popularity with consumers" (674). Due to the widespread printing and distribution of these books throughout the country, it's unclear how much influence merchants had on the actual content of the advice within the sections that their advertisements were placed. The primary goal was scientific motherhood, with an added benefit of gaining customers, under the assumption that audiences would "buy" into the expert rhetoric.

The placement of advertisements opposite clinical advice in the back half of the book further separates scientific from nostalgic motherhood. The childcare advice section (back half) of *The Book of Baby Mine* contains advertisements for local merchants targeting new parents.

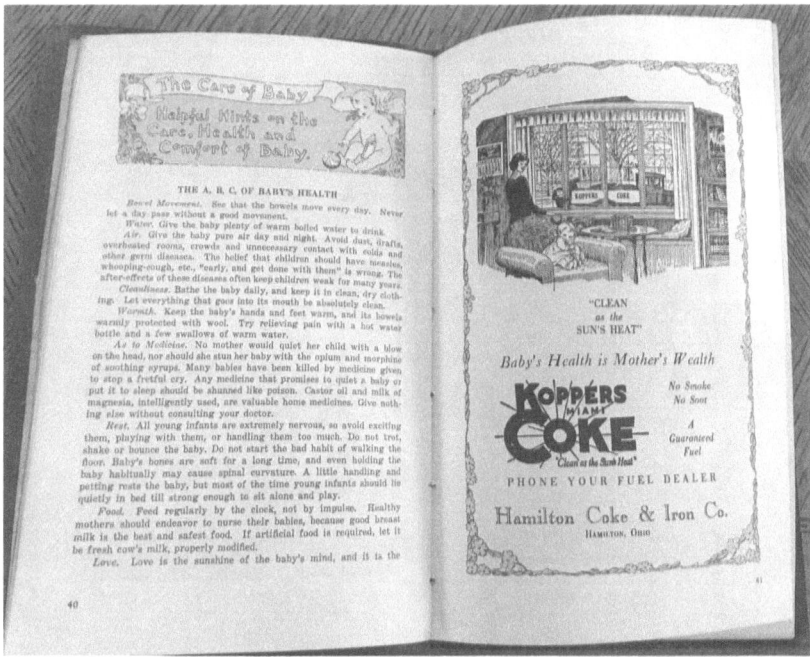

Figure 5.5. "The Care of Baby" parenting advice placed opposite a targeted advertisement touting "Baby's Health is Mother's Wealth," pages 40–41 in The Book of Baby Mine. *Photo Credit: Emilie Merrigan.*

Though the advertisements often employ logic reflecting the ideals of scientific motherhood, there is still a disconnect between this section and the first half of the book with baby's records. In the case of Mary's book from Hamilton, Ohio, it appears that merchants placed advertisements on pages corresponding to relevant information on childcare.

The content from merchants and medical experts seems to lean on one another, and as distributors, the merchants ultimately communicated the expert voice to mothers. Interestingly, since the advertisements feature both logical and emotional appeals, merchants positioned themselves to reach potential customers whether mothers were more receptive of the scientific or nostalgic aspects of motherhood. As the content of the advertisements bridges the expert scientific content and nostalgic portions of the book, the effect seems to lessen the strength of the scientific motherhood by implying that mothers can engage in the content and artifact either clinically or nostalgically.

One aspect of *The Book of Baby Mine* to consider regarding its singularization is the local advertisements placed in the back advice section of the book. While other printings of this book in this time/place would

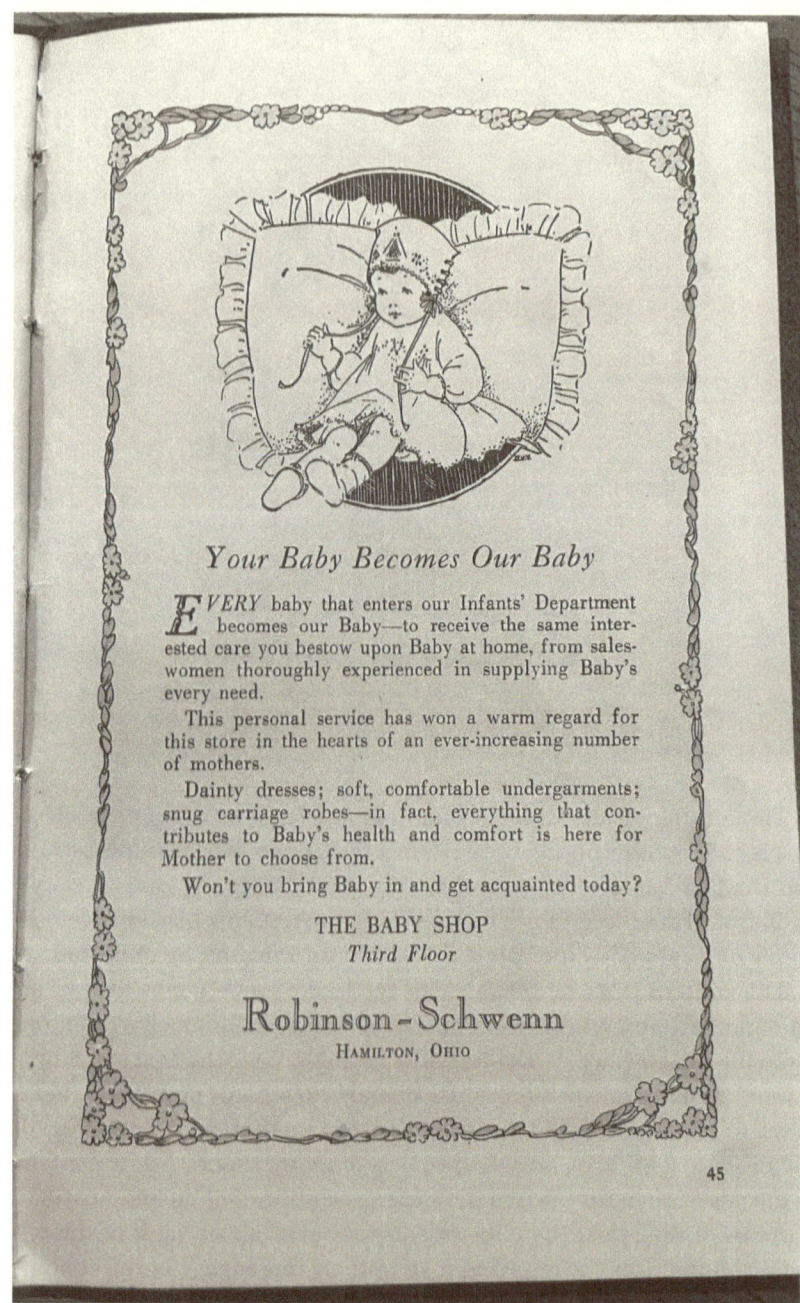

Figure 5.6. "Your Baby Becomes Our Baby" advertisement for The Baby Shop, including language pointing toward both scientific motherhood ("Baby's health and comfort") and nostalgic motherhood ("Dainty dresses"); page 45 in The Book of Baby Mine. Photo Credit: Emilie Merrigan.

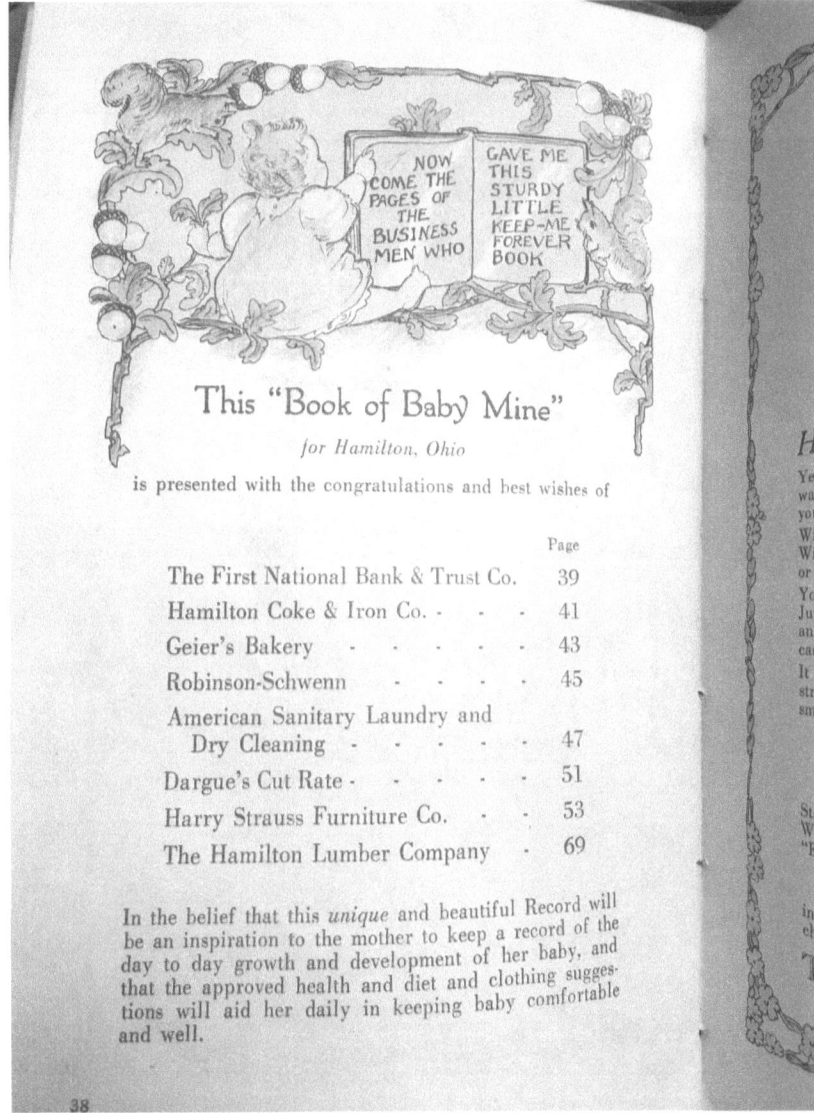

Figure 5.7. Advertisement index of local businesses who sponsored this printing of The Book of Baby Mine *(page 38)*. Photo Credit: Emilie Merrigan.

have had the same advertisements, these are unique to this time and place and therefore contribute to the unique makeup of Mary's book.

As with other baby books, the advertisements in Mary's book appear disconnected from her records, even in the most possible category of "gifts," which do not name brands nor stores.

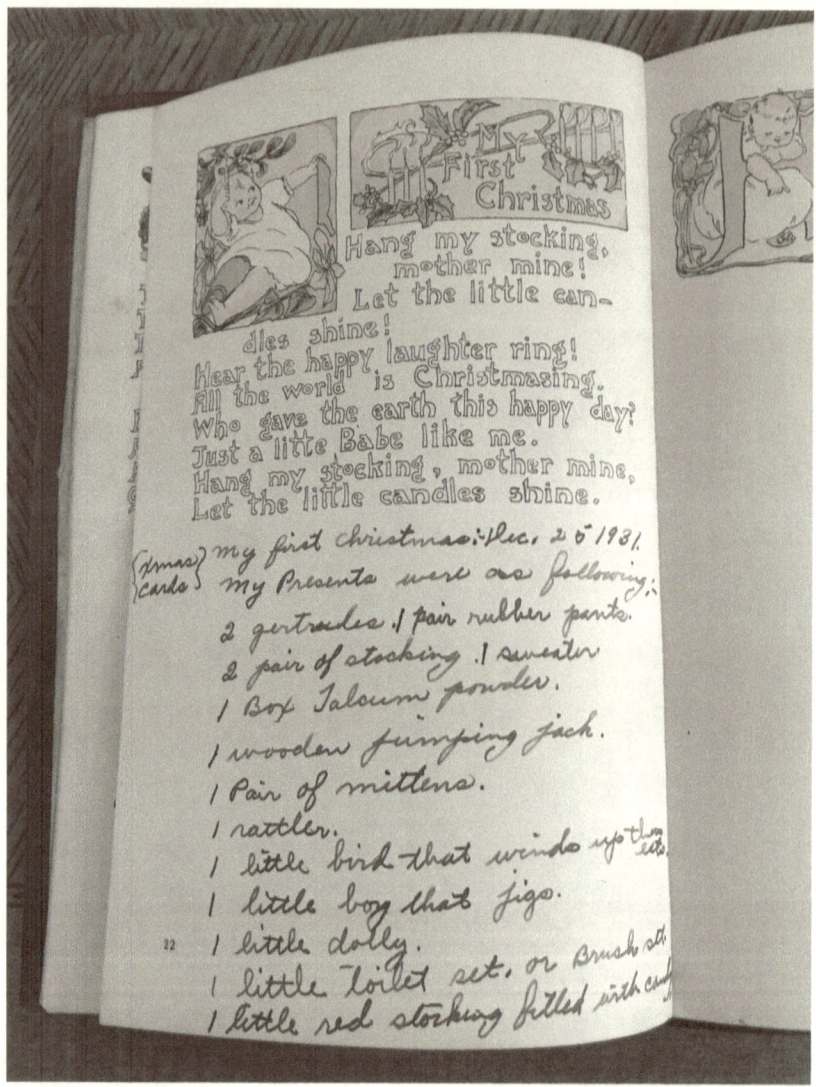

Figure 5.8. Mary's First Christmas list of gifts given to this book's subject, Mary Louise Grabel; page 22 in The Book of Baby Mine. Photo Credit: Emilie Merrigan.

Although the mother details many gifts in keeping with advice and advertisements in the latter half of the book, further information about the Grabel family later in this chapter will point to this page more as evidence of a life well-lived rather than in keeping with the book's advice. Again, it seems that singularization of this artifact is the solidifying factor in disconnecting scientific from nostalgic motherhood. As merchants sometimes served as the "middle man" between these two realms of motherhood, therein lies the disconnect in this material artifact: the book is in the mother's possession, in the family's home, subject to scientific motherhood only as much as the mother and family allow. Jessie's interaction with this artifact allowed her to define her identity as a mother outside the voice of scientific motherhood. The ultimate significance of this material artifact lies in its singularization and continued existence well beyond the time period's medical experts and their advice.

Analysis of a singularized copy of *The Book of Baby Mine* by Jessie Grabel, mother of infant Mary, demonstrates the disconnect of scientific and nostalgic motherhood. One way Jessie does this is by employing the rhetoric of positivity that typifies baby books as a genre of self. At a time when families could credit medical advances to a decrease in infant mortality, this change in the inclusion of children within families was expressed nostalgically, making an emotional connection to children that families and mothers of previous generations were hesitant to do. Golden and Weiner explain:

> [Baby books'] growing popularity and use among middle- and working-class families over the twentieth century certainly reflected the perception that babies were increasingly likely to survive. . . . A material reflection of this transition occurred as families replaced infant postmortem photographs with snapshots of living babies. (670)

The pleasure a mother might gain from relishing her baby's memories was likely a very real appeal of the baby book for the mother/recorder, especially of the baby book I studied. In Mary's book, notes on a page dedicated to baby's other siblings indicate that Mary's mother, Jessie, had given birth two years earlier, but the child died the same day. Jessie's willingness to record this event, unlike modern propensity to be more introverted about deceased infants, reflects the past tradition of keeping photographs or records of deceased infants, yet also suggests Jessie's positivity toward her role and accomplishment in being a mother while acknowledging a past setback and disappointment, not to be confused with failure. This entry and its implications are far from clinical and demonstrate the importance to her in the nostalgic experience of motherhood.

Jessie also demonstrates agency over her nostalgic motherhood in a "My First Outing" entry that reflects the positive, nostalgic rhetoric of baby books and the resulting disconnect from scientific motherhood. On page ten, Jessie describes a visit to Mary's Grandma and Grandpa Hayes and some neighbors. Her mother includes observations of their environment and her personal reflection of the trip: "The day was beautiful & I heard something say 'tweet' 'tweet' and I knew it was the little birdies glad to see me take my first ride. And, oh, how mother held me close to her side. So afraid I would get a little bump" (Denny 10). In many ways this entry is nostalgic. The "outing" seems uneventful at face value, though is conveyed as exciting for baby and anxiety-producing yet successful for mother. The mother achieves nostalgia by creating a picture of the day, describing details like the "little birdies" that would be novel and exciting to a newborn's first outing. Furthermore, rather than simply explaining that Mary rode with her mother, the writer specifies "how mother held me close to her side," expressing the mother's care and protection for the baby despite her desire to expose her to the world. The overall effect is nostalgic for baby Mary for as much as her mother could know about her experience, not to mention the joy they shared in bringing Mary out to experience their world and loved ones.

The "First Outing" entry contains hints of a connection to scientific motherhood in basic ways such as exposing infants to fresh air and protecting from injury ("So afraid I would get a little bump."). But in more ways, this entry helps disconnect the book's first half from the second. It is the first extended entry in Mary's book, following pages to list general birth information. The factual portion of recording baby information is abruptly done and moved onto a clearly different purpose as this entry and most successive entries contain similar space for extended entries and photos, as well as poems to complement them. In this entry, the mother doesn't list their destinations and visitors but rather details the day. With the bottom two-thirds of the page empty, the mother could have included a photograph or memento, either alone or accompanying writing, but Mary's mother fills the space with an extended account of the day.

Finally, the "First Outing" entry contains a note that they went in "daddy's Dodge Sedan" that is an example of a consumer item being noted for its nostalgic value. This could be read as a blatant effect of marketing. However, none of the medical material in the back of the book addresses car travel or any kind of transportation, and Mary's regional copy of *The Book of Baby Mine* contains no automotive advertisements. The drawing on the top of the page is also clearly sentimental, showing fairies and small children escorting a baby carriage through a field. This drawing implies the importance of the loving relationships enjoyed in one's first outing rather than the importance of material objects.

We must consider how intentions, such as displaying positivity, play into our understanding of an artifact. Prown argues, "Style is most informative about underlying beliefs when their expression is least

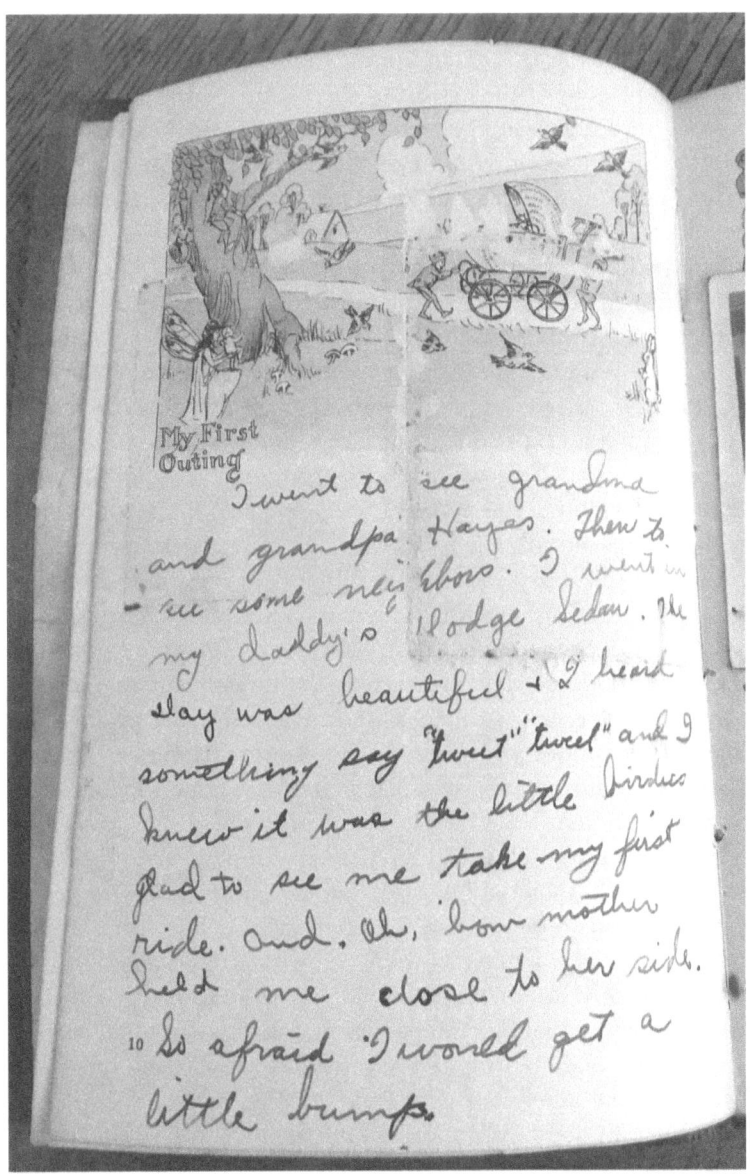

Figure 5.9. "My First Outing" anecdote of baby Mary's first outing written by her mother, Jessie; page 10 in The Book of Baby Mine. Photo Credit: Emilie Merrigan.

self-conscious" ("The Truth" 5). Analysis and understanding of artifacts requires a critical eye as artifacts "may be intended to deceive as well as inform" (5). Knowing more about Mary's family offers an example of considering what information (textual or physical) is absent from an artifact; specifically, information about Mary's family from outside this artifact helps show that this "First Outing" entry is likely more nostalgic than nodding toward materialism. My research into Mary's family revealed that her father, George, worked at times as a truck driver and public worker and was in and out of jail for theft during the time he was married to Mary's mother, Jessie. Eventually Mary's parents divorced, and she moved in with her maternal grandparents along with her mother and younger sister. Knowing this sheds light on a few reasons Jessie may have included this bit of information in this sentimental entry. George's ability to provide the vehicle to transport Mary and her mother to visit loved ones shows his presence both financially and nostalgically. Though partially a financial support, it seems George's largest role in this outing was to provide transportation for his wife and daughter; given his apparent spotty presence in the home, this contribution to and mere participation in the outing would have been of great nostalgic value to the entry's author, Mary's mother. "Deceit" is perhaps a strong word to apply to this entry, but less severely we can certainly see this an example of preferencing positive content in a baby book's entries.

The completion or incompletion of baby books supports the disconnect of scientific and nostalgic motherhood, and it appears that incomplete baby books present as much if not more resistance to scientific motherhood than more complete books. In her extensive analysis, Pascali observes that the majority of baby books are largely incomplete, indicating mothers' tendency to not follow prescriptive suggestions by experts and creators, thereby exerting their agency of their motherhood identity through this material item (7). Yet, the continued existence of baby books in an incomplete or even unused state signifies their importance in our culture and suggests that in any state of completion they hold some kind of value to the materiality of childhood (7). On one hand, we could argue that incomplete baby books leave original patriarchal structure in this genre with no evidence of the mother's application or rejection. On the other, Pascali suggests that, in fact, more complete baby books typically demonstrate stronger adherence to scientific motherhood and, thus, less singularization and exertion of agency over motherhood (12). I would argue that a mother could complete a baby book and exert agency and resistance against scientific motherhood, but I do agree that it is precisely the lack of completion and singularization, or even the rogue and sporadic completion of these baby books, that supports the disconnect between scientific and nostalgic motherhood. In the case of Mary's book, Jessie keeps few records, few of which are even remotely related to the aims of scientific motherhood.

Baby books and other related written genres and material memorabilia employ a common nostalgic rhetorical purpose. This is conveyed through both the text and objects with which they are singularized. In many cases this attention to a positive, successful image appears to affect what or how mothers choose to record or omit information in baby books. The lack of recorded accounts of events such as accidents "most likely says more about cultural beliefs about good parenting than about the experiences of babies" (Golden and Weiner 675). Examination of baby books does not clearly reveal whether information is included or excluded intentionally to fulfill this rhetorical goal of the book, or rather if the books' owners simply abandoned their task. But researchers' reviews of hundreds of baby books nevertheless suggests that inclusion/exclusion overwhelmingly fits this rhetorical criteria of positivity (Golden and Weiner; Pascali; Katriel and Farrell). Furthermore, this rhetoric of positivity is overwhelmingly related to the goal/purpose of nostalgia rather than medical record, showing the cultural value of milestones such as holidays rather than success with growth and development. In fact, even when information exists regarding growth and development, it contains the most positive rhetoric when it accompanies a cultural milestone and/or pleasant social interaction with another child or adult (Katriel and Farrell).

Interestingly, Jessie is in some ways more focused on her mother identity. Just as writers in traditional roles or settings use their writing-related objects (in this case, baby books) as "sets or props for desired purposes," I found that mothers-as-writers seemed just as likely to use these objects for purposes such as to assert identity and agency over their role as mother (Alexis 33). In one entry, Jessie explains an argument with Mary's father over choosing Mary's name. On its face, this entry is fairly negative, especially knowing Mary's parents would ultimately split. However, if the goal of this object is to form positivity and success, this entry does so toward Jessie's identity as she won the baby's naming rights. The anecdote would be an interesting story for Mary about the origin of her identity, and certainly serves to support a positive view of Jessie as a strong-willed woman. Additionally, writing objects can perform identity work but also serve as obstacles to identity work. In her study of individuals' use of the Moleskine notebook, Alexis raises a question about "what happens when our narrative around an object consumes our ability to use it," pointing to the "tension of wanting to become something" and "trying to access it" (43). This distraction and tension feels rampant in baby books as the writer would be confronted with the ideals of an identity in the very object in which they must attempt to navigate and perform their identity work. Although this entry is too brief to be indicative of the parents' ultimate split, including it shows Jessie's willingness to express challenges in her marriage in deference to a desire to portray her success as a power-wielding woman in the role of mother.

CONCLUSION

My findings of the disconnect between scientific and economic influences on nostalgic motherhood are significant because they highlight the opportunity singularization allows for individuals to claim or reclaim an identity such as mother. This identity has deep cultural associations, evident in material artifacts such as baby books; each singularized book enables mothers to accept or reject societal influences and solidify their mother identity through the artifact. My research into baby books and the cultural influences on them brought me to the not-surprising conclusion that the creation and intentions of baby books are laden with the gendered expectations of parenting—motherhood—in American society, especially in the early twentieth century. This tension of gendered power and agency of creators and users that comes into play in baby books is especially evident with the influence of the male-dominated medical profession. While told to use the information and artifact of a baby book in a prescribed way for an established purpose, mothers have frequently done otherwise. By documenting diversions from professional childrearing advice, diverting from or even failing to complete prescribed page content, mothers like Jessie successfully singularize the artifact in both content and materiality separate from its patriarchal intent of scientific and consumer-driven motherhood.

While some like Pascali have studied baby books in large quantities, there are numerous influences of culture and instances of singularization left to examine. One interesting pattern Pascali noted was the desire to record positive experiences of childrearing and infancy that resulted in entries that contradicted popular medical advice, further associating baby books with genres of self. As medical advice (in baby books and elsewhere) became available to more audiences of mothers, a collective, cultural identity of mother was strengthened by women "transcending or challenging expertise" (Vandenberg-Daves). In the case of baby books, mothers choosing to record "violations" of these specific infant-care instructions demonstrates mothers deferring to instinct in caring for children in ways that eventually proved preferable to the advice of that time (Katriel and Farrell). It wasn't until the last half of the twentieth century that feminists and women outwardly confronted parenting literature intending to "de-center the patriarchal voice" (Dobris and White-Mills 35; Vandenberg-Daves). Although baby books are prescribed with cultural ideals, this genre of self allows for owners to singularize this important artifact beyond its homogenous cultural identity. Singularized baby books demonstrate the small ways in which women began to challenge scientific motherhood, recording these events that, despite their rule-breaking, had a clearly positive outcome for the child as well as a positive experience for the adult who witnessed and recorded these events.

The influence of science on motherhood in early-twentieth-century America cannot be discounted, and in fact played a large role in the shift in families' treatment of childhood as an existence worthy of attentions such as through baby books. But my examination of an artifact of material culture highlights the power of singularization that lends agency to the singularizer, allowing them to reclaim any identities connected to the material artifact. Though this book contained a disconnect of science and nostalgia prior to its singularization by the Grabel family, Jessie's entries in this artifact further separate Mary's records from the section on scientific motherhood. There are many more connections to be made between the baby book and other written genres and material artifacts, which may in turn offer more evidence of the influence of society and culture on motherhood, and vice versa.

NOTES

1. The concept has also been studied in cultures around the world (Argentina, Korea, Canada, to name a few), for its effects on countless socially constructed identities including race, socioeconomic class, and able-bodiedness. While there are numerous similarities amongst cultures and identities, particularly as influenced by scientific motherhood, my scope is limited to the early-twentieth-century United States and the singular copy of *The Book of Baby Mine* due to the wealth of cultural insight available from this singularized copy.
2. Denny appears to be the author of the poems and introductions to the baby records section of the book; the author or source of the parenting advice is unattributed/unclear.
3. Although my research of *The Book of Baby Mine* is inconclusive as to the author or source of the childcare section of the book, I argue that it can still be considered scientifically based, as much of the content echoes the medically supported recommendations on topics such as feeding and physical development noted by numerous sources on scientific motherhood and baby books (Aysan and Thompson 2146; Golden and Weiner 673–675; Apple 58–68).

WORKS CITED

Alexis, Cydney. "The Symbolic Life of the Moleskine Notebook: Material Goods as a Tableau for Writing Identity Performance." *Composition Studies*, vol. 45, no. 2, Fall 2017, pp. 32–54. Web.

Apple, Rima D. *Perfect Motherhood: Science and Childrearing in America*. Rutgers UP, 2006.

Aysan, Ferda, and Dennis Thompson. "Professional Child Rearing Advice in the Early 20th Century: American and International Perspectives." *Procedia Social and Behavioral Science*, vol. 1, no. 1, 2009, www.sciencedirect.com. Accessed Dec. 2016.

Bartlett, Lesley. "To Seem and to Feel: Situated Identities and Literacy Practices." *The Teachers College Record*, vol. 109, no. 1, 2007, pp. 51–69.

Belk, Russell W. "Possessions and the Extended Self." *Journal of Consumer Research*, vol. 15, no. 2, 1988, pp. 139–168. *JSTOR*, http://www.jstor.org/stable/2489522. Accessed 1 Apr. 2017.

Csikszentmihalyi, Mihaly, and Eugene Rochberg-Halton. *The Meaning of Things: Domestic Symbols and the Self.* Cambridge UP, 1981.

Deetz, James. *In Small Things Forgotten: The Archaeology of Early American Life*. Anchor-Doubleday, 1977.

Denny, Melcena Burns. *The Book of Baby Mine*. Compiled for Mary Louise Grabel, born 1931. The Simplicity Company, Baby Mine Company, 1915.

Dobris, Catherine A., and Kim White-Mills. "Rhetorical Visions of Motherhood: A Feminist Analysis of the *What to Expect* Series." *Women and Language*, vol. 29, no. 1, 2006, pp. 26–36. *ProQuest*. Accessed 25 Mar. 2018.

Emig, Janet. *The Composing Processes of Twelfth Graders*. NCTE, 1971.

Epp, Amber, and Linda Price. "The Storied Life of Singularized Objects: Forces of Agency and Network Transformation." *Journal of Consumer Research*, vol. 36, no. 5, 2010, pp. 820–838. *JSTOR*, http://www.jstor.org/stable/10.1086/603547. Accessed 1 Apr. 2017.

Frederick, Angela. "Risky Mothers and the Normalcy Project: Women with Disabilities Negotiate Scientific Motherhood." *Gender and Society*, vol. 31, no. 1, Feb. 2017, pp. 74–95, https://doi.org/10.1177/0891243216683914.

Glassie, Henry. *Material Culture*, Indiana UP, 1999.

Golden, Janet, and Lynn Weiner. "Reading Baby Books: Medicine, Marketing, Money and the Lives of American Infants." *Journal of Social History*, vol. 44, no. 3, 2011, pp. 667–687. *EBSCOhost*. Accessed Dec. 2016.

Grant, Julia. *Raising Baby by the Book*. Yale UP, 1998.

Hollenbeck, Bryn Varley. *Making Space for Children: The Material Culture of American Childhoods, 1900–1950*. 2008. University of Delaware, dissertation. ProQuest Dissertations Publishing. UMI 3325489. Accessed Dec. 2016.

Katriel, Tamar, and Thomas Farrell. "Scrapbooks as Cultural Texts: An American Art of Memory." *Text and Performance Quarterly*, vol. 11, no. 1, Jan. 1991, pp. 1–17. *EBSCOHost*. Accessed 2 Dec. 2016.

Klausner, Kim. "Worried Women: The Popularization of Scientific Motherhood in the 1920s." *The History Journal: Ex Post Facto*, vol. 4, no. 2, spring 1995, pp. 51–69, https://history.sfsu.edu/sites/default/files/EPF/1995_KimKlausner-ilovepdf-compressed.pdf.

Kopytoff, Igor. "The Cultural Biography of Things: Commoditization as a Process." *The Social Life of Things: Commodities in Cultural Perspective*, edited by Arjun Appadurai, Cambridge UP, 1986.

Lemus, Cheryl. "Save Your Baby, Save Ten Percent: National Baby Week, the Infants' Department, and the Modern Pregnant Woman, 1905–1925." *Journal of Women's History*, vol. 25, no. 3, 2013, pp. 165–187. *ProQuest*. Accessed 25 Mar. 2018.

Pascali, Lara. *Baby Books and Childhood Narratives: Writing the Self through Material Culture.* 2007. University of Delaware, dissertation. ProQuest Dissertations Publishing. UMI 1444689. Accessed Dec. 2016.
Prown, Jules David. "Style as Evidence." *Winterthur Portfolio*, vol. 15, no. 3, 1980, pp. 197–210.
Prown, Jules David. "The Truth of Material Culture: History or Fiction?" *History from Things: Essays on Material Culture*, edited by Steven D. Lubar and W. D. Kingery, Smithsonian UP, 1993, pp. 1–19.
Prown, Jules, and Kenneth Haltman, editors. *American Artifacts: Essays in Material Culture.* Michigan State UP, 2000.
Stearns, Peter N. *Anxious Parents: A History of Modern Childrearing in America.* New York UP, 2003.
Stearns, Peter N. "Challenges in the History of Childhood." *Journal of the History of Childhood and Youth*, vol. 1, no. 1, 2008, pp. 35–41. *ProQuest.* Accessed 2 Dec. 2016.
Vandenberg-Daves, Jodi. "Twentieth-Century American Motherhood: Promises, Pitfalls, and Continuing Legacies." *The American Historian*, The Organization of American Historians, https://tah.oah.org/november-2016/twentieth-century-american-motherhood-promises-pitfalls-and-continuing-legacies/.
Wolf, Jacqueline H. *Dont Kill Your Baby: Public Health and the Decline of Breastfeeding in the Nineteenth and Twentieth Centuries.* Ohio State UP, 2001.
Wyche, Susan. "Times, Tools, and Talismans." *Essays on Writing*, edited by Lizbeth A. Bryant and Heather M. Clark, Pearson, 2009, pp. 52–64.

PART TWO

Writing Work

As we noted in our postscript to the introduction, the global COVID-19 pandemic has restructured for many what it means to work. For many whose work rapidly shifted online, the home became not just a domestic and social space but a workplace, as local and state governments enforced stay-at-home orders, forcing people and work inside. Numerous journalistic articles have addressed some of the consequences of this reality, including homes being rearranged or reframed to account for the need for private space to work. The housing market has boomed, rather than declined, with some hypothesizing that it is the need for more space when all family members are home, or the need for reimagined space, that accounts for this boom (Gopal; Sarnoff). In the academic world, journals have reported record lows for article submissions from women, a presumed consequence of their domestic roles, as proximity, homeschooling, and the ability to rely on childcare diminished for many (Flaherty). Journalistic essays abound on the ways home and work life have been transformed by working from home and have begun detailing the ways the home and office will be reimagined due to the pandemic (Kennicott; Chayka; Svaldi). People, in other words, have experienced novel relationships to the spaces and objects in their home and to the ways these affordances and technologies impact their ability to work. And close study of these relationships, spaces, and objects is critical. As Brian McNely writes, "The things near us and with us matter to the work we do, to how we perceive that work, and to who we are. In other words, the systemic contexts of our everyday work environments are by no means trivial" (50).

Connections between writing work and environmental and material contexts motivate the studies in this section. Each demonstrates the promise and possibilities for studies of the material culture of writing work, contemporary and historical. Focused on a university design studio, the writing suite of a historical writer, and a multimodal genre and object central to museum curation, this section interrogates the impact of workspaces and the objects within them on writing work, the ways objects and spaces work on us as we write, and the need to reconceptualize what constitutes writing work based on the context within which it is situated.

Continuing her efforts to bring MCS into technical communication, Deborah C. Andrews leads the section with her research on the material design of a contemporary work space, the Design Studio in the department of mechanical engineering at the University of Delaware. Drawing together theory and methods from MCS and WS, Andrews explores how such open plan spaces designed for twenty-first century knowledge workers might (or might not) "foster innovative problem-solving and new writing strategies emerging in response to these new environments." Andrews tests the idea that space and stuff shape human (writing) behavior via the participatory role of the layouts of, and features and objects within, workspaces. In another edited collection (Moore and Richards), Andrews phrases her hypothesis this way: "Do the buildings work?" (Andrews 257). Do well-designed buildings and spaces facilitate, or even participate in, processes of problem-solving, collaboration, innovation, and composing? And do spaces and buildings—as well as laptops, furniture, chairs, files—do work of their own? We think Andrews, and this section, answers *yes* (and, from some vantages, in a flat ontological sense).

Andrews's question provokes examination of how the material surrounds and objects of writing work act upon and collaborate with human actors. Her question reflects a new material sensibility, one carried also into the final chapter in this section. In "Assembling the File, or, How Conservation Works," Anne MacKay, archivist and head of restoration at the McCord Museum in Montreal, examines a familiar object in her daily work: the conservation file, an under-examined professional object that includes "multiple texts written by conservators, along with a host of contextual information, visual references . . . [and] material fragments" related to works on museum display. MacKay considers these files a "fundamental element of material culture studies" and leverages a new materialist approach to conservation practice in order to argue for the file as object, as writing, and as assemblage. MacKay asks what the conservation file does in its own trajectories at the same time that, hearkening back to the previous section on identity, she experiences the file as "the core of [her] professional practice and identity." In part, MacKay's chapter, and this section, illustrates how new material and MCS frameworks might overlap or complement rather than mutually exclude.[1] We can recognize that human beings have strong psychological connections to objects at the same time that we recognize that people work, and objects work, and people and objects work together. As Barnett and Boyle write in *Rhetoric, through Everyday Things*, "Things provoke thought, incite feeling, circulate affects, and arouse in us a sense of wonder" (1) at the same time that they are themselves "vibrant actors, enacting effects that exceed (and are sometimes in direct conflict with) human agency and intentionality" (1).

Chapters also show what is gained when we keep focused on a situated writing artifact. This section's middle chapter by Diane Ehrenpreis, associate curator of decorative arts at Monticello, illustrates this attention to context. Ehrenpreis closely examines the self-engineered and systematic letter-writing station of fraught historical figure Thomas Jefferson. Her analysis draws out different dimensions of the complex context of Jefferson's writing life and the life of his furniture, revealing Jefferson inseparably as a writer, enslaver, inventor, and politician. Her analysis depicts Jefferson as a historical correspondent obsessed with his "workflow"[2] for reading, composing, filing, and retrieving huge volumes of letters. Though it's easy to assume that information overload or data management is a recent challenge, Jefferson's furniture shows that writers have long struggled to manage their work environments and the technologies they use to manage and store information.

Ehrenpreis shows how it is not a meticulously designed set of letter-writing furniture alone that makes Jefferson "one of the world's most prolific correspondents" of his day: it was the brutal exploitation of slavery that made his writing space and practices possible. It was his racial, gendered, and monied privilege that granted unfettered access to materials, time, and domestic space. And it was his economic means, coupled with a legacy curated by multiple stakeholders, that worked to meticulously preserve his things, as well as the storytelling and mythmaking attached to them. These are the circumstances enabling us to know about Jefferson's writing life. The writing life of enslaved worker at Monticello, Israel Gillette, whom Ehrenpreis also features in her chapter, remains more remote, even as his voice and life are inextricable from Jefferson and Monticello. We are left wanting to know more about Gillette's writing life—his tools, his literacy history, and the space and ways he found to write. This curiosity reminds us of the sociomaterial circumstances and cultural compulsions that allow certain artifacts, practices, and histories to be preserved while others remain remote or silenced.

NOTES

1. Readers in writing studies interested in Latour's actor-network-theory might be interested in Epp and Price's work, mentioned in the collection introduction, which draws on this framework in consumer research studies.

2. We invoke the modern concept of workflow intentionally as a way to describe the challenging information work of this historical figure. We credit our thinking about the term to the recent work of Lockridge and Van Ittersum, who describe workflows as "a lens to examine the often omitted tools, material conditions, and activities of writing" (n. pag.).

WORKS CITED

Andrews, Deborah C. "Investigating the Workplaces of Science." *Posthuman Praxis in Technical Communication*, edited by Kristen R. Moore and Daniel P. Richards, Routledge, 2018, pp. 255–280.

Chayka, Kyle. "How the Coronavirus Will Reshape Architecture." *The New Yorker*, 17 June 2020, https://www.newyorker.com/culture/dept-of-design/how-the-coronavirus-will-reshape-architecture.

Flaherty, Colleen. "No Room of One's Own: Early Journal Submission Data Suggest COVID-19 Is Tanking Women's Research Productivity." *Inside Higher Ed*, 21 Apr. 2020, https://www.insidehighered.com/news/2020/04/21/early-journal-submission-data-suggest-covid-19-tanking-womens-research-productivity.

Gopal, Prashant, and John Gittelsohn. "Urban Exiles Are Fueling a Suburban Housing Boom Across the U.S." *Bloomberg Quint*, 21 Aug. 2020, https://www.bloombergquint.com/businessweek/covid-pandemic-fuels-u-s-housing-boom-as-urbanites-swarm-suburbs.

Kennicott, Philip. "Designing to Survive." *The Washington Post Magazine*, 13 July 2020, https://www.washingtonpost.com/magazine/2020/07/13/pandemic-has-shown-us-what-future-architecture-could-be/?arc404=true.

Lockridge, Tim, and Derek Van Ittersum. *Writing Workflows: Beyond Word Processing*. https://processedword.net/writing-workflows/index.html.

McNely, Brian. "Taking Things Seriously with Visual Research." *Communication Design Quarterly*, vol. 3, no. 2, 2015, pp. 48–54.

Sarnoff, Nancy. "How 'Pandemic Buyers' Are Keeping Houston's Struggling Real Estate Market Humming during COVID." *Houston Chronicle*, 16 July 2020, https://www.houstonchronicle.com/business/article/pandemic-buy-houston-real-estate-market-home-covid-15412759.php.

Svaldi, Aldo. "Backyard Sheds and Extended Mountain Stays: Coloradans Adapt as Remote Work Becomes the New Reality." *The Denver Post*, 27 Aug. 2020, https://www.denverpost.com/2020/08/27/remote-work-home-offices-colorado-studio-shed/.

6

NEW WRITING IN NEW SPACES
"Social Writing" in an Interdisciplinary Academic Makerspace

Deborah C. Andrews

Today, many corporate CEOs, tech entrepreneurs, management consultants, and academic administrators believe workplaces and learning spaces can be designed explicitly to foster the communication activities that will help individuals and organizations innovate. A material turn in writing studies, accompanied by the incorporation of the design thinking developed by engineers and architects, is at the same time acknowledging the agency of things in enhancing the functional, aesthetic, and motivational experiences of writers. Such thinking in particular is helping to identify new strategies for collaborative communication, seen as a driver of innovation when individuals and organizations face the messy, ambiguous problems and opportunities in the twenty-first-century global economy.

This chapter describes one site in my ongoing research about how writers collaborate in workplaces explicitly designed to be agents in collaborative communication. It is the interdisciplinary Design Studio in the department of mechanical engineering at the University of Delaware, a makerspace that is evolving in parallel ways to the open-plan commercial workplaces many students will eventually inhabit, and write in, as technical and business professionals. My research on those sites, particularly research in the commercial literature about designing such sites, thus informs the discussion (Andrews, "Investigating"; Andrews, "Physical Environment"; Andrews, "A Space for Place").

In its focus on what Nedra Reynolds calls "the *where* of writing," this chapter further investigates, in Paul Prior and Jody Shipka's terms, the "environment selecting and structuring practices" of writers, including their "self-structuring through environmental structuring" (180). In their research, Prior and Shipka tend to emphasize how individuals craft the spaces in which they write or accept the space as more or less incidental to their writing. This chapter emphasizes the role of environmental structuring. Writer's rooms, both those of famous literary figures as well as other writers whose composing processes are of interest, are a significant thread in writing studies research (e.g., Alexis; Pigg; Rule). This chapter differs from this thread, which largely deals with individual writers, in at least two ways. The first is its focus on writing as a collaborative activity. The four writers whose case studies form the core of Prior and Shipka's study, for example, including an undergraduate engineering major, wrote individually in environments they selected or shaped individually. This chapter concentrates on teams of writers. The second is the chapter's focus on writing less as a literary or academic endeavor and more as a way to solve problems in the world. The workplaces, including the Design Studio, in my research are filled with people who don't think of themselves as writers, while they often write extensively to get their work done. In this sense, the chapter accords with Ehrenpreis's discussion (this volume) of the desk that Thomas Jefferson designed to accommodate his system for carrying out an extensive correspondence. It was the "workstation" from which he conducted his global political affairs.

After a brief introduction to academic makerspaces and the Design Studio, the chapter turns to larger implications for the design of environments that foster innovative problem-solving and new writing strategies emerging in response to these new environments. In the Design Studio, this means that students are learning to take on an entrepreneurial identity as they apply design thinking to collaborative writing in a maker exercise.

ACADEMIC MAKERSPACES

A growing trend on university campuses is the design and implementation of spaces—sometimes called design studios, invention studios, idea factories, or, more generally, makerspaces—that support project-oriented collaboration among students in engineering, science, and other fields. An early and important model for an academic makerspace is the Hasso Plattner Institute of Design, popularly known as the d.school, at Stanford. As David Kelley, a cofounder of the d.school and of the international space design consultancy IDEO, argues

> space should be thought of not as something fixed-as-given, a facilities project or a showcase. It should instead be considered an "instrument for innovation and collaboration. . . . a valuable tool that can help you create deep and meaningful collaborations in your work and life" (quoted in Doorley and Witthoft 5).

A makerspace offers a physical location with fabrication resources and support for students to learn and work in a hands-on environment. More than just a fabrication facility, however, a makerspace aims to promote a sense of community. As Dustyn Roberts, one of the creators of the Design Studio notes, people matter just as much as (or more so than) machines. A participatory culture that encourages informal interactions among the communities the makerspace serves is what distinguishes it from a facility used only for fabrication. The space also serves to grow a culture of "helping others" as students share expertise as well as design, leadership, and administrative responsibilities (Andrews and Roberts).

The growth of academic makerspaces is coming at the same time as academic administrators, boards of trustees, and architects are designing new, purpose-built "innovation centers" on or near university campuses aimed at launching new eras in interdisciplinary scientific and technical research (Andrews, "Investigating"). In a useful categorization developed by Stewart Brand, such buildings often take a "high road" approach: polished, architect-designed, promoted by authorities who won't work there but have "lofty expectations" for researchers who do. Makerspaces, while sometimes incorporated within such buildings, are more likely to be "low road," in Brand's terms. The model for the low road approach is the iconic Building 20 at MIT, a temporary (although long lasting) building that housed an interdisciplinary group of researchers who produced major scientific breakthrough for more than fifty years. These building are rough, often just sheds or reused industrial spaces, shabby but spacious. The occupants are in charge and can personalize the space in ways that are empowering and forgiving. As W. O. Roberts, founding director of the National Center for Atmospheric Research in Boulder, Colorado, noted in his prospectus for its new building (using the pronoun "he" for "scientist" as was common at the time): "The scientist must feel free to tack things on the wall, or anchor things to the floor, or tear out a part of a wall to house some piece of equipment he is using, or create a clutter . . . an air of incompleteness, of non-finality, is essential to a good scientific environment" (quoted in Leslie 186).

The study of collaboration among students in the Design Studio presented in this chapter began as a byproduct of my research on two new innovation centers, one at the University of Delaware—the Harker Interdisciplinary Science and Engineering Laboratory—and the "Discovery Building" at the University of Wisconsin (Andrews, "Investigating"). During my field research on Harker Lab, in a rainstorm, I took a short-cut through the mechanical engineering building, where I was intrigued by the makerspace. I knew the context. For several years, I collaborated with the senior design faculty in mechanical engineering to partner students in my technical editing classes with teams of mechanical engineering students working to solve industry-sponsored projects. I also learned that a colleague in the department of art and design had a hand in shaping the Design Studio and talked with him about a course he teaches there that enrolls both engineering and art/design students. This chapter's discussion of collaborative writing in the makerspace derives from these conversations with engineering and art/design faculty; direct observations from time to time over several years, including taking photographs; a questionnaire circulated to participants in an entrepreneurial project class whose work was conducted in the studio; and informal conversations with students on several occasions. The goal was to see how students experienced its environment as fostering (or not) their ability to collaborate as a project team and to write collaboratively.

THE DESIGN STUDIO

The Design Studio at Delaware is decidedly low-road. A 5,500 square foot, student-run enterprise, it connects several existing rooms on the ground floor of a building used primarily to house the offices and labs of the department of mechanical engineering (see fig. 6.1).

Jenni Buckley and Dustyn Roberts, two department faculty, spearheaded the design. They were joined early on by students who collaborated on the design, constructed many of the features of the space as a maker exercise, and created coherence among the rooms through signage and the common look of several elements, for example, plywood cutouts on the walls (see fig. 6.2).

The terms used to designate areas (the hive, the nook, the clubhouse, the pit), as well as toys, posters, and comments written on the walls ("We Build Engineers"), confirm student ownership and tie the various rooms together (see fig. 6.3).

Starting in 2012 with a former storage area, the organizers negotiated strategically to add more space. It was officially opened as a makerspace in March 2014 and has been evolving in both the amount of space and in its furnishings and technology since then. Like other makerspaces, the basic setting is easily reconfigurable for multiple users and uses. Much of the furniture, on wheels or otherwise movable, was purchased inexpensively and assembled by the students (see fig. 6.4).

As Jenni Buckley notes, the space offers students the ability to "roll around and collaborate." They work mostly in public. Vertical surfaces

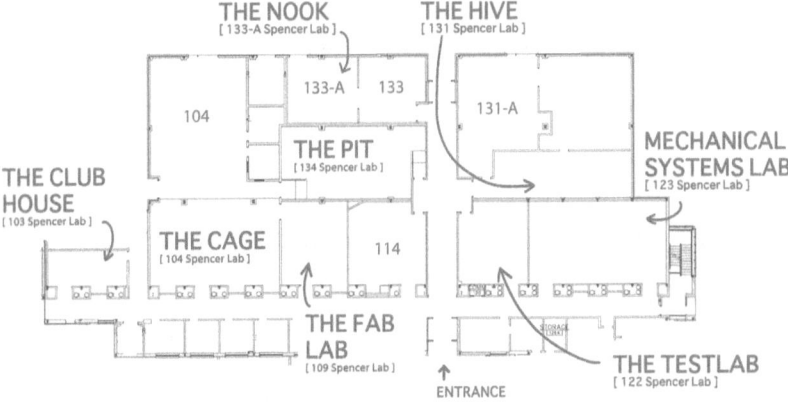

Figure 6.1. Floor plan of the Design Studio in 2017. Photo credit: Dustyn Roberts.

Figure 6.2. The Hive. Note the design of the perforated plywood on the wall that incorporates the name of the room. Photo credit: Deborah C. Andrews.

for writing abound, like the chalkboard in figure 6.3 and the movable panels, created inexpensively as a maker exercise, shown in figures 6.2 and 6.4. These "make thinking tangible," an important practice in interdisciplinary collaboration (Doorley and Witthoft 157). "Thinking of walls

Figure 6.3. The Fab lab. A large writeable blackboard covers the back wall. The logo for students in the department ("We build engineers") is prominently written on another wall. Teams work on projects in an open, social setting with lots of equipment. Photo credit: Dustyn Roberts.

Figure 6.4. The Pit, a more casual area. The low table has large wheels so that it can be easily moved around. The white boards, like the table made inexpensively by students, also have wheels. The bottom wall shelf serves as a counter for computer users; the upper shelves store equipment. Photo credit: Deborah C. Andrews.

Figure 6.5. The large object suspended from a wall in this open area is a rowing shell, which serves as a reminder of a several semester team project to develop ways to adapt shells for use by persons with disabilities. Photo credit: Deborah C. Andrews.

as surfaces rather than separators helps inform when, where, and how they can be used" (Doorley and Wittoff 177). Designers from the Stanford d.school argue, "Actively invite people to look at your secrets" (Doorley and Wittoff 174). What's written on the boards and the walls—sketches, key phrases, unresolved ideas—establishes the team's common ground. The team sees each other's work as they fulfill mutual responsibilities to the project, building trust and gathering momentum and motivation. Making their work broadly visible also serves as a positive source of learning and information sharing among teams. An abundance of computers, including those with large and multiple screens to aid collaboration, augment the laptops and smart phones students bring individually. Visible storage of prototypes and examples of finished projects—what has been called the "reinvention of storage"—provide inspiration (see fig. 6.5).

Creatively housing such items as tools, supplies, and archives offers sites for conversation. The setting welcomes the mess that often accompanies innovation. A range of cheap materials, sometimes called "cruft," and 3D printers allow for easy prototyping and iterative testing of design solutions.

THE AGENCY OF PLACE

That a setting can inspire and motivate as well as foster desired behaviors squares with long-held theory in material culture studies, which argues that objects create subjects, sometimes even more than the other way around. The assumption behind such studies is that, as philosopher Pierre Bourdieu, quoted by anthropologist Danny Miller, notes: "Things, not, mind you, individual things, but the system of things, with their internal order, make us the people we are" (53). Architectural historian Sarah Goldhagen, among other environmentalists and designers, takes this argument even further. She sees consciousness and cognition as the product of a "three way collaboration of mind, body, and environment" (47). Much of our "internal cognitive lives" takes place "outside of language and below the level of conscious awareness," making us less the "imperially sovereign agents over our experiences" than previously thought (47). In other words, humans and things co-constitute each other, even when we are not aware of that.

Recognition of this collaboration between humans and things underlies several recent publications in rhetoric and writing studies (e.g., Prior and Shipka, Moore and Richards, Barnett and Boyle, Packer and Crofts Wiley). Rejecting the notion of a static dualism between the material and the immaterial, Jennifer Slack, for example, sees communication not just as a human-to-human interaction using technology to exchange meaning but as something that exists at the molecular level. Like Goldhagen, she sees cognition as distributed in networks and systems of meaning across a human-machine *assemblage*. Slack defines this as a "dynamic collection or arrangement of heterogeneous elements (structures, practices, materials, affects, and enunciations) that express a character or identity and assert a territory" (152). In calling such an approach *posthuman*, Carl Herndl notes that it offers

> new ways to figure the relation between [rhetorical] action and what had heretofore been seen only as context or background. As the posthuman decenters the human agent and reconceptualizes human subjectivity, it also re-enchants the material world. (Moore and Richards, xii)

Things thus have agency, that is, they offer affordances or otherwise collaborate with people in critical assemblages. They have a purpose in human use, sometimes a very obvious one, like a desk or a whiteboard for writing. Sometimes the affordance is less obvious. It is any "action possibility available in the environment to an individual, independent of the individual's ability to perceive this possibility" (Cole).

Collaborative Learning in Makerspaces

While it may not "re-enchant the material world," the Design Studio does provide affordances that support a pedagogy of collaborative learning, an approach sometimes called (although there are subtle differences) "problem-based learning," "active learning," or "peer-to-peer learning." Makerspaces reflect the theory that "students learn better when questioning and explaining problems and processes to each other" (Andrews and Roberts). As more and more of the technical capacities once taught as core engineering skills are "downshifted" into the machinery itself, professional preparation requires increasing attention to interpersonal skills and higher-order reasoning. Bringing students together in a makerspace fosters collaboration largely through personal, face-to-face communication, centered on objects and making, communication skills not often explicitly addressed in engineering classrooms. Teaching each other as members of the team also provides practice in performing one's expertise for audiences beyond the team, especially on interdisciplinary teams whose members don't share the same context. Team members challenge each other's assumptions, cycling between divergent and convergent patterns of thinking and questioning. This activity requires students to develop a language for talking-about-what-they-are-talking-about, that is, meta-cognitive abilities to explain how their contribution to a large project will be situated as they integrate the various elements being contributed by team members.

The Design Studio is particularly open to collaborations that help students learn across disciplines and differences. Aside from areas where special skills are needed in a supervised environment, other settings, particularly those with more casual furnishings, welcome students who seek an inviting place to learn informally about making things. The presence of students in art and design, fashion, biology, education, and physical therapy, among other disciplines, has sometimes led to more sustained cooperation on projects.

Problem-based learning strategies embrace a now widely held theory that "innovation—the heart of the knowledge economy—is fundamentally social" (Gladwell 2). In a classic study, Bill Hillier ties the spatial configuration of research labs, particularly the kinds of movement fostered in the space and the degree to which its settings are preprogrammed, as they support what he characterizes as two kinds of knowledge. One, Knowledge A, "ideas we think with," centers on a set of "rules that allow us to *act* socially in well-defined ways" (246). The spatial configuration that supports Knowledge A is highly structured, hierarchical, and conservative; it is hard to move around and make changes in the physical setting. Individuals within the space tend to resemble one another and learn the same ideas at the same time through ritual behavior that eliminates the random (245).

The other, Knowledge B, aims at innovation and the problem solving sought in the contemporary knowledge economy. It is "language with think of," language that creates the new. The configuration for Knowledge B leaves room for random, less programmed movement, for the "generation of new relational patterns by maximizing the randomness of encounter through spatial proximity and movement" (245). Hillier's categorization is useful in understanding learning environments as well. Traditional pedagogy is largely focused on Knowledge A, while active learning pedagogies aim at Knowledge B. A recent report by the Society for College and University Planning (SCUP) suggests some important criteria for academic spaces that support active learning: replacing fixed seating with user-centered design, increasing mobility for teachers and students to increase interaction, heightening student engagement through group work and other forms of interactivity, and helping them feel comfortable in the space as they move furniture around and have a sense of ownership. The setting encourages the social learning that creates new ideas and favors a model that knowledge is co-constructed and not simply "delivered" by an authority/teacher (Painter et al.).

The Design Studio more than meets these criteria. In doing so, it creates a neighborhood, a concept evoked often by a growing number of space planners, architects, and critics of the built environment. Like Brand, they quote the economist Jane Jacobs on the virtues of her neighborhood, Greenwich Village, New York. A lively "street ballet" brought individuals together in both commerce and play, establishing connections that build trust and good will across diversity. Following the lead of innovation-oriented tech companies in Silicon Valley and creative branding agencies internationally, the new workspaces, both academic and commercial, encourage the casual contacts and improvising that are thought to breed innovation, especially contacts among those in different disciplines or with different expertise. Speaking to people in one's own area of expertise only reinforces the old. New insights, so the thinking goes, come from the outside, through a wide circle of impromptu interactions. Herman Miller, the office furniture and design consultancy, argues that collaboration "increases the chances that ideas will meet and recombine in unique ways" and cites a study by Google that found an 81 percent correlation between collaboration and innovation (2). As Laing and Bacevice argue, "The workplace has evolved from rationally designed spaces that reinforce bureaucracy, specialization of skills and hierarchical knowledge flow to places that stimulate improvised routines, creative reinterpretation of tasks and multidirectional knowledge flow" (39)

DESIGNING LEARNING SPACES FOR COLLABORATIVE WRITING

While the positive effects of makerspaces on collaboration and innovative thinking are well-documented, the particular effects of the setting on collaborative *writing* remain less so. Two studies, one of engineering teams and one of teams of writers, provide some tentative answers. Eric A. Grulke, Dan C. Beert, and Derek R. Lane tested the effect of the physical environment on the performance of six multidisciplinary teams of engineering students working on a timed problem-solving task. Three teams worked in a newly constructed room with flexible furnishings designed to "accommodate interaction and electronic communication" (319). The other three teams could work anywhere else in the engineering building. No team chose to work in a traditional classroom. They evaluated the teams' final communication product (a memo) and surveyed the teams concerning their experiences of the spaces they worked in along several design criteria (325). In general, the treatment teams did better both in developing technical content and creating a communication product.

Amanda M. Bemer, Ryan M. Moeller, and Cheryl E. Ball conducted a usability study of three different groups of technical communication students in a redesigned computer lab developed by the department of English at Utah State University (USU). Early labs tended to support a view that writing is something engaged in independently. Desktop computers were aligned in rows facing a teacher's station in the front. But more recent pedagogy sees professional and technical writing in particular, like design, as often collaborative. Writing studies research has increasingly demonstrated the need to subvert the traditional row-on-row configuration of a computer lab. The redesigned lab at USU aimed to take advantage of mobile technology and movable furniture to support writing as a "socially active, collaborative practice" (139). The researchers looked at how the sample student groups physically used the new lab to complete a task scenario. They employed pre-and post-test questionnaires and videotaped students as they moved about.

Both Grulke and colleagues and Bemer and colleagues concluded that collaborators were better able to complete writing tasks, with better results, in spaces that provided ease of interaction; a variety of different settings within the larger space for different forms of technology and informal conversations; mobility among those settings with some boundaries for privacy, confidentiality, and a feeling of control; and flexibility in furnishings and arrangements. Grulke and colleagues also suggested that the physical environment of classrooms, whether intentionally or not, has come to be considered "administrative overhead" and not "a strategic part of educational planning." But properly designed, a physical environment "can actually communicate to students that teamwork is a valued part of their learning culture" (328).

The Design Studio represents a significant subversion of typical classroom design well beyond the environments tested in these two studies. As such, it resembles, in approach if not in polish, open-plan, contemporary commercial workplaces. Characterized by such terms as "flexible," "agile" or "mobile," these new workplaces include similarly flexible furnishings and a variety of setting through which workers, supported by mobile communications technology and wide broadband access, move as their work demands. The space provides a sense of community that is "the physical manifestation of the net culture . . . that values sharing, openness, and co-creation as well as accelerated serendipity" (Herman Miller 5). In both academic and workplace contexts, the aim is to accommodate what one consultancy, Gensler, calls the four modes of twenty-first-century work: *"collaborate, socialize, learn,* and focus" [emphasis added]. The fourth, focus, is largely individual and generally requires privacy, but the rest are interactive and public. At its major office in London, for example, the international bank UBS has created "thin desks" available to all workers throughout the building rather than tying workers to the same desk, phone, and computer. A managing director of UBS sees "being chained to a desk in a singular environment" as "restrictive" (Bray). "Working together, talking to each other, working in a more agile way. People are probably not so fixed any more in their working environment," notes UBS's head of group corporate services and sourcing, "They work much more in projects" (Bray).

NEW WRITING: FLEXIBLE, AGILE, MOBILE

They work in projects. Aided by mobile technology, they move about in work settings, talking as they take on problems and investigate opportunities. These workplace activities parallel those in makerspaces. Research in writing studies is now developing insights into writing strategies appropriate to these new workplaces and learning spaces. In an important study of workplace writing, Jim Henry briefly traces the history of the field, particularly the connection between pedagogy and research. Characterizing a mid-twentieth-century approach, he quotes James Berlin on the dominance of a "current-traditional" rhetoric that "makes the patterns of arrangement and superficial correctness the main ends of writing instruction" (2). This rhetoric accords with the "impersonal written communication needed for the rationalization of management systems," reinforced in the composition classroom and in the workplace (4). Individual writers were made subordinate to impersonal styles and formats. The twenty-first-century workplace, focused on collaboration and innovation, needs new writing strategies. One source of these is the process of design thinking that has informed the creation of the makerspaces and the new workplaces themselves as well as the conduct of projects in those spaces.

Design thinking advances through five iterative phases: empathizing with the audience/user/client, defining a problem or opportunity, ideating around a solution, prototyping, testing, and evaluating. This process has clear parallels in the traditional writing process (audience analysis, thesis selection, planning, drafting, revising) and in the five cannons of traditional rhetoric. But design thinking enriches the process at each phase and as a collaborative practice.

James P. Purdy, for example, explicitly references the Stanford d.school in seeing the new writing approach as generative rather than tied to traditional styles and formats. Moreover, while rhetoric has served mainly as a strategy for individual writers, the new approach is, fundamentally, collaborative. It is also flexible and adaptable to writing on different forms of technology, including laptops and smartphones, and on different surfaces and planes, not only the horizontal, the most common for individual writers, but also the vertical, prominent in the Design Studio. It does so in ways that "reunite things and words" (Kostelnick 185). The new rhetoric is interdisciplinary and not limited to any specific content, but is, as Richard Buchanan notes, a metadiscipline that manifests itself in writing studies as a way to see writing as both activity and practice. It responds dynamically to twenty-first-century problems, which are messy, ambiguous, "wicked," not tame and predictable (Kostelnick 272). Mathew Newcomb sees "creating, with design" as not essentially a matter of expression "but rather an innovative response to a perceived situation and need." Design, he notes, "makes more than an object or arrangement—it makes new contexts and associations" (594). The process aims to achieve "textual action" that "does something" in the world (Purdy 634). It is driven by situations, not by formats. Charles Kostelnick sees invention and discovery—the first cannon of rhetoric—as "a social extension of the environment in which the writer . . . communicates" (273). He further emphasizes the need to "externalize decision making in invention" by bringing in other voices (271). The sense that composition is a community function reinforces the pedagogy of collaborative learning.

James Reither argues that the "top-down" approach to collaborative writing often taught in classrooms, basically coauthoring or peer-to-peer editing, doesn't hold up in workplace practice. It misses the "circumstances" that motivate writing as a social process, writing that gets work done and moves readers to action (196). He notes that workplace writing begins in other texts and in conversations not aimed to produce a document but to solve a problem, to make new knowledge, to bring together multiple voices. That is the situation in a makerspace. Writing helps manage and negotiate leadership of the projects being undertaken and integrate the contributions of team members as they iterate both the products they are prototyping and the texts and visuals that document and advance the process. As they make the turn from writing as students to writing as professionals, particularly as entrepreneurs completing innovative projects for clients, their writing strategies need to keep up.

Clay Spinuzzi provides a distinction between two types of labor as each relates to writing that helps creative professionals, including students becoming such professionals, think about their work. One type of labor is that exercised by "self-programmable specialists" who have "authorial discretion" to "exercise their authoritative voice, bringing in beliefs, logics, traditions, and ideologies to operate in a given activity" (Spinuzzi, "Genre" 492). They also have "operational discretion" to identify problems, search and recombine information from a wide range of sources, and exercise creativity in developing innovative, one-of-a-kind, custom approaches to the arrangement and delivery of a writing product. The other, generic labor, however, as the term implies, can be largely automated, increasingly outsourced to a content management system or a lower-cost labor market, and embedded in preset instructions for executing tasks that solve known problems. To increase productivity and make the new more routine, specialists turn the results of their self-programmable labor into something generic like standardized text, templates, genres, and protocols. Workplace collaboration software like Slack and file-sharing applications like Google Docs (the major platform in the Design Studio) and Dropbox support the creation and circulation of such texts, both within an organization and among writers distributed widely across organizations.

"SOCIAL WRITING" IN THE DESIGN STUDIO

Students in the Design Studio, future "self-programmable specialists," are developing their skills at writing customized products for clients and other users as well as completing more generic documents that track their projects. Design thinking helps them do both. One student, without prompting, called this process "social writing." The Design Studio offers a setting for social writing by bringing together resources, both people and

> various forms of material inscriptions that are part of the cognitive creative process, such as visual representations and diagrams of different kinds, symbolic expressions, models, charts, or images. . . . Space enhances productivity when it provides an intelligible framework within which copresence, coawareness, and interaction patterns become engaged in the exploration, representation, interpretation, and transformation of collective knowledge. (Peponis et al. 816)

The "transformation of collective knowledge" into communication products and performances is, of course, a central activity of workplaces and makerspaces. Copresence and coawareness, a measure of the physical environment, is part of the process. In conversations and answers to a questionnaire circulated in a course, Prototype to Product, taught in Spring 2017, students largely agreed. Here are some comments they provided on the questionnaire. They felt that being aware of others in the framework of the Design Studio was more productively immersive than invasive; interruptions were sometimes a good thing. This "ambient awareness" provided a sort of "peripheral vision." As students developed their networking skills, "anyone is fair game to learn from or teach," noted one. The open layout of the space was credited with fostering "the formation of relationships with other students and faculty," and with providing the opportunity "for other groups to chime in and share knowledge/skill" as well as to overhear "someone working on the same thing you are." All of these affordances make it easier to collaborate.

In addition to the functional affordances for doing their project work, including team communication, students also cited the aesthetics of the space as motivational. They noted the "inspiration" provided by "all the different types of materials around me when I work." "Being in the Design Studio gives me the feeling that I'm in an environment where creativity is more stimulated. I feel like I think more 'freely/creative' [than in a regular classroom] (maybe it is just seeing the tools/other projects, not really sure)."

While recognizing the positive features of social writing in the Design Studio, students also mentioned downsides. As in other open-plan workplaces, noise can be a major problem, especially when the space is crowded, sometimes countered by people shutting themselves off by wearing earbuds or large headphones, thus negating the options for face-to-face interactions. Students also complained about distractions and a lack of privacy when they needed to focus or produce "any kind of intellectual design work" and the lack of natural lighting. Such complaints, in turn, have become a source of problems to be solved as a project for teams in the makerspace. A course enrolling both engineering and design/art students, for example, took some on. Students prototyped a variety of smartphone apps that would provide real-time information about crowding and the availability of resources to alert users remotely about timing their work there. They also investigated lighting technology that would compensate for the lack of natural light in the studio, and ways to create movable walls that could be put in place easily to ensure more privacy when needed for focused work or for conversations with clients.

Prototype to Product

With their focus on creating knowledge collaboratively and on innovating, academic makerspaces ultimately help students turn from thinking like students to thinking like entrepreneurs. Through a series of courses over their undergraduate years, student teams advance from solving given, "tame" problems to identifying new problems and opportunities on their own, in the greater marketplace. In the studio-based "Prototype to Product" course, for example, student teams turned early stage prototypes they had developed in prior courses into real-world products. As the course instructors noted, that process involved learning advanced prototyping techniques, designing products for manufacture, and gaining skills in such entrepreneurial activities as "end user profiling, market size estimation, cost-of-goods analysis, and building basic business models in order to guide commercialization decisions."

Successful students persuaded themselves to take on an entrepreneurial identity. That entailed developing, as noted on the course syllabus, "self-efficacy and self-confidence in utilizing resources, both human and capital, external to the department and the University in commercializing a design" and "gaining experience 'pitching' design and business concepts to a range of audiences," not just faculty or fellow students, and not just engineers.

The opening assignment was a proposal and business plan. Students had to follow guidelines established for the "Hen Hatch," the University-wide startup funding competition (www.udel.edu/henhatch). The assignment immersed teams immediately in an interdisciplinary context in which they tried to persuade potential sponsors and investors of the value of their concept. The proposal required a detailed profile of the likely customers for the product, a discussion of the "unmet need" the product aimed to serve, a product description that also attested to its "unique value proposition," information about its basic business economics, and a description of the "relevant experience, skills, and resources of the team." It was a marketing piece that engaged students in particular in the first phase of the design thinking process: empathy with the client or customer or user. Mid-term, in both writing and oral presentations, students articulated where they were with their prototype and the path forward, as well as their level of understanding of the product's possibility for commercialization, at what scale. The writing could be a text entry box, website, or file upload; they could also do a video. The required deck of slides for the presentations, documents in themselves, included both text and images. Their final pitch was evaluated on the basis of its being professional and practiced as well as clearly showing the need for the product in the world. A final written report archived the work.

Having to frequently "nutshell" their work to others in informal conversations went a long way toward helping students focus on and refine core ideas. Team members often kept individual physical notebooks about their project. But they brainstormed over a prototype and then took pictures of their common notes on a whiteboard or chalkboard to post, along with modules of documents, on Google Docs.

Writing Like an Entrepreneur

In moving from prototype to product, student teams circled back to their initial concept of a product. The final test was whether it worked for the customer or client. In a productive categorization, Jennifer Bay, Richard Johnson-Sheehan, and Devon Cook refer to a spectrum of, at one end "empathizers," who are well able to understand "the needs and feelings of others and respond appropriately" and "systematizers," those who "tend to analyze, build, and utilize structures, preferring order and predictability" (182). Engineers and other technical professionals are often systematizers; as entrepreneurs, they must be flexible and empathetic. This requires deep understanding of the perspective, priorities, values, and bodily experiences of those who will use their products. What stories do they tell? How do *they* see a problem or opportunity—which may be very different from the way the team developing the product does.

The interpersonal skills and social ties students develop in the Design Studio play a strong role in helping them empathize with users. In impromptu as well as more directed conversations arising in the settings of the makerspace, they incubate ideas, negotiate possibilities, and formulate text and visuals to capture their thinking. Through a cycle of learning and performance, they see what works and what doesn't. They fail and then make sense of their failures while they in turn enhance their self-confidence. That self-confidence derives as well from a sense of studio ownership that reinforces their role as active collaborators with faculty and likely or confirmed users of their products in cocreating knowledge. The work process is flexible and resource-oriented, not task-based and hierarchical, as in more traditional courses.

In their survey of 101 entrepreneurs about their writing habits, attitudes, genres, and skills, John M. Spartz and Ryan P. Weber identified significant differences between writing common in existing organizations and the strategies needed by entrepreneurs, whose writing "shapes emerging organizations" (430). Their findings have resonance in the kinds of writing to be encouraged in new spaces like makerspaces and in courses that prepare students for entrepreneurial careers, whether within larger organizations focused on innovation or as independent professionals. Entrepreneurs, note Spartz and Weber, need to "plot their own selves" as they create their companies. To do so, they create a compelling narrative, a story to tell, that frames their ideas as both "plausible and revolutionary" and align their communication efforts with it (431). Storytelling, once considered the province of English majors and fiction writers, becomes a core skill. That narrative also reflects empathy with the customer. It fits a story about how their problem will be solved in their context—how *they* might tell the story—or how, for example, a new application they had never thought about will serve them well.

"Social writing," as practiced in the Design Studio, takes on the dimensions of a maker exercise aligned with other products being developed there. As Spartz and Weber argue, a chief difference between entrepreneurial documents and those common in more traditional organizations is their intensive focus on the client or customer, at least in the beginning. They need to be customized, inspired by individual, one-of-a-kind needs. In Spinuzzi's terms, it's the writing of self-programmable specialists. It's unlike the traditional approach to an academic report that places more emphasis on what the team did, a narrative of their hard work, than on what their hard work achieved. Once the emerging organization is established, however, Spartz and Weber, like Spinuzzi, see writing strategies as more generic and format driven. For students who are learning about writing as a maker exercise, a major strategy is carrying over the design thinking that grounds their technical work to the writing that accompanies that work, especially the focus on the customer or user. Writing then becomes integral to product design. It enhances the process at every stage in a fluid, write-and-test way. Text and documents accumulate, both custom and generic ones, across semesters and years.

As projects evolve in the Design Studio, the studio spaces themselves are changing. Some of the change comes from institutional needs, particularly trying to keep the access open and welcoming while also addressing university concerns for health and security. As the space has evolved, and its usage expanded, more controls have been put in place, including locks on all major entrances. Some areas are still available to those without training, but there are various levels of control on others that offer special equipment. As Jenni Buckley noted in a recent conversation, they are trying to preserve some of the original DIY atmosphere while adding a degree of polish and more sophisticated, and expensive, technology and furnishings. Funding from the university and alumni, including a potential major donor, is advancing the process. The evolution neatly traces the design trajectory from a prototype space, with low fidelity materials, to a more mature entity. In addition, as the makerspace itself evolves, students and faculty are inspired to think about how common areas on other floors of the building could be redesigned to support its core concepts. Social writers will find new environments in which to thrive.

WORKS CITED

Alexis, Cydney. "The Material Culture of Writing: Objects, Habitats, and Identities in Practice." *Rhetoric, through Everyday Things*, edited by Scot Barnett and Casey Boyle. U of Alabama P, 2016, pp. 83–95.

Andrews, Deborah. "Investigating the Workspaces of Science." *Posthuman Praxis in Technical Communication*, edited by Kristen R. Moore and Daniel P. Richards, Routledge, 2018, pp. 255–280.

Andrews, Deborah. "The Physical Environment for Communication in 21st Century Workspaces: A Research Model." *The Ins and Outs of Business and Professional Discourse Research*, edited by Glen M. Alessi and Geert Jacobs, Palgrave Macmillan, 2016, pp. 37–62.

Andrews, Deborah. "A Space for Place in Business Communication Research." *International Journal of Business Communication*, vol. 54, no. 3, 2017, pp. 325–336.

Andrews, Deborah, and Dustyn Roberts. "Academic Makerspaces: Contexts for Research on Interdisciplinary Collaborative Communication." *SIGDOC '17: Proceedings of the 35th Annual Conference on Design of Communication*, ACM, 2017.

Barnett, Scot, and Casey Boyle, editors. *Rhetoric, through Everyday Things*. U of Alabama P, 2016.

Bay, Jennifer, Richard Johnson-Sheehan, and Devon Cook. "Design Thinking via Experiential Learning: Thinking Like an Entrepreneur in Technical Communication Courses." *Programmatic Perspectives*, vol. 10, 2018, pp. 172–200.

Bemer, Amanda M., Ryan M. Moeller, and Cheryl E. Ball. "Designing Collaborative Learning Spaces: Where Material Culture Meets Mobile Writing Processes." *Programmatic Perspectives*, vol. 1, no. 2, 2009, pp. 139–166.

Brand, Stuart. *How Buildings Learn: What Happens after They're Built.* Penguin, 1994.

Bray, Chad. "Your Desk? Take Your Pick. UBS Rethinks Work Space in Its London Offices." *The New York Times*, 4 Nov. 2016, p. B6.

Buchanan, Richard. "Design and the New Rhetoric: Productive Arts in the Philosophy of Culture." *Philosophy and Rhetoric*, vol. 34, no. 3, 2001, pp. 183–206.

Cole, Teju. "On Photography: Take a Photo Here." *New York Times Magazine*, 27 June 2018, https://www.nytimes.com/2018/06/27/magazine/take-a-photo-here.html. Accessed 10 Sep. 2018.

Doorley, Scott, and Scott Witthoft. *Make Space: How to Set the Stage for Creative Collaboration.* John Wiley and Sons, 2012.

Gensler. *2019 US Workplace Survey/Key Findings.* 2019, www.gensler.com/research-insight/workplace-surveys/us. Accessed 25 July 2019.

Gladwell, Malcolm. "Designs for Working: Why Your Bosses Want to Turn Your New Office into Greenwich Village." *The New Yorker*, 11 Dec. 2000, pp. 1–6.

Goldhagen, Sarah W. *Welcome to Your World: How the Built Environment Shapes Our Lives.* HarperCollins, 2017.

Grulke, Eric A., Dan C. Beert, and Derek R. Lane. "The Effects of the Physical Environment on Engineering Team Performance: A Case Study." *Journal of Engineering Education*, vol. 90, no. 3, July 2001, pp. 319–330.

Henry, Jim. *Writing Workplace Cultures: An Archaeology of Professional Writing.* Southern Illinois UP, 2000.

Herman Miller. *Insight: What It Takes to Collaborate.* 2014, http://www.HermanMiller.com/research/topics/all-topics/what-it-takes-to-collaborate.html. Accessed 14 Aug. 2014.

Herndl, Carl. "Foreword." *Posthuman Praxis in Technical Communication*, edited by Kristen R. Moore and Daniel P. Richards, Routledge, 2018, pp. xi–xiv.

Hillier, Bill. *Space Is the Machine: A Configural Theory of Architecture.* Cambridge UP, 1996.

Jacobs, Jane. *The Death and Life of Great American Cities.* Random House, 1961.

Kostelnick, Charles. "Process Paradigms in Design and Composition: Affinities and Directions." *College Composition and Communication*, vol. 40, no. 3, 1989, pp. 267–281.

Laing, Andrew, and Peter Anthony Bacevice. "Using Design to Drive Organizational Performance and Innovation in the Corporate Workplace: Implications for Interprofessional Environments." *Journal of Interprofessional Care*, vol. 27, sup. 2, 2013, pp. 37–45. https://doi.org/10.3109/13561820.2013.792043.

Leslie, Stuart W. "'A Different Kind of Beauty': Scientific and Architectural Style in I. M. Pei's Mesa Laboratory and Louis Kahn's Salk Institute." *Historical Studies in the Natural Sciences*, vol. 38, no. 2, 2008, pp. 173–221.

Miller, Daniel. *Stuff.* Polity, 2010.

Moore, Kristen R., and Daniel P. Richards, editors. *Posthuman Praxis in Technical Communication.* Routledge, 2018.

Newcomb, Matthew. "Sustainability as a Design Principle for Composition: Situational Creativity as a Habit of Mind." *College Composition and Communication*, vol. 63, no. 4, 2012, pp. 593–615.

Packer, Jeremy, and Stephen B. Crofts Wiley, editors. *Communication Matters: Materialist Approaches to Media, Mobility and Networks.* Routledge, 2012.

Painter, Susan, et al. *Research on Learning Space Design: Present State, Future Directions.* Society for College and University Planning, 2013.

Peponis, John, et al. "Designing Space to Support Knowledge Work." *Environment and Behavior*, vol. 39, no. 6, 2007, pp. 815–840.

Pigg, Stacey. "Emplacing Mobile Composing Habits: A Study of Academic Writing in Networked Social Spaces." *CCC*, vol. 66, no. 2, 2014, pp. 250–275.

Prior, Paul, and Jody Shipka. "Chronotopic Lamination: Tracing the Contours of Literate Activity." *Writing Selves/Writing Societies*, edited by Charles Bazerman and David Russell, 2003, http://wac.colostate.edu/books/selves_societies/. Accessed 24 July 2019.

Purdy, James P. "What Can Design Thinking Offer Writing Studies?" *CCC*, vol. 65, no. 4, 2014, pp. 612–641.

Reither, James A. "Bridging the Gap: Scenic Motives for Collaborative Writing in Workplace and School." *Writing in the Workplace*, edited by Rachel Spilka, Southern Illinois UP, 1993, pp. 195–206.

Reynolds, Nedra. *Geographies of Writing: Inhabiting Places and Encountering Difference*. Southern Illinois UP, 2004.

Rule, Hannah. "Writing's Rooms." *CCC*, vol. 69, no. 3, 2018, pp. 402–432.

Slack, Jennifer D. "Beyond Transmission, Modes, and Media." *Communication Matters: Materialist Approaches to Media, Mobility and Networks*, edited by Jeremy Packer and Steven B. Crofts Wiley, Routledge, 2012, pp. 143–158.

Spartz, John M., and Ryan P. Weber. "Writing Entrepreneurs: A Survey of Attitudes, Habits, Skills, and Genres." *Journal of Business and Technical Communication*, vol. 29, no. 4, 2015, pp. 428–455.

Spinuzzi, Clay. "Genre and Generic Labor." *International Advances in Writing Research: Cultures, Places, Measures*, edited by Charles Bazerman, et al., WAC Clearinghouse and Parlor Press, 2012, pp. 487–505, https://wac.colostate.edu/books/perspectives/wrab2011/. Accessed 3 Sep. 2018.

7

"EVERY CONVENIENCE FOR A MAN OF LETTERS"
Thomas Jefferson's Writing Suite

Diane Ehrenpreis

Among Thomas Jefferson's accomplishments and complex legacies, including that he both drafted the Declaration of Independence and enslaved nearly six hundred people over the course of his life ("Slavery"), his standing as a prolific and informed correspondent is often missed. Tens of thousands of letters originated from his writing table at Monticello, many intended for correspondents who kept him informed about current events and ideas, enabling him to maintain his position as an active participant in the international political and intellectual spheres, even when writing from his remote mountaintop home. While he often found it time consuming, when Jefferson was kept from his correspondence, he lamented "I am losing sight of the progress of the world of letters" ("Letter to Benjamin Rush" *PTJ:RS*, vol. 1, 558–59). Writing, recording, and storing tens of thousands of letters spurred him to seek new means to draft his correspondence, as well as systems to keep these documents organized, readily accessible, and safe for posterity.

As part of a major new study of Jefferson's private rooms at Monticello, I undertook a close study of his original writing objects and the rooms where they were used. The findings yielded surprising new information about Jefferson's attempts to create an ideal writing practice for himself, which he hoped would provide an exemplar for other correspondents. This essay will show how the statesman applied rational and reason-based methods, honed from Enlightenment philosophy, to become the most efficient and effective writer possible. To that end, he devised a personalized work arrangement that included a suite of writing furniture in purpose-designed rooms, as well as a personalized system for tracking the myriad letters that formed the paper biography that he hoped to leave for posterity. To undertake a correspondence of such immense proportions and import, Jefferson benefited from a patriarchal social structure at Monticello where the labor, most significantly, of enslaved workers as well as of family members, many of them women, made his life as a writer possible. The Thomas Jefferson Foundation, which owns and operates Monticello, has long addressed the complex issue of Jefferson and slavery directly; indeed, slavery cannot be disentangled from conceptions of Jefferson, or his writing suite specifically. Every visitor to Monticello learns about slavery and how it was central to the financial and social structure of this working plantation. In describing the issue of slavery, foundation president Leslie Greene Bowman states, "Monticello was also a working plantation—where the paradox of slavery stands in stark relief to the ideals of liberty expressed by Jefferson in the declaration. As a result of Jefferson's assiduous record keeping, and more than 50 years of scholarly research by curators, historians, and archaeologists, Monticello is among the best documented, best preserved, and best studied plantations in North America. Our work illuminates the lives of those enslaved at Monticello—their families, work, skills, hopes, and dreams" (6). Later in the essay, I return to the contexts of slavery that undergirds Jefferson's writing work.

As project leader and curator for the multi-year reinstallation of Jefferson's private rooms, I collaborated with a team of specialists to determine specifics about their function, finish, and furnishings as he might have known them.[1] The space he allotted for himself at Monticello, his home outside Charlottesville, Virginia, is substantial, including a bedchamber, a cabinet or study, library with an annex, greenhouse, and, until 1815, a reading room which he called a book room. Jefferson conceived of a distinct function for each room. The greenhouse and bedchamber were devoted to relaxation and repose, leaving the remaining rooms, which contained his renowned book collection and an array of writing furniture and implements, as a place for work. I became particularly interested in the library and cabinet because this is where Jefferson did most of his writing. I spent hours in these tandem rooms, studying what literary scholar Diana Fuss called the "theatre of composition," familiarizing myself with what she describes as "the artifacts, mementos, machines, books and furniture that frame intellectual labor" (1).

Beginning in 1923, when Monticello became a museum, curators began to collect and install many of the original objects Jefferson used for writing. The most familiar example of the material culture linked to Jefferson as a writer is the copying or polygraph machine he used to compose identical duplicate letters (Bedini, *Thomas*). Today an original polygraph, which has been on loan from the University of Virginia since

Figure 7.1. Cabinet with Writing Workstation at Monticello. Courtesy Thomas Jefferson Foundation. Photo Credit: Walter Smalling Jr.

1949, is situated prominently in the cabinet and is a highlight of every Monticello tour (see fig.7.1). That he used a distinctive arrangement of furniture when writing, including a revolving chair, revolving stand, and a converted table, in conjunction with the polygraph machine is well-documented through early accounts and articles (Stockton; Stein, *Worlds* 103–105, 366–368; Crowley 199).

My research has shown that in addition to this writing arrangement, Jefferson utilized two groups, one for writing and one to manage incoming mail, indicating that Jefferson had distinct and innovative ideas about the objects in these rooms and how to arrange his writing space. In her study of the material culture of writing, writing studies scholar Cydney Alexis argues for what she calls "writing identity," noting that "people who write develop an identity around writing, one that manifests and is expressed largely through material objects" (85). In the case of Jefferson, the list of material objects associated with writing is lengthy and primed for a close reading. The collection includes writing paper, letters and envelopes, sealing wax and seal, various pens and knives to sharpen them, lap desks, a journal of letters, and odd scraps with his handwriting. Such ephemeral items rarely survive, but through the privileges of financial capital, even as his estate was in debt at the time of his death, as well as social standing, his family was systematic in collecting the stuff of writing, to be preserved at Monticello, a nearly complete record of the material culture of Jefferson's writing practice. That there is such a high survival rate of writing objects may reflect how the descendants and relic-keepers thought of, or pictured, Jefferson, as a correspondent at work with his letters. Perhaps they understood, as we do today, that letters and the exchange of ideas via the written word were incredibly important to Jefferson. For him, being able to effectively communicate ideas through the means of letter writing was an essential skill that educated citizens needed. He challenged his grandson to:

> write a letter to somebody every morning, the first thing after you get up[,] as most of the business of life, & all our friendly communications are by way of letter, nothing is more important than to acquire a facility of developing our ideas on paper; and practice alone will give this. ("Letter to Thomas Jefferson Randolph" *PTJ:RS*, vol. 2, 335)

While he didn't make much headway with this correspondent, Jefferson himself remained a dedicated letter writer. The job of writing was so important to him, that he created objects, recording and filing systems, rooms, all built within a social structure of slavery that would make his work as a writer not only efficient but possible.

In this essay I will focus on four pieces of furniture from Jefferson's material objects of writing: a tabletop desk called a *pupitre*, writing table, reading stand, and a revolving chair. These objects form the nucleus of what I will call his writing suite, and while there were adjustments over time, these four pieces remained key elements that he used for nearly half of his life as a writer. My working method for this project started with a close reading of the original furniture associated with Jefferson's library and cabinet, studying them individually as works of art, as well as part of an integrated interior scheme. I began with object analysis, considering art historian Jules David Prown's thesis that "style is inescapably culturally expressive, that the formal data embodied in objects are therefore of value as cultural evidence" (197). I visualized various arrangements of objects, and what it would have been like to physically work at each component of the writing suite. This evaluation yielded new information about scale, function, and structure, and in some cases, shortcomings. In addition to capturing the information imbedded within the objects, I used primary documents, some only recently made available, including inventories, account books, family letters, and Jefferson's own letters that he struggled to preserve, to expand what we know about a seemingly straightforward writing room and its inhabitant. This methodological approach is derived from the influential work of historian Laurel Thatcher Ulrich who studies humble objects and previously dismissed documents to better understand the social history of things.[2]

In considering Jefferson's habits as a writer, I investigated not only how he dealt with incoming and outgoing letters, but what methodology he applied to devise new objects and processes for writing. Here, the statesman called upon an Enlightenment world view that valued efficiency, convenience, and reason-based solutions for conceiving his routines, as well as for designing the rooms where he worked, and his writing suite of furniture. Visitors to Monticello now see both where Jefferson wrote his letters as well as where he tracked and filed them. It is reasonable to look at these two complementary settings as precursors to a modern workstation, with the entire setup illustrative of Jefferson's ideas about convenience, or fitness for its purpose, time-saving work systems, and furniture designed to facilitate writing. One way he did this was by freely sharing ideas and innovations, including the material things of writing, like inventive furniture and copying machines. By introducing his special writing suite with the public, Jefferson presented himself as an innovator and man of science while offering these objects as models. Supporters and family members perpetuated this vision of a creative thinker throughout his life and into the twentieth century. But his Enlightenment notions, exemplified in his prized revolving chair, also became an easy target for his political enemies who ridiculed him as an eccentric and philosopher. By reading the objects and space most closely associated with Thomas Jefferson's writing practice, this essay will offer new ways of thinking about how such a prolific correspondent succeeded at his self-appointed mission. I will analyze Jefferson's writing practice through the lens of his writing suite, considering the ideas and motivations behind its creation, as well as situate it within the physical environment at Monticello, an environment built on the institution of slavery, which freed Jefferson from onerous responsibilities, but at a tremendous cost to those with the least power. Finally, with the revolving chair as a focus, I will also show how Jefferson and his detractors used objects to both self-fashion a personae and to denigrate an opponent in the philosophical battle over how to shape the new nation.

ENLIGHTENMENT IDEALS

From the beginning of his political career, Jefferson showed a strong interest in writing objects. While serving as a delegate to the second

Continental Congress, Jefferson found the time to design and commission a desk, one that would best fulfill his role as a writer of both letters and declarations. He settled on a small portable version fashioned in imported mahogany. The so-called Declaration of Independence desk, which resides in the Smithsonian Institution, is rectangular with an adjustable lectern or stand, and a drawer for implements, and is similar to other examples from this period (Stein, "Thomas"; Bedini, *Declaration*; Bemis; Burstein). In a letter written near the end of his life, Jefferson wrote:

> It was made from a drawing of my own. . . . And I have used it ever since. It claims no merit of particular beauty. It is plain, neat, convenient, and taking no more room on the writing table than a moderate 4to. volume, it yet displays it self [*sic*] sufficiently for any writing. ("Letter to Joseph Coolidge")

Historian Amanda Vickery defines neatness in this context as "simple elegance of form, finely made and proportioned, free from unnecessary embellishments" (180). That such a small and simple desk, the size of an open book, was adequate for "any writing" and that he continued to use it throughout his life, indicates the extent to which Jefferson committed himself as a writer to the ideals of efficiency, utility, convenience, and neatness. According to Nicholas Trist, grandson-in-law and aid to the statesman, Jefferson was "an economist of space" who sought the most efficient, and even compact, solution for how to arrange the physical space he occupied when writing, and how to make the objects he used when writing suit his need for convenience and functionality (Trist). That Jefferson took these ideals that were common to the age and applied them to the betterment of his writing practice is to be expected, but the lengths to which he went to create a strategy that included furniture design to aid in his writing is distinct, reflecting his understanding of Enlightenment ideals.

Jefferson's preference for the "plain, neat, and convenient" is based on Enlightenment philosophy, which he studied as a student in Virginia and continued to explore throughout his life (Adams 30–32). Jefferson chose the ideas of English philosopher Francis Bacon, an advocate of reason through observation, as the framework to process his world. With Bacon at the forefront, Jefferson also praised Isaac Newton and John Locke, calling them "my trinity of the three greatest men the world had ever produced" ("Letter to Benjamin Rush" *PTJ:RS*, vol. 3, pp. 304–8). Bacon and Locke championed rational inquiry, as well as systematizing knowledge by seeking a common language, and by using images to illustrate concepts (Pannabecker). Jefferson used the Baconian method to observe, measure, and sketch innovative furniture he saw on his travels, later referring to these examples when assembling his group of writing furniture. For Jefferson, who developed a particularly wide range of interests, nearly everything was worthy of inquiry and analysis. This was true of his writing, where he reevaluated and redesigned the setting, furniture, and implements, as well as recordkeeping that made up the material culture of his practice.

Jefferson also owned the greatest exemplar of Enlightenment thought, the monumental *Encyclopédie* edited by Denis Diderot and Jean Le Rond d'Alembert (Pannabecker; Jaucourt). With this project, the editors were the first to attempt to compile and share reason-based information on myriad topics. It consists of twenty-eight volumes of text and plates offering definitions and illustrations of a hierarchy of subjects including "Mechanical Arts," a classification that Jefferson found useful, but others had dismissed as a minor art not worthy of consideration. Within this category, he may have read about cabinetmaking, upholstery, papermaking, as well as penmanship, with plates illustrating the equipment for writing, how to correctly hold a quill pen, and what posture to assume when undertaking the "art of writing" (Jaucourt). Jefferson considered penmanship an important skill, telling his grandson to "write a neat round, plain hand, and you will find it a great convenience through life to write a small & compact hand as well as a fair & legible one" ("Letter to Thomas Jefferson Randolph" *PTJ:RS*, vol. 2, 335). Judging from his own handwriting, Jefferson was not a particularly dedicated practitioner of artful penmanship.

SOLVING THE PROBLEM OF WRITING LETTERS

As a prominent correspondent in the Republic of Letters, including the exchange between America and Europe, Jefferson's epistolary output was unmatched in scope among his peers (Van Miert). During his lifetime, he dealt with a staggering estimated 47,000 letters, of which approximately 19,000 were written by him—the remaining 28,000 were letters he received (Looney). The cost of such a lively correspondence was substantial, as John Adams pointed out in 1822: "Your stationary bill alone for paper, Quills, Ink, Wafers, Wax, sand and sound, must have amounted to enough to maintain a small family" ("Letter from John Adams"). These statistics also reveal that Jefferson spent hours nearly every day with his correspondence, at times lamenting that "From sun-rise to one or two o'clock, and often from dinner to dark, I am drudging at the writing table" ("Letter to John Adams" *PTJ:*RS, vol. 10, pp. 657–58). Such dedication enabled him to connect with his extensive network of family, friends, and associates in the private and public spheres, but it also saddled him with an unprecedented collection of paper that needed to be organized and accessible upon demand (Cogliano). Necessity, and his optimistic Enlightenment belief that problems could be studied and improved, spurred him to create a personalized writing method that was reliant on specialized furniture and equipment to resolve what to do with an ever-expanding mass of paper.[3]

Jefferson had another reason for taking such care with his epistolary record. He intended to secure his legacy as a politician and statesman, a thinker and founder of the University of Virginia, and a loving patriarch, by leaving his collection of select letters for later generations. His short-lived effort to write an autobiography focused on the years from the revolution until 1790 (*Autobiography*). Perhaps he lost interest when he realized that his letters and documents would better tell his life story. Indeed in 1823, when historian Robert Walsh wrote asking him to help author a history about the founding of the nation, Jefferson declined, arguing that "The letters of a person, especially one whose business has been chiefly transacted by letters, form the only full and genuine journal of his life" ("Letter to Robert Walsh"). For the statesman, the letters functioned as both written communication and vital historical documents that he sought to organize and preserve. How "genuine" the epistolary journal that Jefferson left is questionable. Knowing that he was shaping his biography while corresponding in his daily life, he may have selectively omitted or destroyed letters, like those to his wife.

By the mid-1780s, Jefferson seemed to decide that he needed a better arrangement to handle the sensitive correspondence he dealt with when serving as minister to France for the United States. Jefferson was receptive to ideas and innovations that he thought might be useful, finding inspiration nearly everywhere he ventured. Numerous notes with reminders, sketches, and dimensions survive in Jefferson's hand, available as reference tools or source material for his own projects. The most complete example of his method remains *Notes of a Tour through Holland and the Rhine Valley*, with jottings taken on his 1788 trip (Jefferson, "Notes"). It includes descriptions, measurements, and sketches of buildings, bridges, furnishings, and tools. Some of these notes were later translated into fully realized projects for Monticello, adaptations of useful things like a set of seven drop-leaf dining tables that are only four inches in depth when closed (Stein, *Worlds* 288–289). The notes and sketches, the reason-based study, and reenvisioned objects reveal how Jefferson thought through problems, and how he reached solutions.

148 DIANE EHRENPREIS

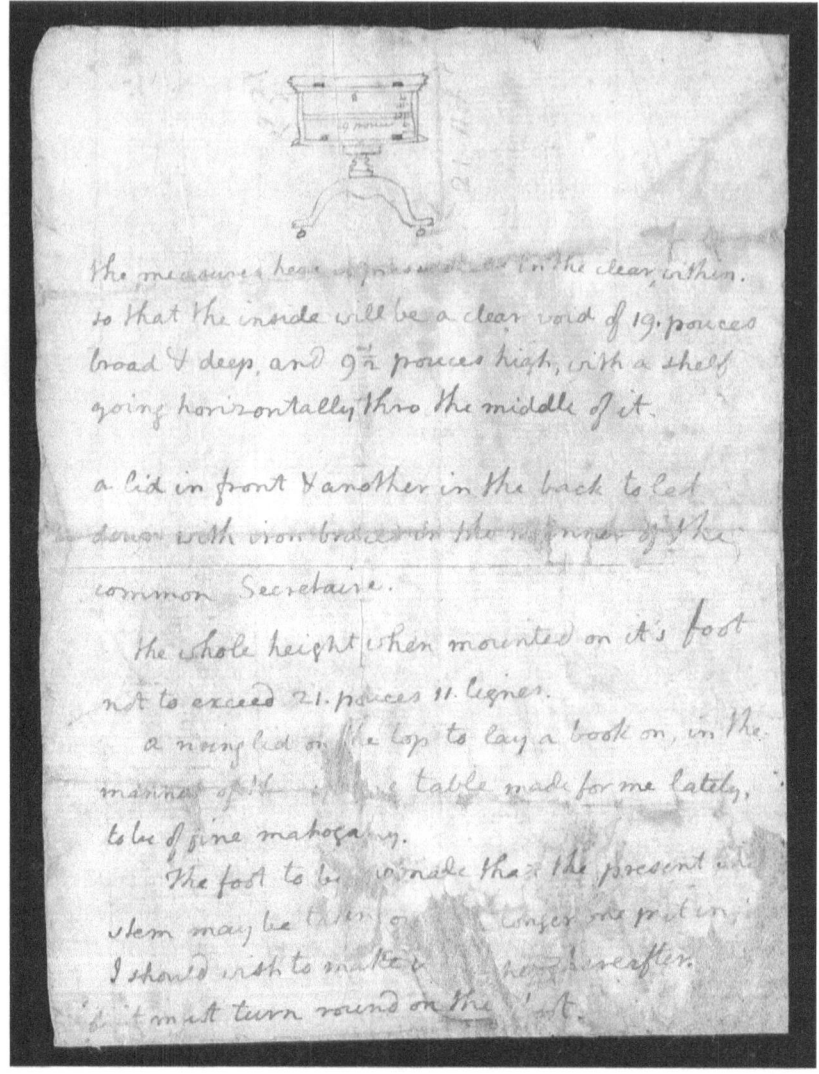

Figure 7.2. "Design for a Desk." Paper CX, 4½" × 6", Thomas Jefferson Papers, Albert and Shirley Small Special Collections Library, University of Virginia.

THE WRITING SUITE

One such document has recently been identified as a commission that relates to Jefferson's early attempts to create a new system to handle his letters (Nichols 44). Jefferson wrote this document, providing a cabinetmaker working in Paris detailed directions on how to craft his idiosyncratic version of a *pupitre en cartonnier* (see fig. 7.2).

An unusual form even for novelty-mad Parisians, this specialized desk was used by officials who generated large amounts of paper (de Reyniès 1036–1037). These desks, or *pupitre*, offered storage for paper-board file boxes or *cartonnier*, and often featured an adjustable lectern. Jefferson's annotated drawing is his interpretation of this useful form. The original *pupitre* has not been located, but the notes tell us that it was small compared to French examples, essentially a square wooden box with a lectern to hold documents. It had two doors that when opened revealed a void divided by a single horizontal shelf to hold *cartonnier*. At only 23 inches tall, Jefferson's vision of an improved *pupitre* was a rotating tabletop desk on a pedestal base where he could both write documents and safely store them with the minimum amount of effort.

This *pupitre* and its *cartonnier* were the first components of what would eventually become Jefferson's writing suite, a group of furniture that he redesigned and commissioned to fulfill his needs as a writer. Jefferson retained the odd *pupitre*, using it as the site for processing his incoming correspondence. With this object in regular use, Jefferson expanded his writing suite after his return to the United States in 1789. He commissioned New York cabinetmaker Thomas Burling to make an entire group of furniture associated with writing. A recently discovered packing list in Jefferson's hand tallies what he purchased, including a variety of objects used for writing (*List of Packages*). From this group, which included a secretary bookcase that has not been located, three key objects stand *in situ* at Monticello: Jefferson's original writing table, revolving armchair, and reading stand (Goodman).[4] These three new pieces of furniture, plus the *pupitre*, comprised Jefferson's writing suite.

That Jefferson conceived his writing suite as an integrated unit, intended to function in tandem rather than as independent elements, can be seen in both the design and timing of their creation. The writing suite evidences the innovation and efficiency of design that Jefferson saw in the best furniture being made in Europe, paired with the "plain, neat, and convenient" qualities first seen in the portable desk that he used in Philadelphia to draft the Declaration of Independence fifteen years earlier.

In conceiving his writing suite, Jefferson seems to have considered his typical writing practice, and then devised furniture to make his method more efficient. One of the most necessary objects for any writer is a surface to work on. Because of the crate dimensions on the packing list, the "writing table" can now be positively identified as the octagonal table on loan to Monticello since the 1920s (see fig. 7.3).

Figure 7.3. Jefferson's Octagonal Writing Table, Formerly Rent Table. Attributed to Thomas Burling, New York, 1790. MHS Furniture 049. Collection of the Massachusetts Historical Society.

Jefferson's choice of a pedestal table with drawers is adapted from the more common English versions with circular tops (Stein, *Worlds* 252–253; Gloag 553–554). For his own example he opted for an octagonal top, a shape that Jefferson favored and frequently turned to as an architect because it optimized space (Fletcher). For his redesigned table, he managed to utilize the entire interior space by devising eight triangular and rectangular drawers. They are labeled "A B C," "D E F," and so on, for storing in alphabetical order his folded letters. The body is made of mahogany, and it revolves on a pedestal base, enabling the correspondent to remain stationary while the necessary drawer conveniently glides into place.

That Jefferson thought of his writing suite as a set of geometrically shaped units which could be used together or singly is evidenced in his pairing of the square-shaped *pupitre* with the octagonally shaped writing table. Having two objects, both representing the ideal geometric forms he favored, may also connect to his burgeoning ideas about architecture, as well as complement one another as to function. By using the two objects together, each with storage for letters, Jefferson could consolidate his incoming correspondence into one streamlined arrangement. This pairing became the locus for incoming mail, one that economized space and reduced wasted movement by centralizing like tasks with a pair of interrelated objects. To more accurately represent how Jefferson paired the writing table and *pupitre*, curators commissioned an exact reproduction of the latter, installing the objects together in the library at Monticello.

The writing suite included a specialized chair with a circular-shaped seat, offering comfort, convenience, and style (see fig. 7.4). Jefferson found a padded revolving armchair ideal for writing, and he became so closely associated with the form that he is incorrectly credited with inventing it (Stein, *Worlds* 266–267). Derived from a French *fauteuil de cabinet* or office chair, it was used exclusively by gentlemen when working at a writing table or desk (Koeppe 167–169). Jefferson's adaptation follows the formula by relying on a circular base and seat atop four tapered mahogany legs with casters. However, he redesigned his example to have a taller back, making it more imposing as well as practical. The body is upholstered in red leather. The armrests feature candleholders, but these are probably not original. The armchair rotates, making it the third object in the writing suite to revolve. His Americanized version of the *fauteuil* offers a "neat and plain" appearance with no ornamentation. With this chair, Jefferson could turn in space and shift his position by activating the casters or the rotating mechanism, offering a novel and efficient way to sit.

The final component of Jefferson's writing suite is a cube-shaped reading stand, an idiosyncratic interpretation of the common lectern (see figs. 7.5 and 7.6). A standard piece of furniture for centuries, lecterns or reading stands were used to hold books, pamphlets, and papers at eye-level (Gloag). Typically, reading stands had two sides and looked much like a modern music stand. Many examples had a pedestal base that could be raised when the reader worked standing. Not satisfied with what his contemporaries deemed adequate, Jefferson reinvented his own reading stand into a five-sided version in the shape of a perfect cube (Stein, *Worlds* 290). When closed, the twelve-inch cube on a pedestal base does not telegraph its purpose, looking much like a box. However, when open, its five adjustable wings can hold multiple documents upright on its thin ledger strips or supports. Whether open or closed, the stand rotates on a shaft, enabling access to information without requiring the author to move to

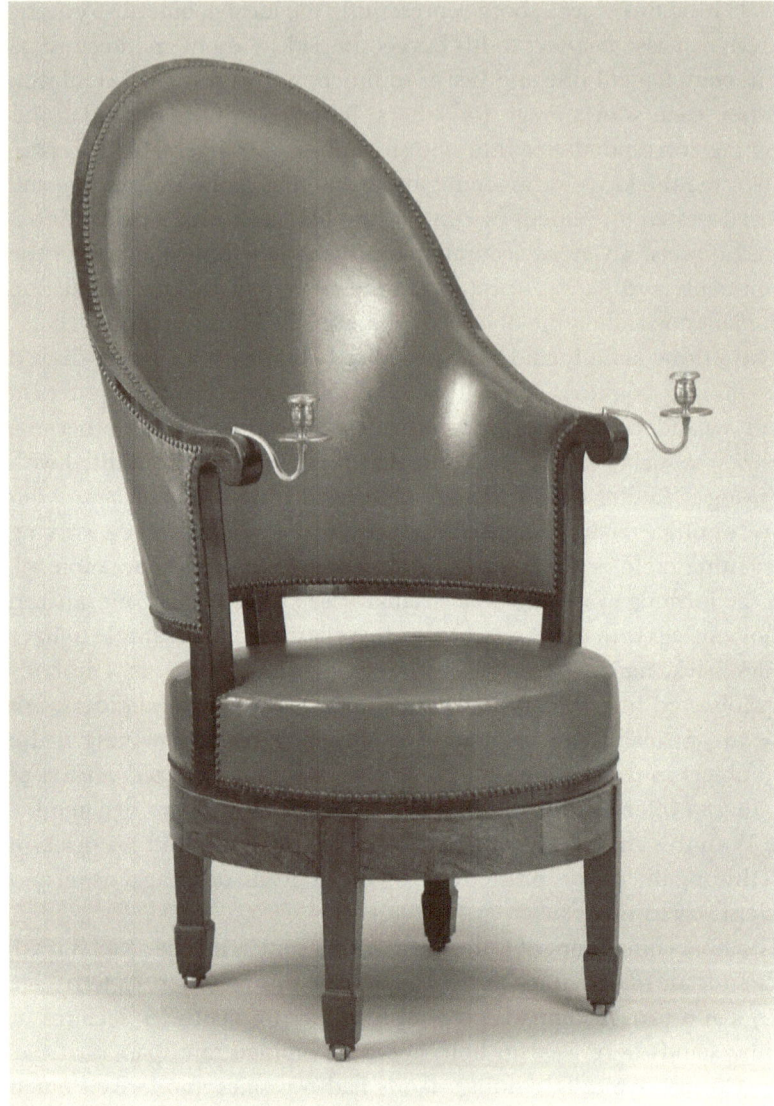

Figure 7.4. Revolving Chair. Attributed to Thomas Burling, New York, 1790. ©Thomas Jefferson Foundation at Monticello. Photo Credit: Edward Owen.

claim it. The base with its casters ensured that the stand could be easily moved to be near the writing table, or wherever Jefferson chose to write. It complemented the act of writing, providing easy visibility of referenced letters or documents, leaving the table uncluttered and reserved for sole purpose of writing.

Figure 7.5. Revolving Stand, closed (reproduction base). Attributed to Thomas Burling, New York, 1790. ©Thomas Jefferson Foundation at Monticello. Photo Credit: Walter Smalling Jr.

Figure 7.6. Revolving Stand, open (reproduction base). Attributed to Thomas Burling, New York, 1790. ©Thomas Jefferson Foundation at Monticello. Photo Credit: Walter Smalling Jr.

With this stand, Jefferson devised an efficient and innovative way to access multiple documents at once, in some ways foreshadowing folders on today's computer desktop. The reading stand's adjustable base features a telescoping post, which allowed Jefferson to set the correct height whether working seated or standing. Ink stains on the top surface indicate that it also served as a writing table. In 1887, the reporter Frank Stockton stayed with a Jefferson descendant, where he encountered the reading stand. He noted with delight the stand's function and its usefulness:

> a small table with four curious wings, which can be spread out at the sides to hold books of reference, that was used by Mr. Jefferson as a writing-stand, and on which yet remain some blots of ink which declared their independence of his pen. (Stockton 654)

Jefferson's willingness to experiment with new ideas, and his commitment to fully realize an innovative writing suite, ultimately provided him with the labor-saving work arrangement he sought. Additionally, we now understand that this suite, with furniture either adapted or by his own design, is corollary to his better-known experimentation with ideal geometric forms in architecture: the square, octagon, circle, and cube. Jefferson devised and commissioned the entire writing suite between the mid-1780s and 1790, while simultaneously reimagining Monticello based on French neoclassical and Palladian architecture. The timing reveals that Jefferson applied the same design vocabulary to his furniture as well as his buildings. He continued experimenting with this geometrical vocabulary in his later design for his retreat called Poplar Forest, where he used an octagonal plan that encloses a centralized square-shaped cellar and dining room, demonstrating Jefferson's celebration of the beauty found in ideal geometric forms (McDonald). His working method not only reveals his delight in geometric forms, but also references the traditional connection between architecture and furniture and its reliance on ideal proportion (Morley 219–223). Jefferson and other furniture designers would have known of this relationship through pattern books, particularly Palladio's *Four Books of Architecture*, and Vitruvius, who included classical ornamentation and information on ideal proportion in his work. Jefferson's exercise in devising his writing suite as a group culminated with the addition of movement into his three-dimensional objects. By ensuring that the entire writing suite rotated in space, Jefferson the designer and architect pushed their potential beyond merely time-saving features toward a dynamic and interconnected operation of moving shapes.

THE WRITING SUITE AND JEFFERSON'S CORRESPONDENCE SYSTEM

As we have seen, the writing suite provided the base of operations for the actual labor of writing, but it was not conceived in isolation; rather it probably developed in tandem with his radically new ideas about how to handle the thousands of letters he processed. Because of my recent work on Jefferson's private rooms, I discovered the full extent of how he organized his writing practice and where this work took place. The basis for his arrangement consisted of two distinct workstations, one for mail received and one for writing. While workstation is a twentieth-century term, I use it because it best describes Jefferson's intent in separating and centering like epistolary tasks in one place. As Jefferson grew older, he adjusted his writing workstation to include a bench that would ease his aching legs and a repurposed table to hold the ever-present polygraph machine (Stein, *Worlds* 264–265, 286–287; Ehrenpreis and Tay).

With its varied labeled drawers, the octagonal writing table served as the nexus for the first workstation, which was devoted to incoming mail. Here Jefferson opened and alphabetized his mail before recording each item into his log, known as his Summary Journal of Letters (*Epistolary*). This small book probably sat on the lectern of the *pupitre*, which in turn, sat squarely on the writing table. Jefferson refolded the new letters securing them in the alphabetical drawers in the table. When ready to reply, he retrieved the folded letter and flattened it on his screw press, a device commonly found in libraries. The correspondence then went into the *cartonnier*, later Americanized to carton, designated for letters to be answered.

With letters and carton in hand, Jefferson moved to his second workstation, this one dedicated to writing. The operation centered on the polygraph machine, which Jefferson considered "the finest invention of the present age" ("Letter to James Bowdoin"). He first acquired one in 1804, remaining an active proponent for the rest of his life. The machine features two arms outfitted with pens, allowing him to write a letter while simultaneously making an exact copy, resulting in an efficient and private way to control his correspondence. In contrast to most of his contemporaries, Jefferson did not use a letterbook system, where the text of the letter was hand copied, often by a secretary, into a bound and indexed book (Boonshoft).

Author Frank Stockton, who interviewed Jefferson descendants in 1887, offers a sense of how the writing station worked:

> In his study, stood Mr. Jefferson's writing-chair which was made to suit his peculiar needs; the chair itself was high-backed, well rounded, and

cushioned, and in front of it extended a cushioned platform, on which Mr. Jefferson found it very pleasant to stretch his legs, being sometimes troubled with swellings of the smaller veins of these limbs. The writing-table was so made that it could be drawn up over this platform, legs, and all, and pushed down when it was not in use. The top of this table turned on a pivot; on one side of it were his writing materials and on the other was the little apparatus by which he made copies of all his letters. By this side was another revolving table, on which his books of reference lay, or were held open at proper angles. (654)

This description clarifies how Jefferson used these objects, including his need for comfort and reliance on movement. But it also upholds the idea promoted by Jefferson's descendants that their patriarch was an ingenious inventor.

Once a letter was completed the resulting polygraph copy was carefully filed, Jefferson returned to his Summary Journal and logged in the date of his reply, then mailed the outgoing letter. Copies of letters were typically filed chronologically according to where Jefferson was living at the time. Eight filing presses or cupboards filled with labeled cartons stored the correspondence that would eventually document his life.

The effectiveness of Jefferson's correspondence and filing systems was tested when contacts asked for information or documents from his past. In 1820, a young gentleman enquired after an old law record, recounting in amazement:

> Mr. Jefferson immediately informed him that it would be no trouble at all, for if he had the paper . . . he could put his hand on it in 'less than one minute.' He stepped to a case, opened the door, run his eye over the letters of the pigeon holes, drew forth a package of ancient papers, glanced at their "files," and in less than one minute put the paper in the hands of his astonished visitor. (Randall 231–32)

The documentary systems and the well-ordered presses with cartons enabled Jefferson to efficiently organize his papers, apparently allowing him to secure any document with ease. Jefferson's plans and innovations for his writing practice apparently worked for him, but few contemporaries, if any, adopted his improved writing system.

The Cabinet

I have looked closely at the objects, ideas, and systems that Jefferson used to organize his writing practice with an emphasis on his writing suite. But it is equally important to situate the writing suite physically into what Jefferson called the cabinet at Monticello. For this, I have drawn on the work of literary scholar Diana Fuss, who identifies a connection between architecture and the psychological interior, one that can be accessed through the "human sensorium," including sight, sound, and touch (Fuss 17). Based on new information about Jefferson's cabinet, I will discuss how the room looked and what it might have felt like to write within its confines. And in considering the cabinet, the space most closely connected to Jefferson and his ideas, it is essential to discuss the role enslaved people and the system of slavery which made Jefferson's writing practice possible.

Jefferson sorted out his epistolary systems and furnishings years before he was finally able to use his redesigned cabinet at Monticello, c. 1800 (see again fig. 7.1). Jefferson's choice of the term "cabinet" probably refers to the cabinets or *studiolo* first popularized by wealthy gentlemen in Renaissance Italy. Developed as scholar's retreat, it was often the final and most intimate space in an *enfilade*, or series, of adjoining rooms. Historian Joan DeJean notes that a "writing room" was fashionable in France during the years that Jefferson lived there. Such rooms had their origins in the small studies first developed in the Renaissance. Different than the social "reading room" or library becoming popular in England, writing rooms and cabinets provided privacy, and new specialized furniture (DeJean 60–61; Thornton). In the early nineteenth century, furniture designer Thomas Sheraton described the cabinet as a room "set apart for writing, studying, or preserving anything that is precious" (Gloag 167). Jefferson doesn't comment on why he called his writing room the cabinet, but evidence of how he used this space suggests that it was appropriately named. As a man dedicated to Enlightenment reason and scientific analysis, the idea of a cabinet in the spirit of the Renaissance may have appealed to him.

His cabinet functioned as a traditional scholar's retreat, offering Jefferson the secluded workspace he required for his writing practice. In rebuilding Monticello, Jefferson reserved the entire south side of the ground floor as his private domain, which as a privileged landowner and family patriarch he was able to claim. An account by Margaret Bayard Smith, a friend and supporter who visited in 1809, notes that "This suite of apartments opens from the Hall to the south. It consists of 3 rooms for the library, one for his cabinet, one for his chamber, and a green house" ("Winter" 227). She provided one of the few contemporaneous descriptions, noting that the cabinet "is furnished with every convenience for a man of letters" ("Account"). The cabinet remained his preferred place to write for the remainder of his life. And upon his death, granddaughter Ellen Randolph Coolidge ventured there to gather from

"Every Convenience for a Man of Letters"   159

his table "some small relics, memoranda and scraps of written paper which I still preserve" ("Letter to Henry Randall, 1857").

Typical of a retreat, Jefferson insisted on controlling access to his private rooms by locking the doors. He demanded privacy as part of his writing practice, so no one was allowed entry without permission. Smith called the cabinet and its adjoining rooms his *sanctum sanctorum*, or holy of holies, and noted that while she gained entry, "it is very seldom any one is admitted" ("Winter" 227). Jefferson succeeded in controlling access to his writing room and his person because he had an entire system of locks, and the authority to establish such a perimeter between himself and the greater household. But for the rest living at Monticello, those many who were enslaved, as well even as Jefferson's extended family, who lived in the main house and elsewhere on the plantation, space was limited and privacy nearly impossible.

The cabinet where so many hours were spent writing was especially designed by Jefferson to accommodate his working method. It is semi-octagonal in plan, echoing his own octagonal writing table. Surprisingly small with limited wall space, the cabinet is just large enough to hold the writing workstation, a sofa, filing presses, and two wall-mounted lecterns. The walls were covered in pea green wallpaper, and the floral paper borders added to the overall effect of sitting and writing in a bower. Jefferson installed folding doors across the bed alcove that opens to both the cabinet and bedchamber. With the doors closed, he could create two private but adjoining spaces, delineating spheres designed for the intellectual self and one for the private self.

Jefferson created what is essentially a wall of glass in his cabinet, and these windows had a significant impact on how he used the room and what it felt like to work there. To harness the abundant natural light, he often situated his writing table near a window. In a letter to his son-in-law Thomas Mann Randolph, Jefferson directs:

> I have left a bundle of papers at home the want of which distresses me infinitely. I think it must be in one of the cartoons in the Cabinet window near which I usually sit to write, that is to say near the red turning chair. the cartoon has a label with these words "to be answered or acted on." ("Letter to Thomas Mann Randolph")

This passage evokes what it was like for Jefferson to work in the cabinet, and the types of things that he came in daily contact with. He routinely handled the paper-covered cartons with their cotton pull tabs, and the spidery metal pens of the polygraph. The tabletop was slightly rough to the touch, while the red leather on the revolving chair felt smooth but stiff. He spent hours touching the leather bindings that protected his books, as well as hand-laid paper, reams and scraps of it, drafts and copies, folded and unfolded.

When seated at his writing workstation, Jefferson would have seen the stacks of books, cartons, and papers that cluttered the room. If he looked straight ahead to the library, a vista of book-lined walls and the writing workstation were visible. When the folding screen was open, he could see into the bedchamber with its French commode and looking glass, and he could glimpse his garden through his louvered porch. Jefferson could easily see and use the writing apparatus on his table, even after the light faded. It seems the business of letters was not confined to daylight hours, as when Jefferson noted, "I received your letter at dusk when no candle was lighted" ("Letter to James Monroe"). Artificial light sourced from oil lamps and candles offered enough light for him to write on into the night, if so wished.

The windows that offered such abundant light also created temperature extremes. A lack of wall space meant there was only room for a portable cast iron stove as a heat source. Heavy wool curtains and shutters offered some protection from the cold, as well as privacy. The tall back of the revolving chair shielded him from drafts. Some years the chill in the cabinet was relentless, making it impossible to keep the frail statesman warm. When Francis C. Gray visited Monticello in the winter of 1815, he noted that "Mr. Jefferson took us from his library into his bed chamber where on a table before the fire stood a polygraph with which he said he always wrote" (232–38). The Virginia summers created the equally troublesome problems of heat, humidity, and pests. Jefferson had wire window screens enabling him to write with the windows open, but at times it was stifling. Regardless of the conditions, Jefferson favored his cabinet, with his writing suite and polygraph machine, as the ideal place to undertake his correspondence.

Jefferson spent hours writing, mostly in silence, but when "in the intervals of his occupations" his granddaughter Ellen Randolph Coolidge could "hear him humming old tunes, generally Scotch songs but sometimes Italian airs or hymns" ("Letter of Henry Randall" 1853). Despite being sequestered in his cabinet, Jefferson would have heard the sounds of an active household, because sound traveled easily through the four-story stairwells and open windows. He certainly heard footfalls on the stairs, voices from inside and outside of the house, the crash of dishes, the Chinese gong sounding the hours, and the wail of babies. The sounds within the cabinet were calmer, like the chiming of clocks, the scratch of two pens of the polygraph, the song of his pet mockingbird, Dick, and perhaps most significantly, the sounds made by his enslaved personal servant, Israel Gillette, who was responsible for taking care of this space, even when Jefferson was writing. In his autobiography titled "Life Among the Lowly, No. 3" published in 1873, Israel Gillette (who later took the surname "Jefferson") explained that at Monticello he "made the fire in [Thomas Jefferson's] bedroom and private chamber, cleaned his office, dusted his books, run of errands, and attended him at home" (I. Jefferson).

When visitor Margaret Bayard Smith wrote that it was a rare privilege to enter Jefferson's *sanctum sanctorum*, she was certainly not thinking about the enslaved servants who cared for this space every day. And while Smith may have encountered Israel Gillette in the cabinet, because of his status as both inferior and enslaved, he would not have merited mention in her account. Gillette's candid personal recollection provides a necessary counterbalance to Bayard's romanticized description of visiting the cabinet. His rare account not only offers the telling details concerning how he cared for this room but demonstrates how the system of slavery was integral to Jefferson's writing practice, and how it impacted the life of one enslaved individual.

Gillette introduces himself as one of thirteen children born to Jane and Edward Gillette who were themselves enslaved at Monticello. He was born in 1800, and by the age of eight "began the labors of life" as a waiter, serving meals at the Jefferson family table. A few years later, he acted as coachman and postillion when Jefferson used his carriage. Sometime after the statesman retired in 1809, Gillette began working as his enslaved personal servant, which included hours in the cabinet. While Gillette mentions Jefferson's private space, he says nothing about his own living conditions. At the time, he would likely have been living in a rough cabin near Mulberry Row, the plantation street to the south of the main house. Eventually Israel Gillette married Mary Ann Colter, who was also enslaved at Monticello, and they had four children. But at the time Israel Gillette wrote this account, in 1873, he had lost contact with all of them. Gillette writes, "As they were born slaves they took the usual course of most others in the same condition of life. I do not know where they now are, if living; but the last I heard of them they were in Florida and Virginia" (I. Jefferson). Gillette is also very clear about the devastation of the enslaved community after Jefferson's death in 1826, stating that only a few individuals were freed in the will. "All the rest of us," he writes, "were sold from the auction block." The Gillette family were among the approximately two hundred enslaved people sold to pay down the enormous debt left by Jefferson. In Gillette's case he was sold to a neighbor in Albemarle County, and in 1844 he bought his own freedom, later marrying a second time and moving to Ohio.

While his normal demeanor when working was to be seen and not heard, there was one particular conversation Gillette remembered well and recounted in detail. It took place during the Marquis de Layette's visit in 1824. The Frenchman "remarked that he thought that the slaves ought to be free, that no man could rightfully hold ownership in his brother man" (I. Jefferson). Gillette, who had been enslaved his entire life, recalled Jefferson replied "that he thought the time would come when slaves would be free, but did not indicate when or in what manner they would get their freedom. He seemed to think that the time had not then arrived" (I. Jefferson). For Gillette and nearly all the enslaved people at Monticello, freedom never materialized during Jefferson's lifetime. Instead, Gillette wrote, he spent nearly thirty years "retained about the person of our master as long as he lived" (I. Jefferson).

That Jefferson could work in his cabinet, undisturbed, free from the responsibilities and realities of plantation life was made possible through the system of forced labor, slavery. His privileged position as gentleman, patriarch, and enslaver meant that he controlled the social structures and economic engine that supported his large plantation. Those Jefferson enslaved were used for labor of every description, whether in the fields, kitchens, workshops, or in the main house. The women in Jefferson's family included his daughter and granddaughters, who were highly educated and dedicated writers as well, rotated running the household one month at a time. The male members of the family and hired overseers undertook the daily management of the plantation, freeing Jefferson from innumerable duties and problems. This social structure with Jefferson at the apex made it possible for him to retreat to his *sanctum sanctorum* to write, leaving responsibilities and hard realities of plantation life for others to carry out.

OBJECTS AS PROPAGANDA

In the previous sections, I have shown that Jefferson determined he needed a plan for managing his voluminous correspondence, settling on an arrangement that featured a writing suite and workstations, an efficient new system for handling paper, and a writing room in the form of a gentleman's cabinet. The social dynamics at Monticello, where others, especially the enslaved workers, undertook most of the daily tasks, also favored Jefferson as a writer. But stepping out of the closed world of Monticello and Jefferson's cabinet, what happened when the writing suite entered the public realm? Jefferson used the revolving chair while in public office in Philadelphia, where it became a symbol of his character, for good or ill. To Jefferson and his supporters, this innovative chair telegraphed the owner's positive attributes, that of an Enlightenment thinker, a man of science, and hopefully, a man of the people. To his critics, Jefferson's revolving chair showed him up as an out of touch dreamer, a philosopher unfit for high office, making it a useful tool for political propaganda. Eventually, the image of Jefferson as an innovator and man of science prevailed, with the writing suite and the polygraph serving as worthy exemplars for his supporters to champion.

Before being installed at Monticello, the writing suite saw three years of service in Philadelphia, from 1790–1793, when Jefferson served as secretary of state. It is during this time that the public became familiar with his revolving chair. In 1793, frustrated with the rancorous political situation and with Alexander Hamilton in particular, Jefferson resigned from office and shipped home his belongings. He claimed to be done with politics, content to enjoy the pastoral life, but by 1796 he was ready to run for president. It was the first election where political parties featured in the process, pitting Thomas Jefferson and his Democratic-Republicans against the Federalists and John Adams. Historian Andrew Burstein wrote that Jefferson "believed the Federalists to be monarchical in tendencies, pro-British in spirit and politically effete." Conversely, Jefferson positioned "his own Democratic-Republican program as more representative of the simpler, homespun republican principles that animated the Americans of 1776" (39). Federalists had a vocal advocate in Alexander Hamilton, who wrote propaganda pieces at Jefferson's expense, singling out the revolving chair as symbolic of his opponent's failings and idiosyncrasies.

It is possible that Jefferson used his revolving chair to help shape the public image he began cultivating when he returned to politics. Costume historian G. S. Wilson has shown that Jefferson was keenly aware of his image, and that he adjusted how he presented himself according to the political climate (Wilson 102–128). She notes that "Jefferson created his public image and directed his self-fashioning to support his political vision for the early American republic" (6). Presenting himself in simple suits, walking and greeting fellow citizens on the streets, and using an innovative chair that revolved, all helped foster his chosen image as a man of the people, one who sought out new ideas for the good of society. Perhaps to Jefferson, the chair represented what reason-based study and American ingenuity could create, but to his enemies this same chair became cudgel in the fight for the heart and soul of the nation.

The first reference to the revolving chair appears in the Phocion essays written by Alexander Hamilton in the fall of 1796. Hamilton ridiculed him as a philosopher "contriving turn-about chairs for the benefit of his fellow citizens and mankind in general" (Chernow 513). His attack on the "philosopher" and his revolving chair became copy for a pamphlet entitled *The Pretensions of Thomas Jefferson to the Presidency Examined.* Using Hamilton's jibe William Loughton Smith argued that Jefferson should continue "in his philosophical retirement, employing his fertile genius in discoveries and improvements in the useful arts, and contriving turn-about chairs, for the benefit of his fellow citizens, and mankind in general" (4). Smith returned to make a second and third attack on the revolving chair and Jefferson. Smith imagined that if the Virginian was president, he would be "contriving with assiduous perseverance an easy chair of new construction" (4). And finally, "Who has not heard from the Secretary the praises of his wonderful Whirligig Chair, which had the miraculous quality of allowing the person seated in it to turn his head, without moving his tail" (16). The term "whirligig chair" is infantilizing, referencing a child's spinning toy. Smith argued that Jefferson was ill-equipped to keep track of both the head and tail of government, and that as a man he was childish, two-faced, and untrustworthy.

Jefferson's revolving chair could only be drawn into the fray if the public understood the nature of the attack, and this was possible because they were aware that Jefferson favored it above all others. Contemporaries understood the ceremonial function of chairs as symbols of authority, and more abstractly, they may have recognized that chairs could serve as physical extensions of the sitter. Art historian Jules David Prown argues that chairs "are particularly revealing of cultural values because they so easily become human surrogates" (199). By attacking Jefferson's revolving chair in their propaganda, his enemies denigrated both his authority, his ideology, and his person. The "whirligig chair" approach may have found an audience, because Jefferson lost the election, instead becoming vice president under John Adams.

CONCLUSION

It was Jefferson's optimistic hope that Americans, namely free white males, would embrace the innovative writing suite he pioneered, but his contemporaries failed to see the benefit in it. However, in his role as a writer, Jefferson became one of the most prolific letter writers this country has produced. His view that letter writing was an important duty that every educated person should perform, meant that he was a motivated writer and he encouraged others to pursue letter writing. To better accomplish his correspondence, he designed or adapted a writing suite of furniture, workstations for incoming mail and writing, systems for filing and retrieving letters, a cabinet at Monticello in which to write, and social and economic structures based on slavery that supported his writing. He saw himself as a thoughtful innovator, creating new objects based on Enlightenment principles, and he promoted this attribute as part of his personae as a politician. His political enemies sought to discredit him by ridiculing his revolving chair, and initially they were successful. Eventually, the idea put forward by supporters that Jefferson was a dedicated writer and a man of ingenuity prevailed, with the polygraph, revolving chair, and the writing suite serving as the physical manifestation of these ideal attributes.

The struggle over what type of society Americans would choose for themselves shifted toward Hamilton's vision that emphasized commerce and cities, over Jefferson's ideal of an agrarian society with an educated citizenry. Jefferson did, however, prevail in the battle over at least some of his image, successfully removing the taint from labels like "philosopher" and "fertile genius." Friends like Margaret Bayard Smith served as boosters, promoting his image as an inventive genius, using his scholar's cabinet as an example. After his death, Jefferson's family furthered the idea of the genius Jefferson in recollections and interviews. In one instance, granddaughter Ellen Randolph Coolidge corresponded with biographer Henry Randall, describing Jefferson's character "as a theorist, a man of projects, an innovator. He certainly had a good deal of ingenuity in contrivance" ("Letter to Henry Randall" 1856). Thirty years later, descendants welcomed author Frank Stockton to use the writing suite, who later lauded Jefferson's ingenuity by focusing on the idiosyncrasies of the arrangement. When it comes to the discussion of Jefferson and writing, the majority of sources and previous historical interpretations have emphasized the notion of him as a fertile genius, while ignoring the complexity, even brutality, of what made his life as a writer possible. In part, this project attempts to broaden the perspective of his writing practice, introducing a corrective that shows both the correspondent and the enslaver.

Jefferson's cabinet at Monticello has been reinstalled to better represent the way it looked and functioned during his later life, telling not only his story but that of the enslaved individuals who literally built and cared for his private suite. Papers, pens, spectacles, and scissors are arranged on his writing table. Letter drafts sit on the reading stand, and his revolving chair is turned slightly, as if Jefferson was there moments earlier. These same objects also evoke the presence of Israel Gillette, and all of the enslaved servants who labored, some for their entire lives, at Monticello. Alongside these writing implements is a facsimile of a document written by Jefferson in his own hand. It is a slave inventory from 1820, listing the names of every enslaved man, woman, and child at Monticello, and the clothing allotted to each one. It serves as a reminder of the human cost that so many letters and fine rooms demanded, promoting a dialog about Jefferson as an enslaver, who despite his words that all men are created equal, could not or would not resolve the issue of slavery at Monticello. For many who come to Monticello today to consider Jefferson's complex legacies, the direct experience with these objects and spaces can both inspire and dismay. It's these carefully preserved writing artifacts and the stories we tell about them that help shape our understanding of Jefferson, even as his legacy is being debated and reframed.

NOTES

1. I served as project leader for the interior and furnishing component of the Mountaintop Project at Monticello. Beginning in 2013, we researched and reinstalled all the rooms on the second and third floors, as well as Jefferson's private rooms. The reinstallation was possible through the generosity of our donors, and the brilliance of my talented colleagues. This chapter benefited from the careful reading and suggestions from this volume's editors, Cydney Alexis and Hannah Rule. I extend sincere thanks to colleagues: Kay Arthur, Niya Bates, Anna Berkes, Leslie Greene Bowman, Tabitha Corradi, Aurelia Crawford, Andrew Davenport, Brandon Dillard, Lauren Greene, Linnea Grim, Gardiner Hallock, Emilie Johnson, J. Jefferson Looney, Gail Pond, Robert L. Self, Cinder Stanton, Susan R. Stein, Endrina Tay, and Gaye Wilson, and special appreciation goes to David Ehrenpreis.
2. My approach has also been shaped by time working with Edward S. Cooke Jr. and Brock Jobe, scholar-curators who specialize in furniture and the material culture of makers. Recent works of scholarship by Margaretta Markle Lovell and George Boudreau, as well as Jennifer Van Horn, have been helpful resources for working methods and models in material culture studies.
3. Part of this research appears in Diane Ehrenpreis and Endrina Tay, "Enlightened Networks: Thomas Jefferson's System for Working from Home," *The Spirit of Inquiry in the Age of Jefferson*, Proceedings of the American Philosophical Society, 2022.
4. Goodman describes secretaries as a personalized and private form of writing furniture, suitable for only one writer at a time, where private correspondence was written and stored. Jefferson may have stored his intimate letters here.

WORKS CITED

Adams, John. "To Thomas Jefferson from John Adams." 12 July 1822. *Founders Online*, National Archives, founders.archives.gov/documents/Jefferson/98-01-02-2948.

Adams, William Howard. *The Paris Years of Thomas Jefferson*. Yale UP, 1997.

Alexis, Cydney. "The Material Culture of Writing: Objects, Habitats, and Identities in Practice." *Rhetoric, through Everyday Things*, edited by Scot Barnett and Casey Boyle, U of Alabama P, 2016, pp. 83–95.

Bedini, Silvio A. *Declaration of Independence Desk: Relic of Revolution*. Smithsonian Institution Press, 1981.

Bedini, Silvio A. *Thomas Jefferson and His Copying Machines*. UP of Virginia, 1984.

Beltramini, Guido, and F. Lenzo. *Jefferson and Palladio, Constructing a New World*. Officina Libraria, 2015.

Bemis, Bethanee. "Laptops That Powered the American Revolution." *Smithsonian.com*, 3 Mar. 2016, smithsonianmag.com/smithsonian-institution/laptops-powered-american-revolution-180958253/. Accessed 16 Aug. 2020.

Boonshoft, Mark. "Letterbooks, Indexes, and Learning about Early American Business." New York Public Library Blog, 20 July 2015, nypl.org/blog/2015/07/20/letterbooks-in-early-american-business. Accessed 16 Aug. 2020.

Boudreau, George W., and Margareta Markle Lovell. *A Material World: Culture, Society, and the Life of Things in Early Anglo-America*. Penn State UP, 2019.

Bowman, Leslie Greene. "Introduction." *Monticello: The Official Guide to Thomas Jefferson's World*, Thomas Jefferson Foundation and National Geographic Society, 2016.

Burstein, Andrew. *Letters from the Head and the Heart: Writings of Thomas Jefferson*. Thomas Jefferson Foundation, 2002.

Chernow, Ron. *Alexander Hamilton*. Penguin Books, 2004.

Cogliano, Frank D. *Thomas Jefferson: Reputation and Legacy*. U of Virginia P, 2006.

Coolidge, Ellen W. Randolph. "Letter to Henry Randall." Letterbook, 1853 (ViU: Ellen Wayles Randolph Coolidge Correspondence). Published in "Jefferson Quotes and Family Letters," Thomas Jefferson Foundation, 2019, tjrs.monticello.org/letter/1432.

Coolidge, Ellen W. Randolph. "Letter to Henry Randall." Letterbook, 22 Feb. 1856 (ViU: Ellen Wayles Randolph Coolidge Correspondence). Published in "Jefferson Quotes and Family Letters," Thomas Jefferson Foundation, 2019, tjrs.monticello.org/letter/1966.

Coolidge, Ellen W. Randolph. "Letter to Henry Randall." Letterbook, 16 May 1857 (ViU: Ellen Wayles Randolph Coolidge Correspondence). Published in "Jefferson Quotes and Family Letters," Thomas Jefferson Foundation, 2019, tjrs.monticello.org/letter/466.

Crowley, John E. *The Invention of Comfort: Sensibilities and Design in Early Modern Britain and Early America*. Johns Hopkins UP, 2001.

DeJean, Joan. *The Age of Comfort*. Bloomsbury, 2009.

De Reyniès, Nicole. *Le Mobilier Domestique*, vol. 2, Imprimerie Nationale, 1992.

Ehrenpreis, Diane, and Endrina Tay. "Enlightened Networks: Thomas Jefferson's System for Working from Home." *The Spirit of Inquiry in the Age of Jefferson*. Transactions of the American Philosophical Society, vol. 110, part 2, 2022, pp. 197-218.

Fletcher, Rachel. "Thomas Jefferson's Poplar Forest." *Nexis Network Journal*, vol. 13, no. 2, 2011, pp. 487–498.

Franklin, Benjamin. "A Proposal for Promoting Useful Knowledge, 14 May 1743." *The Papers of Benjamin Franklin*, edited by Leonard W. Labaree, vol. 2, Yale UP, 1961, pp. 378–383.

Fuss, Diana. *The Sense of an Interior: Four Writers and the Rooms That Shaped Them*. Routledge, 2004.

Giordano, Ralph G. *The Architectural Ideology of Thomas Jefferson*. McFarland, 2012.

Gloag, John. *A Complete Dictionary of Furniture*. The Overlook Press, 1990.

Goodman, Dena. "The *Secrétaire* and the Integration of the Eighteenth-Century Self." *Furnishing the Eighteenth Century: What Furniture Can Tell Us about the European and American Past*, edited by Dena Goodman and Kathryn Norberg, Routledge, 2007, pp. 183–203.

Gray, Francis C. "Account of a Visit to Monticello, 4–7 February 1815." *The Papers of Thomas Jefferson: Retirement Series (PTJ:RS)*, edited by J. Jefferson Looney, vol. 8, Princeton UP, 2011, pp. 232–238.

Jaucourt, Louis, chevalier de. "Writer." *The Encyclopedia of Diderot and d'Alembert Collaborative Translation Project*, translated by Erik Anspach, Michigan Publishing, University of Michigan Library, 2011.

Jefferson, Israel Gillette, and S. F. Wetmore. "Life Among the Lowly, No. 3." *Pike County Republican*, December 25, 1873. Transcription, *Encyclopedia Virginia*, Virginia Humanities Foundation.

Jefferson, Thomas. *The Autobiography of Thomas Jefferson, 1743–1790*. Edited by Paul Leicester Ford, U of Pennsylvania P, 2011.

Jefferson, Thomas. *Epistolary Record or Summary Journal of Letters, 1783–1826*. Series 1: General Correspondence, The Thomas Jefferson Papers at the Library of Congress. Manuscript.

Jefferson, Thomas. "Letter to John Adams." *The Papers of Thomas Jefferson: Retirement Series (PTJ:RS)*, edited by J. Jefferson Looney, vol. 10, Princeton UP, 2013, pp. 657–658.

Jefferson, Thomas. "Letter to James Bowdoin." 10 July 1806. *Founders Online*, National Archives, founders.archives.gov/documents/Jefferson/99-01-02-3997.

Jefferson, Thomas. "Letter to Joseph Coolidge." 18 Nov. 1825. *Founders Online*, National Archives, founders.archives.gov/documents/Jefferson/98-01-02-5674.

Jefferson, Thomas. "Letter to James Monroe." 27 Sep. 1821. *Founders Online*, National Archives, founders.archives.gov/documents/Jefferson/98-01-02-2342.

Jefferson, Thomas. "Letter to Thomas Jefferson Randolph." *The Papers of Thomas Jefferson: Retirement Series (PTJ:RS)*, edited by J. Jefferson Looney, vol. 2, Princeton UP, 2005, p. 335.

Jefferson, Thomas. "Letter to Thomas Mann Randolph." 4 Oct. 1808. *Founders Online*, National Archives, founders.archives.gov/documents/Jefferson/99-01-02-8784.

Jefferson, Thomas. "Letter to Benjamin Rush." *The Papers of Thomas Jefferson: Retirement Series (PTJ:RS)*, edited by J. Jefferson Looney, Princeton UP, vol. 1, 2004, pp. 558–559.

Jefferson, Thomas. "Letter to Benjamin Rush." *The Papers of Thomas Jefferson: Retirement Series (PTJ:RS)*, edited by J. Jefferson Looney, Princeton UP, vol. 3, 2006, pp. 304–308.

Jefferson, Thomas. "Letter to Robert Walsh." 5 Apr. 1823. *Founders Online*, National Archives, founders.archives.gov/documents/Jefferson/98-01-02-3436.

Jefferson, Thomas. "List of Packages, 31 August 1790." Curatorial Department, Thomas Jefferson Foundation, Charlottesville, VA. Manuscript.

Jefferson, Thomas. "Notes of a Tour through Holland and the Rhine Valley, 3 March–23 April 1788." *The Papers of Thomas Jefferson (PTJ)*, edited by Julian P. Boyd, vol. 13, Princeton UP, 1956, pp. 8–36.

Koeppe, Wolfram. *Extravagant Inventions: The Princely Furniture of the Roentgens*. Metropolitan Museum of Art, 2012.

Looney, J. Jefferson. "Number of Letters Jefferson Wrote." Thomas Jefferson Foundation, 24 Mar. 2008, https://www.monticello.org/site/research-and-collections/number-letters-jefferson-wrote. Accessed 16 Aug. 2020.

McDonald, Travis C., Jr. "Constructing Optimism: Thomas Jefferson's Poplar Forest." *Perspectives in Vernacular Architecture*, vol. 8, 2000, pp. 178–179.

Morley, John. *The History of Furniture, Twenty-Five Centuries of Style and Design in the Western Tradition*. Bulfinch Press, 1999.

Nichols, Frederick Doveton. *Thomas Jefferson's Architectural Drawings, Compiled and with Commentary and a Check List*. Massachusetts Historical Society, Thomas Jefferson Memorial Foundation, and UP of Virginia, 1984.

Pannabecker, John A. "Diderot, the Mechanical Arts, and the *Encyclopédie*: In Search of the Heritage of Technology Education." *Journal of Technology Education*, vol. 6, no.1, fall 1994, pp. 45–57.

Prown, Jules David. "Style as Evidence." *Winterthur Portfolio*, vol. 15, no. 3, 1980, pp. 197–210.

Randall, Henry Stephens. *The Life of Thomas Jefferson*, vol. 1, Derby and Jackson, 1858.

"Slavery at Monticello, FAQ's-Property." Thomas Jefferson Foundation, tjrs.monticello.org/slavery/slavery-faqs/property/.

Smith, Margaret Bayard. "Account of a Visit to Monticello." *Richmond Enquirer*, 18 Jan. 1823.

Smith, Margaret Bayard. *A Winter in Washington: or, Memoirs of the Seymour Family*, vol. 3, E. Bliss and E. White, 1824.

Smith, William Loughton. *The Pretensions of Thomas Jefferson to the Presidency Examined*. Philadelphia, Oct. 1796, pt. I, pp. 4, 16, *Internet Archive*.

Stein, Susan R. "Thomas Jefferson's Traveling Desks." *Magazine Antiques*, vol. 133, May 1988, pp. 1156–1159.

Stein, Susan R. *The Worlds of Thomas Jefferson at Monticello*. Harry N. Abrams, 1993.

Stockton, Frank R. "The Later Years of Monticello." *Century Illustrated Magazine*, vol. 34, no. 5, Sep. 1887, p. 654.

Thornton, Dora. *The Scholar in His Study: Ownership and Experience in Renaissance Italy*. Yale UP, 1997.

Trist, Nicholas P. "Trist Testimonial." 1865–1874? Burke Family Locator File, Curatorial Department, Thomas Jefferson Foundation, Charlottesville, VA. Manuscript.

Ulrich, Laurel Thatcher. "Furniture as Social History: Gender, Property, and Memory in the Decorative Arts." *American Furniture*, Chipstone Foundation, 1995, pp. 39–68.

Van Horn, Jennifer. *The Power of Object in Eighteenth-Century British America*. University of North Carolina Chapel Hill, 2017.

Van Miert, Dirk. "What Was the Republic of Letters? A Brief Introduction to a Long History (1417–2008)." *Groniek*, no. 204, Feb./Mar. 2016, pp. 269–287.

Vickery, Amanda. *Behind Closed Doors: At Home in Georgian England*. Yale UP, 2009.

Wilson, G. S. *Jefferson on Display: Attire, Etiquette, and the Art of Presentation*. U of Virginia P, 2018.

8
ASSEMBLING THE FILE, OR, HOW CONSERVATION WORKS

Anne MacKay

FOREWORD

In early 2017, I took part in a series of strategic planning meetings for the museum where I work.[1] Staff members around the table were tasked with defining a new positioning for the institution, which would be more closely aligned with current museological debate. At one point, we were asked to present an object that would reveal an essential aspect of our work: this object, we were told, should also touch us personally and be at the core of what we believe to be important about what we do. Reflecting on my job as head of the museum's conservation team, I considered and rejected a number of seemingly obvious possibilities (museum objects, conservation test pieces, tools) before finally deciding on a conservation file. Conservators create these files as they examine, research, and treat objects, and a conservation department of any size has thousands of them, which, in our museum, may include multiple texts written by conservators over many years, along with a host of contextual information, visual references, even material fragments. The file I selected was created during the lengthy conservation treatment of a small basket, well known in the museum by its notable accession number, M1.

My object seemed a bit odd when compared with the others. It was not a discrete physical entity, but a hodge-podge of stuff, including documentation I had written, other texts, photographs, drawings, and pieces of the basket itself. Was my object even an object? And how did it describe, reflect, or locate what I do in a meaningful way? This chapter is an attempt to answer these questions, to uncover how the file—with its jostle of texts and other accumulated things—lies at the core of my professional practice and identity.

INTRODUCTION

The practice of conservation is centered on caring for material culture, particularly its treatment and preservation, and has consequently generated a vast corpus of writing about objects. Many of these texts are widely available and can be read in books, conference proceedings and peer reviewed journals, in newsletters and popular magazines, and on web sites and blogs. The subject matter of this writing is diverse and includes the description of conservation treatment practices, studies in material culture, issues in ethical debate, critical and historical enquiry, and aspects of collections care. However, this chapter deals with a very different kind of writing that is even more central to a conservator's work: object documentation in the conservation file. This writing notes material aspects of individual objects, describes and tracks treatment interventions, and records further research on their materiality that often has historical import or an impact on future care. Containing passages of close observation and diarist narrative, its format has evolved though decades of professional prescriptions within the field that have normalized both its language and content. Although voluminous (conservators can easily write thousands of pages over a career) and an obligation of professional practice, these texts are not widely circulated, and are typically accessed only by other conservators, researchers and collectors. This circumscribed consumption, and the often quite arcane and meticulous nature of the texts, plays a role in the perception of conservation by those outside the field as something either mysteriously magical (reviving moribund objects of the past) or entirely technical (using state-of-the-art technology to "analyze" a work of art). But conservation documentation is also vital to a positioning whose bulwarks are professionalism and ethical practice, and is seen by those in the field as ensuring transparency of methodology, reproducibility of procedure, and, perhaps most importantly, accountability to the future (Rivers and Umney 396–98). Furthermore, containing the fruit of material research on objects and collections, it is a fundamental element of material culture studies, and the starting point of much writing about conservation for public consumption.

That said, the conservation file is not merely a textual record of examination and treatment. I believe it to be, and will argue here, that it is itself a rich element of material culture and a writing object that both guides and reflects professional practice. As such, it is the critical third component in a triad of constantly shifting relationships that include the conservator and the object itself. The fluctuations in this triangle are due to the vectors of transmission and reception between conservator and object, conservator and file, and file and object, each component displaying its own kind of engagement and response. Conceiving the file as a complex physical entity with its own agency, and not merely a passive reflection of a conservator's practice or an object's materiality, recognizes its authority and clout in the active role it can assume in driving the conservation process forward.

I will start my critical look at the file by briefly tracing the early history of conservation and tracking the increasing importance of conservation documentation during the construction of the profession at the beginning of the twentieth century. Characterizing the file as material culture, I will further probe the idea of it as an assemblage, with an agentic force in the conservation process. I will then relate the story of a key museum object, M1, a basket from the Indigenous Cultures collection of the museum, from the point of view of its file that was compiled during the course of a conservation treatment. Bringing the history of conservation to the present day, I will finally describe the evolution of a more critical approach to practice, which has been deeply influenced by studies in new materiality, the marks of which can be touched, viewed and read in the multifarious contents of the file.

CREATING A PROFESSION

The slow evolution from artisan to conservation professional began in the eighteenth century, with the shift from royal and private collections to the establishment of large, government-supported museums, such as the British Museum (1753) and the Louvre (1793), which in turn led to the creation of a cadre of museum workers responsible to the public (Whitehead 78–79; McClellan "Restoration Policy" 451–2). Having to answer to public and ministerial criticisms of practice, be they the condition of the works and their display, or issues of classification and collecting, forced these new institutions to defend choices that would have previously remained in the private realm. Only restorations on the most important works in major collections were documented by restorers themselves: what little documentation that survives today is more often found in the correspondence of those responsible for the collections, or in administrative reports describing the results of a procedure (McClellan, "Raphael's *Foligno Madonna*" 82–84; Massing 68). Controversies occurred both in England and in France concerning the appearance of some restored paintings, and in England these disputes led to lengthy parliamentary enquires, whose recorded testimony has left us with a revealing picture of practice in the mid-nineteenth century: heavy-handed, inconsistent in procedure and outcome, and by and large undocumented (Anderson 450–51; Brommelle 178–79). The latter half of the century saw the publication of a number of widely read restoration manuals, which outlined procedures and explained chemical and physical interactions, producing the first indications of a shift toward a minimal standardization of practice (Forni 326–30; Secco-Suardo 331–38; Aschel 80–90). Documentation, however, generally remained an unrecognized aspect of the restoration process (Brajer ix).

During the first half of the twentieth century, changes within cultural institutions brought about what has been described as the "professionalization, specialization and the canonization of museum practices" (Meijer-van Mensch and van Mensch 33). This shift included the addition of conservation departments to museums, which ultimately led to the creation of the modern professional conservator. The twentieth century also saw the realization of a slew of international charters addressing best standards in heritage preservation (the Athens Charter, 1933; the Venice Charter, 1964; the Burra Charter, 1979; the Nara Document on Authenticity, 1994) and national codes of ethics for conservation (Code of Ethics and Guidance for Practice of the CAC). Articles in the codes outline foundational ethical issues—including, for example, the standardization of practice with such fundamental concepts as minimal intervention and reversibility—that reflect a further refining of a professional discipline. Also stressed is the importance of documentation as a requirement of professional practice. For example, the *Code of Ethics and Guidelines for Practice of the American Institute for Conservation of Historic and Artistic Works* contains an article in the code, and a full description in the guidelines, outlining the obligation to document, and what the structure and the contents of that documentation should be ("AIC Code").

This period was also witness to the rapid growth of science and scientific methodologies in conservation practice. As early as 1850 the chemist Michael Faraday, a member of the Select Committee on the National Gallery, looked at the effect of the highly polluted London air on the museum's collection and advised on the mitigation of the alarming rate of change of some of the art (Saunders 77). Later, a more sophisticated understanding of chemical reactions, along with advances in technology, instigated both an increase in more systematic methods in conservation treatment and a sharp rise in the use of technologies in museums (Brewer 137–208). The modern conservator slowly supplanted the artisan/restorer, as a new corps of university-trained specialists took his place. Science and technology both extended and legitimatized conservation's position in the museum, by lending conservators a unique authority that few had the tools to challenge, and providing a way of differentiating their core competencies from those of others. Moreover, with this new paradigm, treatment came to be thought of in terms of material interactions that could be understood with analytical tools and reliably replicated (Clavir 37–38). These profound shifts gave birth to the conservator in the lab coat who no longer worked in a studio, but in a laboratory. Documentation, as a detailed, accurate, and reproducible (i.e., scientific) record of the examination and treatment of an object, was central to this new professional positioning, both defining and being defined by it (Lerner 40).

Written conservation documentation is now quite standardized, following a structured format with rubrics that both order and limit information. Sections flow logically from a basic inventory, to a more detailed material description and a report on condition. A proposed treatment follows, after which the treatment itself is described, either with a summary of procedures and materials or with a daily log of interventions. The documentation concludes with any recommendations for subsequent care that might be necessary (Krueger et al.). This format is commonly followed internationally and is taught in conservation programs (Anastassiades). Terminology has been standardized as well, and lexicons and multi-language dictionaries are available to practitioners ("Condition Reporting"). The contents of the documentation, dealing solely with material preservation issues and treatment-related processes, fit comfortably within the zones of expertise demarcated by the standard tripartite divisions (conservation, curatorial, and collections management) in museum collections departments.

But while this kind of writing is central to the file, for me it does not get to the heart of the conservation process today. The restricted format and scientific gloss of the texts, while buttressing a familiar place of professional competence, impose boundaries that must be transgressed for conservators to inhabit the new territories delineated by recent work in material culture studies.

ASSEMBLING THE FILE

Assemblage (Deleuze and Guattari; DeLanda) is a social theory that describes a process wherein an arrangement of heterogeneous elements, for example objects, bodies, events, or technologies, enter into relationships to exert influence on, and to interact with, other entities. The players in an assemblage do not converge to create a unity but instead exist side by side in changing and complex ways. Elements are independent and can be added and subtracted as necessary. This construct privileges an understanding of the world wherein social, political, and cultural phenomena are viewed as having emergent and dynamic properties, which evolve over time. Examples of assemblages can be anything from humanitarian advocacy campaigns, to popular cultural events, to the relationships between bodies and technologies (Kennedy et al. 49).

This way of understanding the social world fittingly describes the complex processes and things in orbit around the conservation process and opens a window onto the connections and energies in the conservator—object—file construct. In a kind of concretization of these ideas, the file itself can also be thought of as an assemblage, in that it embodies the things that the conservator finds herself associated with, and holds their material expression, manifesting a process that is multi-directional and open-ended. Thomas Nail notes two important concepts in the logic of assemblage: "the rejection of unity in favor of multiplicity, and the rejection of essence in favor of events" (22–24). The file is not an organic whole, wherein all the elements click seamlessly together, but instead contains a multiplicity of very different parts, each of which can stand on their own and may even contradict one another. Over time, as knowledge about an object evolves and conservators add elements (or find others to be no longer pertinent), the things in a file can regroup to create different emerging networks and associations that influence the conservation process. The changeable nature of the file means that it will never produce a final, definitive product, or essence, but that instead it will continue to create a string of contingent things and events. As with all assemblages, the file is better described by what it does, rather than by what it is.

Given the rhetorical power attributable to things (Barnett and Boyle 1), all the contents of the file can be understood to have equal standing and the same discursive power as the texts, creating and dispensing insight and meaning in an equally distributed way. In other words, material remnants and sketches are endowed with the same weight as the written documentation. Discussing how writing works in this context, Laura Micciche describes "agency and energy as emergent not from one site of meaning—that is the text—but from a conglomeration of source material linked in diverse, often unpredictable designs" (495). All the things in the file, and their connections, create a powerful and stimulating tool for conservation, producing a web of connection between the historical, social, and material nature of the object, and linking that to the process of conservation treatment.

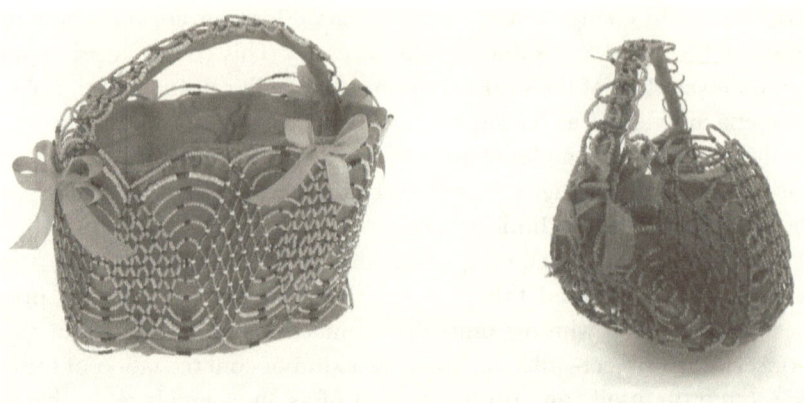

Figure 8.1. Basket, McCord Museum, M1. Before treatment (right) and after treatment (left). Photo Credit: Anne MacKay.

The file also signals a new territory: while the documentation texts are closely connected to the laboratory, with all its disciplinary associations and boundaries, the file moves out and beyond, incorporating other related but more distant places a conservator may encounter. The spaces where writers choose to work have been described as carefully calibrated environments that are structured to afford the things, the rituals, and the activities needed for writing practice (Prior and Shipka 219). These ESSPs, or environment selecting and structuring processes, are in the end "externalizations meant to regulate thought and affect, to channel attention and action" (228). Of course, the file is not a room or an arrangement of furniture, but is nonetheless an intangible, layered space that somehow dwells within the confines of a paper folder. Cydney Alexis refers to the writing habitat is part of an extended self, that provides not only a physical space, but also, more importantly here, "a figural stage for identity performance" (87). The file expands the territory of conservation beyond what the conservator-written texts it contains would imply.

M1 AND ITS FILE: THE STORY OF A BEADED BASKET

In 1915, David Ross McCord, founder of the McCord Museum, acquired a bright pink cloth basket from a buyer in Nova Scotia (see fig. 8.1). Less than four inches high and delicately decorated with tiny glass beads strung on garlands of horsehair, this unusual object was subsequently catalogued as M1 into the fledgling collection. Museum files from that time record that members of the Mi'kmaq community

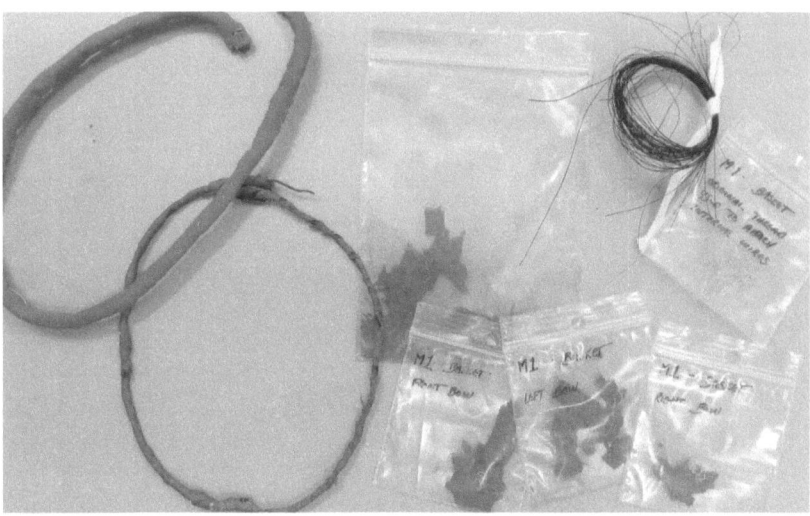

Figure 8.2. Materials in the M1 file. Photo Credit: Anne MacKay.

had given the basket to Amelia Fitzclarence Cary, wife of the lieutenant governor of Nova Scotia from 1840 to 1846, likely as a token of friendship and respect: the fact that Amelia Fitzclarence Cary was an amateur artist, and painted portraits of Mi'kmaq individuals during her residence in Nova Scotia, lends credence to this story (Reinhart). Highly valued on acquisition, the basket was lost at some point, only to be found, unidentified and in a damaged state, during a 1971 move of collections into the current museum building. The basket remained disassociated from its cataloging until 2002, when it was recognized by a museum volunteer working in the collection. The file for M1 was created in 2011, during treatment for an exhibition of treasures from the museum's collections.

The file contains original components of the basket, removed during treatment, as well as materials used for its conservation (see fig. 8.2). The fragments in the M1 file are valuable because they permit freer access to the actual substance of the basket and are the source for both the identification of materials and a closer investigation of their macro- and microscopic properties. Materials in the file include:

- two fabric-covered wire supports from the inside, which were removed because they were weighing down and distorting the shape of the basket.
- the remnants of four silk bows from the rim, which had powdered on contact during treatment.

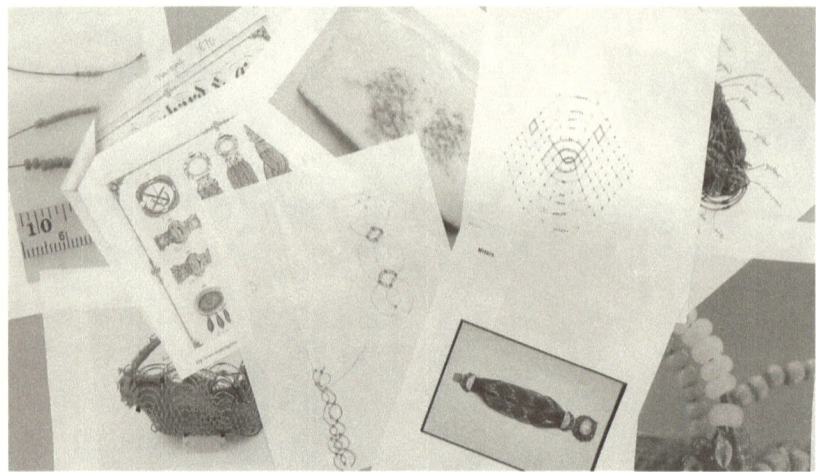

Figure 8.3. Images in the M1 file. Photo Credit: Anne MacKay.

- some of the thread originally used to attach the beaded horsehair band and the wire supports, removed during treatment and saved for comparison with other thread on M1.
- horsehair used to repair losses on the beaded band.

The file contains a plethora of images of M1 and other related objects (see fig. 8.3).

Images in a file create their own kind of story, reflecting the object's passage through time and its associations with other things. Images in the file include:

- a selection of the scores of photographs taken of the object during examination, depicting its unusual material aspects, and during conservation, showing the gradual, but striking evolution of the appearance of the basket through the treatment process. Annotated photographs detail specific condition issues or treatment procedures.
- images of historic Mi'kmaq objects and beading or quillwork patterns.
- a photograph of another museum object, a bracelet made of human hair, bearing the same unusual pattern as the beaded design on the basket.
- sketches and diagrams describing the structure of the basket and its beadwork designs. Several of my drawings piece together the logic of a damaged motif, by sketching different areas where it had been obscured because of loss and damage. Diagrams detail conservation interventions, such as the locations of removed threads or rebeaded sections.

The file contains numerous texts, including the conservation documentation, email correspondence with other conservators, manuscript

Figure 8.4. Texts in the M1 file. Photo Credit: Anne MacKay.

notes, bibliographic references, web page print-outs, and photocopies from books and journals (see fig. 8.4).

Texts in the file include:

- the conservation documentation.
- current Museum catalogue information, with a photocopy of the original 1915 entry identifying the basket as a gift to Lady Falkland.
- a manuscript list of museum objects of Mi'kmaq origin, with dates and storage locations, all of which incorporate horsehair in the beaded decoration, to be examined for comparison with M1.
- a manuscript list of references to books, historic magazines and journal articles.
- notes to self, to-do lists.
- printouts from web sites that investigate Victorian whimsies and hair jewelry, which were consulted for more information on published Euro-Canadian styles and patterns at the time.
- an analytical report on the identification of the dye of the fabric, which identified it as synthetic and not in use until the 1880s, providing a crucial piece of information about M1's constituent materials.

Understanding the M1 file as an assemblage that works, rather than a fixed entity, allows us to reconceptualize it and bring it into a closer relationship with the conservation process. Interesting clusters appear, grouping and regrouping, when cutting transversally across the contents of the file. For example, one such cluster contains the cloth remnants, the museum catalogue entry identifying the basket as a gift to Lady

Falkland at some point between 1840 and 1846, and the analytical report on the dye identifying it as Basic Violet 10. These contradictions between object, text, and technology raise fundamental questions regarding the dating of the basket and its ascribed historical significance as a link between Lady Falkland and members of the Mi'kmaq community, and have repercussions in the world. The photograph of a bracelet with a similar pattern and website printouts depicting nineteenth-century hair work call our attention to a connection that could be made with the basket to the world of Euro-Canadian fashion and nineteenth-century women's past times, underscoring the deeply hybrid nature (Phillips 259–60) of the object. Photographs of the object, before and after treatment, documentation texts, and sketches of a new support system to replace the removed wires, describe a new iteration of the basket, arrived at through the conservation process.

Despite the virtual character of much of its contents, a paper file was created for this complex treatment. The file needs to be in a physical state to be able to function well as an assemblage, in that its material nature emphasizes the fact that it as a life of its own, and will change over time. Touching on the material contents in this way unlocks new doors to reflection. It is that accumulation of things, to be flipped through, handled, or spread out on a table, which affords the associations and disjunctions so fruitful for thinking through an object. Moreover, the physical file makes the absence of something more apparent. For example, the M1 file does not contain any comparable examples of Mi'kmaq beading (strange!), as none have yet to be found.

EVOLVING A PROFESSION

Just before the turn of our current century, it seems that the world became filled with objects, with materials and materiality, and especially with things. The material turn, as it has been called,[2] brought our attention to the stuff of our existence, which was then examined from a myriad of viewpoints, both in popular and academic writing. We traced object lives, situating them within the narrative arcs of global trade and consumerism, as well as in the micro-histories of individuals and communities (Gosden and Marshall). Stable objects mutated into unpredictable things, springing free from their long confinement as the passive half in an imbalanced relationship with a domineering subject (Brown 4). Brokenness became a valued state, revealing a gap or an open door to a deeper understanding of materiality and material interactions theretofore masked by an opaque and unmarked surface

(Jackson 221). And along the way, dull as dishwater matter got invited to the ball, and emerged, dance card full, vibrant and lively (Bennett, *Vibrant Matter* 3).

This new attention to materiality from a (mostly) academic cohort felt to me a bit like a surprise flank attack on territory long assumed secure from acquisitiveness or even passing notice. Although conservators are traditionally considered experts on the physical nature of objects and collections, we now share this terrain with other critical voices whose interests have inevitably deepened our own reflection on our positioning, processes, and outcomes. The more voices added to the debate, from across the spectrum of the humanities and social sciences, the richer, although at times destabilizing, this ground becomes.

Listed below are four ideas about conservation that resonate deeply with issues in material culture studies and that I have found to be revelatory for my practice. Furthermore, they all can be related, in one way or another, to the assembly of things in the M1 file.

CONSERVATORS ENGAGE DIRECTLY WITH THE LIFE OF AN OBJECT

Object biography reveals the way objects can be the material starting point for a deeper understanding of the social, political, or historical dimensions of our world. Igor Kopytoff's seminal article on the cultural biography of things has shown that tracing an object's use and its vectors in space and time provides a rich understanding of its social import, its multiple roles and divergent meanings (87–90). Objects also live lives through their material being: they are made, they physically evolve, and eventually (unless extraordinary measures are taken) they disintegrate and disappear. Conservators work on the body of the object in ways that have significant impact both on our understanding of it and on its continued existence in time, making the act of preservation an important chapter in its biography. This is not a new idea and a number of classic conservation texts use the notion of a life cycle to explore the ways in which conservation is situated within the life of the object (Brandi 61; Baldini 355).

Conservators of contemporary art, who deal with complex artworks, have pushed the idea of object biography further, taking into account events such as the obsolescence of integrated technology or the rapid deterioration of unstable components, which are not controlled by the human subject. This has necessitated certain practices—the reconfiguration of installations, the migration or emulation of out-of-date technological elements of a work, or the wholesale replacement of parts of an object—that challenge our understanding of what should be considered original or authentic (van de Vall et al. 1). The idea of alteration either as something inscribed in the artwork's on-going materiality or as something imposed by a conservator has filtered through to other specialties in conservation and has made conservators think more critically about the use of words like conservation or damage, and to opt at times for terms like different iteration or change.

M1's file speaks to the object's biography in several ways. In the most basic sense, the dye analysis report, providing a *terminus post quem* of 1887 for the pink fabric refutes our century-old understanding of its past life. It throws our beliefs regarding its significance, and by extension, my understanding of what was to be recovered during treatment, into a state of profound questioning. Other elements in the file speak more directly to conservation processes. For example, the conservation photographs, supported by the written documentation, show an almost undecipherable object regaining legibility through treatment. This new iteration reflects our fascination with M1's shifting story and our desire to see it today in a state befitting its complex life and current status as a museum treasure. Finally, drawings made to decipher the original designs of the damaged beading reveal an ingenious twinning of motifs on the handle and the sides of M1 not evident at first glance. The basic pattern of these two parts of the basket is the same, but the motifs appear different, because of variations in the number of garlands in each band and the sequencing of bead colours. Looking toward M1's future, this observation provides a new basis of comparison with other objects and offers an important marker for future paths in the investigation of its story.

CONSERVATORS AND OBJECTS INTERACT WITHIN COMPLEX SOCIAL NETWORKS

Actor-network theory (ANT) provides a way for conservators to better understand and further conceptualize this biographical process. ANT sees social interaction as a collective activity, influenced by a host of entities or actants—people, objects, technologies, and so forth—whose agency is described through their interconnections (Latour). ANT gives the nonhuman as much importance as the human in these networks, and in doing so undermines automatically held assumptions about how the world around us is constructed and how systems function. As Bruno Latour states, while things do not have intentionality, they do enter into causal relations. "In addition to 'determining' and serving as a 'backdrop' for human action, things might authorize, allow, afford, encourage, permit, suggest, influence, block, render possible, forbid and so on" (72). Reflecting on the interactions that occur during conservation in terms of ANT has been fruitful in both reconsidering the relationship of the conservator and the object and in distinguishing other significant actants (van Saaze 147–48). ANT takes into account the complexity and the dynamic quality of any conservation process, where a conservator's input is only one of many forces at play.

M1's file contains an impressive array of things that have exerted influence on the conservation process. The object's material hybridity, whatever the actual history of that may be, put me, as a conservator, in touch with a variety of actants, all present in its file. Nineteenth-century Indigenous communities and Euro-Canadian settlers (and today's members of these communities, drawn to the object through its thought-provoking qualities), researchers, scientists and museum workers, as well as pieces of historic jewelry and Indigenous beaded or quilled objects, are all elements in M1's networks. In a more intimate way, the presence of different hands is clearly displayed on the body of the basket. Photographs of the sewing on the fabric reveal amateurish construction and hasty stitching, while the beading is inventive and skillfully done. This evidence corroborates conflicts in the dating of the synthetic dye (late nineteenth century) and the tiny beads (early to mid-nineteenth century) and supports the idea that the basket was made by at least two different people at two different times.

Our own narratives and beliefs about M1 also impose themselves as actants. Even though we know that the basket was never a gift to Lady Falkland, this story still clings to the object and makes an appearance in the file, lending a notion of anterior richness and significance to an object whose actual history remains shrouded in mystery. Moreover, current interest in the transcultural object (Phillips 16–17) as emblematic of the colonial relationship between Euro-Canadians and Indigenous peoples is a key element in promoting the basket to its current status as a museum treasure and in pushing forward its conservation treatment. Finally, as the conservator who undertook this treatment, I must acknowledge that, in enacting my role, I am not outside these things, processes, and beliefs but, instead, have also been caught up in the web of M1.

WEAR, DAMAGE, AND DECAY ARE CRUCIAL SIGNPOSTS IN A CONSERVATOR'S WORK

Steven Jackson's proposal of "broken world thinking" as a way to counter the "productivist" slant of much current reflection about technology is particularly interesting for conservation (221). According to Jackson, focus on novelty, development, and design has blinded those who deal with technology to the real and significant forces of breakdown and repair: "Breakdown disturbs and sets in motion worlds of possibility that disappear under the stable or accomplished form of the artifact" (230). Thinking about repair as something that is generative and productive, provides rich fodder for reconceptualizing conservation practice. According to Jackson, broken world thinking has "no automatic preference for stasis over change" (233) but instead favors the practice of "articulation"—an activity, like conservation, that occurs in time and attempts to fit together the numerous forces in motion around it.

Valuing breakdown (damage, deterioration) for its positive effects, and repair (conservation treatment) for the ways in which it is creative and generative, shifts conservation discourse away from classic tropes about recovering the original and locating the authentic to a different conceptualization of practice. That conservation actually adds to the world by producing something new and is not simply seeking stasis or a return to a former state is an important element in a more critical approach to received ideas regarding the authenticity of the object. According to conservator Salvador Muñoz-Viñas: "Conservation does not pursue authenticity . . . conservation is done because we do not like the authentic state of some objects . . . because what authentically is does not suit our needs, our tastes, our expectations" (37). This language is interesting and unusual for conservation: Muñoz-Viñas drops the veil of scientific neutrality and admits to liking, and to having needs, tastes, and expectations. Conservation is not about freezing the present, or recovering the past, or worrying about the needs of those amorphous future generations. Treatment as articulation reinforces the idea that conservation—in recognizing the disjunctions and creating the connections that help to make objects work for us anew—produces something inextricably part of our present.

During M1's treatment, it was only through the close observation of damage and deterioration that a pathway could be found back to an accomplished form of the object, which was unknown at the beginning of the process. This articulation involved juggling scraps of evidence, removing some parts and adding new ones, to generate a slowly reconstructed whole, one that created a version of the object that we like and that serves our purposes. The M1 file lays bare the sutures inherent in this process, as opposed to the seamlessness of the basket's presentation in a conserved state. Bits of ribbon and thread, photographs of losses in the beading, and detailed written descriptions attest to this state of disrepair. Brokenness revealed a moment of openness and potential in M1 that disappeared after treatment, a moment that, however, is realized and maintained in the texts and things that comprise the file.

DYNAMIC MATTER IS THE VITAL STARTING POINT FOR A CONSERVATOR'S UNIQUE CONNECTION WITH THE WORLD

New materiality draws our attention to the stuff of things, to the brute materials of which everything is composed. Thing-power materialism and vibrant matter circle back to the core of material culture and speak to the agency that is found in the most basic components of our material world. Tim Ingold asks us to take a step back from the congealed entities that have traditionally been seen as emerging from historical or scientific processes, to engage with the primal dynamism of matter itself, stating "materials . . . do not present themselves as tokens of some common essence—materiality—that endows every worldly object with its inherent 'thingliness,' rather, they partake in the very process of the world's ongoing generation and regeneration." (9). Here, materials are in flux; they do not merely exist but occur. Jane Bennett echoes these ideas: "Thing-power materialism figures materiality as a protean flow of matter-energy and figures the thing as a relatively composed form of that flow" ("The Force of Things" 349). Bennett's things engage forcefully in the world: they are cheeky and cunning; they are movers and shakers (359–60). In describing an ecology of matter, Bennett emphasizes the close networks of human and nonhuman entities, activated and described by the "energetic forces" flowing through them.

Energetic forces, vibrant matter: these concepts have particular resonance for conservators who have long felt the contrariness of objects in their opacity under examination and their stubbornness in treatment. The intimacy of the conservation process is one of its salient features, and being in close contact with the substance of an object, wrestling with its physicality, is truly a humbling process of give and take. Here the material casts off its muteness and engages; thing-power and matter-energy are not constructs for reconfiguring the social but are concretely felt in a quotidian way.

M1 is an object whose matter (keratin chains, silica lattices) and materials (horsehair, glass beads, fuchsia dye) sang an epic tale of being and becoming. The basket pushed back, forcing me to draw its damage, to examine it microscopically, to track every clue, in order to uncover a treatment path. M1 took the lead: text and image in the file describe procedures done slowly and in reaction to the responses of the basket's materials. Horsehair, samples of which are in the file and can be handled, was used to repair the sections that were broken or lost in the beaded horsehair band, even though using the same material would make conserved sections more difficult to locate in the future. The perfect aptness of this material—its thinness, strength and springiness—meant that nothing else would remotely work. I was struck by the marvelous fineness of the beads, about one-half the size of the oldest replacement beads at our disposal, and less than one quarter the size of today's seed beads. While they would have been exceptionally difficult to string with a needle and thread, they slipped with ease onto a length of horsehair, which was then arched and elegantly integrated into the weave of the band.

CONCLUSION

If conservation is really an act of articulation or a conservator's way of participating in the fit of the object in the world, then the file is the hinge that describes that relationship. Materials and materiality are resolved in a very real way within the file, establishing links between the substance of objects and their social and historical lives. Objects cannot undergo treatment otherwise. This breakdown of the standard binary opposition of the tangible and the intangible, through an unbroken chain of association from objects out into the world of ideas, is integral to a closer positioning of conservation with other fields of study.

The file itself is an essential tool, even a prerequisite, for conservation practice today. It is deeply rooted in the creation of a discipline and the gradual professionalization of conservation over the course of the last century. Especially in the museum setting, the file has highlighted the imperative to track and record interventions that change the nature of the object. The written documentation in the file, in both its form and language, connects with many widespread notions about the scientific nature of conservation, its deep focus on the material, and its concern with certain ethical principles and guidelines. However, a closer look reveals something much more complex than that. New materiality has tossed conservators into a constellation of novel ideas relating to their work. Partaking in an object's life, acting within networks, understanding the generative nature of conservation treatment, and extending out into the world from a material center are ideas that are rich for conservation practice. The complexities of the file, the assemblage of all those things, images and texts, echo the indeterminacy and messiness inherent in the conservation process, entangling it in increasingly interesting ways with the connective tissues of material culture debate.

AFTERWORD

I remember well how my colleagues responded to my object choice during our strategic planning meeting, because I saved the comment sheets that were passed around during the exercise. We were asked to think about the other participants' objects, and in addition to writing general observations, to produce ad copy, an exhibition label, and an obituary for them. Interestingly, M1's obituary mourned the imminent loss of the material file (heretofore maintained in a digital afterlife), while the ad copy noted, in breathless tones, the possibility of acquiring an original manuscript document written by a conservator, notes in the margins included. Several colleagues referred to the importance of "understanding objects"; another spoke to "secrets . . . revealed through process." All this is very interesting to me, and has led to the long reflection that has brought about in this chapter. As a result, I have recently decided to add a new section to the museum's treatment documentation form, one that I hope will broaden its scope and relevance. I have decided that the heading of this new section will be "Conservator's Comments."

NOTES

1. I lead a team of five people in the Conservation Department of the McCord Museum, a museum of social history, located in Montreal, Canada. The McCord's collections comprise about 1,500,000 objects in six collections: Indigenous Cultures; Dress, Fashion and Textiles; Photography; Textual Archives; Paintings, Prints and Drawings; and Material Culture.
2. For an investigation of the material turn across the humanities, see Peter N. Miller, editor, *Cultural Histories of the Material World*, U of Michigan P, 2013, https://muse.jhu.edu/book/25312.

WORKS CITED

Achel, Bettina. "*Il Manuale* by Giovanni Secco-Suardo: Its Impact on the Development of Conservation and Restoration in the Nineteenth Century." *Conservation in the Nineteenth Century*, edited by Isabelle Brajer, Archetype Publications, 2013, pp. 80–90.

"AIC Code of Ethics and Guidance for Practice." *American Institute for Conservation*, www.culturalheritage.org/about-conservation/code-of-ethics. Accessed 20 July 2019.

Alexis, Cydney. "The Material Culture of Writing: Objects, Habitat, and Identity in Practice." *Rhetoric, through Everyday Things*, edited by Scot Barnett and Casey Boyle, U of Alabama P, 2016, pp. 83–95.

Anderson, Jaynie. "The First Cleaning Controversy at the National Gallery 1846–1853." *Issues in the Conservation of Paintings*, edited by David Bomford and Mark Leonard, 2004, pp. 441–453.

"Athens Charter." *Getty Conservation Institute*, www.getty.edu/conservation/publications_resources/research_resources/charters/charter04.html. Accessed July 10, 2019.

Baldini, Umberto. "Theory of Restoration and Methodological Unity." Translated by Erikson Translations. *Historical and Philosophical Issues in the Conservation of Cultural Heritage*, edited by Nicholas Stanley Price et al., Getty Publications, 1996, pp. 355–357.

Barnett, Scot, and Casey Boyle. "Rhetorical Ontology, or, How to Do Things with Things." *Rhetoric, through Everyday Things*, edited by Scot Barnett and Casey Boyle, U of Alabama P, 2016, pp. 1–14, https://muse.jhu.edu/chapter/1816437/pdf. Accessed 1 Aug. 2019.

Bennett, Jane. "The Force of Things: Steps toward an Ecology of Matter." *Political Theory*, vol. 32, no. 3, 2004, pp. 347–372. *JSTOR*, www.jstor.org/stable/4148158. Accessed 30 July 2019.

Bennett, Jane. *Vibrant Matter: A Political Ecology of Things*. Duke UP, 2010.

Bonsanti, Giorgio. "Raphael's *Marriage of the Virgin* in Milan and the Restoration by Giuseppe Molteni." *Conservation in the Nineteenth Century*, edited by Isabelle Brajer, Archtype Pulications, 2013, pp. 29–44.

Brajer, Isabelle. Introduction to *Conservation in the Nineteenth Century*, edited by Isabelle Brajer, Archetype Publications, 2013.

Brandi, Cesare. *Theory of Restoration*. Translated by Cynthia Rockwell, Nardine Editore, 2000.

Brewer, Francesca. *A Laboratory for Art: Harvard's Fogg Museum and the Emergence of Conservation in America, 1900–1950*. Harvard Art Museum, 2010.

Brommelle, Norman. "Material for a History of Conservation: The 1850 and 1853 Reports on the National Gallery." *Studies in Conservation*, vol. 2, no. 4, 1956, pp. 176–188. *JSTOR*, www.jstor.org/stable/1504963. Accessed 30 July 2019.

Brown, Bill. "Thing Theory." *Critical Inquiry*, vol. 28, no. 1, 2001, pp. 1–22. *JSTOR*, www.jstor.org/stable/1344258. Accessed 30 July 2019.

"Burra Charter." *Australia ICOMOS*, australia.icomos.org/wp-content/uploads/The-Burra-Charter-2013-Adopted-31.10.2013.pdf.

Clavir, Miriam. *Preserving What Is Valued: Museums, Conservation, and First Nations*. U of British Columbia P, 2002.

"Code of Ethics and Guidance for Practice of the Canadian Association for Conservation of Cultural Property and of the Canadian Association of Professional Conservators." 3rd ed., Canadian Association for Conservation, 2009.

"Condition Reporting—Paintings. Part III: Glossary—(CCI) Notes 10/11." *Canadian Conservation Institute*, www.canada.ca/en/conservation-institute/services/conservation-preservation-publications/canadian-conservation-institute-notes/condition-reporting-paintings-glossary.html. Accessed 16 Apr. 2018.

Delanda, Manuel. *A New Philosophy of Society: Assemblage Theory and Social Complexity*. Continuum, 2006.

Deleuze, Gilles, and Felix Guattari. *A Thousand Plateaus: Capitalism and Schizophrenia*. Translated by Brian Massumi, U of Minnesota P, 1987.

Forni, Ulisse. "Manual for the Painter-Restorer." Translated by Erikson Translations. *Issues in the Conservation of Paintings*, edited by David Bomford and Mark Leonard, Getty Publications, 2004, pp. 326–330.

Gosden, Chris, and Yvonne Marshall. "The Cultural Biography of Objects." *World Archaeology*, vol. 31, no. 2, 1999, pp. 169–178. *JSTOR*, www.jstor.org/stable/125055. Accessed 1 Aug. 2019.

Ingold, Tim. "Materials against Materiality." *Archaeological Dialogues*, vol. 14, no. 1, 2007, pp. 1–16.

Jackson, Steven. "Rethinking Repair." *Media Technologies: Essays on Communication, Materiality and Society*, edited by Tarleton Gillespie et al., MIT Press Scholarship Online, Sep. 2014, pp. 221–239, mitpress.universitypressscholarship.com/view/10.7551/mitpress/9780262525374.001.0001/upso-9780262525374-chapter-11?print=pdf. Accessed 24 Apr. 2018.

Kennedy, Rose, et al. "All Those Little Machines: Assemblage as Transformative Theory." *Australian Humanities Review*, vol. 55, Nov. 2013. *PROQUEST*, literature.proquest.com/searchFulltext.do?id=R04965982&divLevel=0&area=abell&forward=critref_ft. Accessed 11 Sep. 2018.

Kopytoff, Igor. "The Cultural Biography of Things: Commoditization as Process." *The Social Life of Things: Commodities in Cultural Perspective*, edited by Arjun Appadurai, Cambridge UP, 1986, pp. 64–91.

Krueger, Holly, et al. "Written Documentation." *American Association for Conservation*, www.conservation-wiki.com/wiki/Written_Documentation_(PCC)#5.6_Glossary_of _Terms. Accessed 10 July 2019.

Latour, Bruno. *Reassembling the Social: An Introduction to Actor-Network Theory*. Oxford UP, 2005, townsendgroups.berkeley.edu/sites/default/files/reassembling_the_social _selections.pdf. Accessed 12 July 2019.

Lerner, Neal. "Writing Is a Way of Enacting Disciplinarity." *Naming What We Know: Threshold Concepts of Writing Studies*, edited by Linda Adler-Kassner and Elizabeth Wardle, UP of Colorado, 2015, pp. 40–41.

"Lingua Franca—A Common Language for Conservators of Photographic Materials." *Library and Archives Canada*, www.bac-lac.gc.ca/eng/about-us/publications/electronic -books/Pages/title-page-lingua-franca.aspx.

Marcus, George, and Erikan Saka. "Assemblage." *Theory, Culture and Society*, vol. 23, nos. 2–3, 2006, pp. 101–106, journals.sagepub.com/doi/pdf/10.1177/0263276406062573. Accessed 31 July 2019.

Massing, Ann. "Restoration Policy in France in the Eighteenth Century." *Studies in the History of Painting Restoration*, edited by Christine Sitwell and Sarah Staniforth, Archetype Publications, 1996, pp. 63–84.

McClellan, Andrew. "The Politics and Aesthetics of Display: Museums in Paris 1750–1800." *Art History*, vol. 7, no. 4, 1984, pp. 438–464, onlinelibrary.wiley.com/doi/epdf/10.1111 /j.1467-8365.1984.tb00116.x. Accessed 11 July 2019.

McClellan, Andrew. "Raphael's *Foligno Madonna* at the Louvre in 1800: Restoration and Reaction at the Dawn of the Museum Age." *Art Journal*, vol. 54, no. 2, 1995, pp. 80–85. *PROQUEST*, search.proquest.com/pio/docview/1290146110/fulltextPDF/E23A0914C 96C43F8PQ/14?accountid=12339. Accessed 11 Sep. 2018.

Meijer-van Mensch, Léontine, and Peter van Mensch. "From Disciplinary Control to Co-Creation—Collecting and the Development of Museums as Praxis in the Nineteenth and Twentieth Century." *Encouraging Collections Mobility—A Way Forward for Museums in Europe*, edited by Susanna Petterson, Monika Hagedorn-Saupe, Teijamari Jyrkkio, and Astrid Weij, Finnish National Gallery, n.d., http://www.lending-for-europe .eu/fileadmin/CM/public/handbook/Encouraging_Collections_Mobility_A4.pdf. Accessed 11 July 2019.

Micciche, Laura R. "Writing Material." *College English*, vol. 76, no. 6, pp. 488–505. *PROQUEST*, https://literature.proquest.com/pageImage.do?ftnum=3349456361&fmt=page&area =criticism&journalid=00100994&articleid=R05009840&pubdate=2014. Accessed 1 Aug. 2019.

Miller, Peter N., editor. *Cultural Histories of the Material World*. U of Michigan P, 2013, muse .jhu.edu/book/25312. Accessed 11 Sep. 2018.

Muñoz-Viñas, Salvador. "Beyond Authenticity." *Art Conservation and Authenticities: Material, Concept, Context*, edited by Erma Hermes and Tina Fishe, Archetype Publishing, 2009, pp. 33–40.

Nail, Thomas. "What Is an Assemblage?" *SubStance*, vol. 46, no. 1, 2017, pp. 21–37, https:// muse.jhu.edu/article/650026/pdf. Accessed 1 Aug. 2019.

"Nara Document on Authenticity." *ICOMOS*, www.icomos.org/charters/nara-e.pdf. Accessed 17 Apr. 2018.

Phillips, Ruth B. *Trading Identities: The Souvenir in Native North American Art from the Northeast, 1700–1900*. U of Washington P, 1998.

Prior, Paul, and Jody Shipka. "Chronotopic Lamination: Tracing the Contours of Literate Activity." *Writing Selves/Writing Societies: Research from Activity Perspectives*, edited by Charles Bazerman and David Russell, WAC Clearinghouse, 2003, pp. 180–238, www.researchgate.net/publication/241202237_Chronotopic_Lamination_Tracing_the_Contours_of_Literate_Activity. Accessed 11 July 2019.

Reinhart, Melinda. *Lady Falkland's Travel Album: Negotiating Colonial and Feminine Discourses.* 2005. Concordia University, master of arts thesis, spectrum.library.concordia.ca/8594/1/MR10312.pdf. Accessed 20 Aug. 2018.

"Report from the Select Committee on the National Gallery (1853)." *Issues in the Conservation of Paintings*, edited by David Bomford and Mark Leonard, Getty Publications, 2004, pp. 59–68.

Rivers, Shayne, and Nick Umney. *Conservation of Furniture.* Butterworth Heinemann, 2003.

Saunders, David. "London Pollution and the National Gallery in the Nineteenth Century." *National Gallery Technical Bulletin*, vol. 21, 2000, pp. 77–94, www.nationalgallery.org.uk/upload/pdf/saunders2000.pdf. Accessed 11 July 2019.

Secco-Suardo, Giovanni. "The Idea of the Perfect Restorer." Translated by Erikson Translations. *Issues in the Conservation of Paintings*, edited by David Bomford and Mark Leonard, Getty Publications, 2004, pp. 331–338.

van de Vall, Renée, et al. "Reflections on a Biographical Approach to Contemporary Art Conservation." Preprints of the 16th ICOM Committee for Conservation Triennial Conference, Lisbon, Portugal, 19–23 Sep. 2011, edited by Janet Bridgland, Critério, 2011, pp. 1–8, www.hannahoelling.com/wp-content/uploads/2016/09/Reflections_on_a_Biographical_Approach_t.pdf. Accessed 3 Apr. 2018.

van Saaze, Vivian. *Installation Art and the Museum: Presentation and Conservation of Changing Artworks.* Amsterdam UP, 2013.

"Venice Charter." *ICOMOS*, www.icomos.org/charters/venice_e.pdf. Accessed 17 Apr. 2018.

Whitehead, Christopher. *Museums and the Construction of Disciplines: Art and Archaeology in Nineteenth-Century Britain.* Gerald Duckworth and Company, 2009.

PART THREE
Writing Genre

This section focuses on the materiality of everyday genres and historical writing practices. Centering on Renaissance- and Victorian-era Europe, contributors in this section examine acts of inscription in household letters and hotel visitors' books, raising again the question of who gets to write, who is seen as a writer, and whose writing should be studied. In his chapter "The Victorian Visitors' Book as Genre and Artifact," historian Kevin James reclaims visitors' books, or "inn albums" as overlooked material artifacts that index the socio-cultural mores of travel practices and identity in the period. James focuses his analysis initially on a single, much-written-about page of one of these books, the isolated "Montenvers leaf" made famous because of its inscription by the British Victorian poet and traveler, Percy Shelley. He questions commentators' fetishization of the famous inscription, emphasizing how visitors' books and their everyday practices have been largely ignored in historical study. James recontextualizes the inn album as a sociomaterial genre read and written by travelers as "acts of social production and self-fashioning, in this case as part of the choreography of a guest's departure centered on a particular set of objects (the book, the pen, the desk on which it was inscribed)." James' discussion speaks to fellow historians as he demonstrates how historical artifacts get (re)circulated among commentators and take on inflated meaning and life. And via the WS concept of genre as social action (Miller), James counters that dismissive perspective, reading the albums no longer as insufficiently literary or "high art" but instead as enlivened social practices situated in everyday routines.

In her chapter "Gendered Letterwriting in Renaissance England: Genre as Sociomaterial Action," WS scholar Keri Epps analyzes women's Renaissance correspondence and domestic writing spaces to investigate how gendered power is materialized in the letter genre. Focusing on a particular letter of Lady Elizabeth Bagot (along with those written by other Bagot women), archived in the collection of the Bagot family papers (1557–1671) housed at the Folger Shakespeare Library, Epps uncovers "complex intersections of material space and rhetorical genre awareness that reveal tensions among genre, materiality, and prescribed roles for Renaissance women." While letters in this period have been subject to much scholarly discussion (though not necessarily in WS), Epps approaches this expansive archive with interest in the Bagot *women's* letters and specifically on their material conventions and features, as well as the tools used to make them. Such focus on the material features, not just the discoursal, opens up dynamics of gender in domestic and civic power, Epps suggests, that might otherwise go unnoticed. Extending rhetorical genre studies' (RGS) focus on genre as repetitious social performance through discourse conventions, Epps argues for examining genres as "sociomaterial action" because such an approach can reveal "*how* and *why* power gets *materially* reproduced (or not) in specific writing contexts." Here again, Epps demonstrates how focus on the materialities of writing (and genre) reveals the dynamics of power, agency, and social positioning in writing acts.

This section shows us writers in geographical and historical contexts and periods we've not much considered in WS. But, as we've asked throughout this collection, why wouldn't the material culture of historical writers be of interest? As Bazerman has pointed out, there are 5,000 years of writers, practices, and cultures out there for systematic study (36). James and Epps demonstrate how vernacular writing practices are illuminated through careful study of artifacts. They show how material culture is crucial to the operation and circulation of genres. As scholars in RGS like Carolyn Miller and Amy Devitt have shown, WS has come to understand genre no longer as a set of formal features but as something people *do* in recurring situations, situations that are constrained by others, by collaborative aims and needs, and through adherence to and strategic violation of textual and discourse conventions. As Amy Devitt puts it, "Genre entails purposes, participants, and themes, so understanding genre entails understanding a rhetorical and semiotic situation and a social context" (575–76). That social semiotic situation, this section argues, is always a material one; genres are not just social, but socio*material* action. When Victorian inn albums are examined as a social genre and artifact (not just isolated inscriptions held up for textual and historical analysis), a network of social practices centered on the visitors' album are revealed and in turn travel culture of the nineteenth century is better understood. When close attention is given to the tools, material features, and household spaces constituting Renaissance women's genre practices of the letter, "agentive moments" of participation and measures of discoursal authority in spheres of cultural life (civic and royal, household, land transaction) from which we might assume they were otherwise routinely prohibited are revealed.

Genres, after all, are not free-floating semiotic constructions. The work of, as well as access to, genres equally requires objects—volumes, implements, wax seals, rooms, pages, technologies. As Suresh Canagarajah has argued about academic scholarship, genres have myriad and unacknowledged "nondiscursive conventions"; they require and often assume access to certain things like quality paper, postage, electricity or oil lamps, telephones or fax (436). If we want to study how people do genres, we must investigate the material objects people need, use, hack, and modify. Like Epps, we are intrigued by the possibilities for further genre studies that employ an MCS ethos to account for the things involved in, and the things necessary to gain access to, the practice of genre as social action.

WORKS CITED

Bazerman, Charles. "The Case for Writing Studies as a Major Discipline." *Rhetoric and Composition as Intellectual Work*, edited by Gary A. Olson, Southern Illinois UP, 2002, pp. 32–38.

Canagarajah, A. Suresh. " 'Nondiscursive' Requirements in Academic Publishing, Material Resources of Periphery Scholars, and the Politics of Knowledge Production." *Written Communication*, vol. 13, no. 4, 1996, pp. 435–472.

Devitt, Amy. "Generalizing about Genre: New Conceptions of an Old Concept." *CCC*, vol. 44, no. 4, 1993, pp. 573–586.

Miller, Carolyn. "Genre as Social Action." *Quarterly Journal of Speech*, vol. 70, 1984, pp. 151–167.

9
THE VICTORIAN VISITORS' BOOK AS GENRE AND ARTIFACT

Kevin James

Reflecting on inn albums and visitors' books—bound volumes of "empty" pages that invited signatures and commentaries—the Earl of Crewe remarked in 1898 that Charles Lamb had neglected to include them in an 1822 enumeration of false claimants to the dignity of a "book." Lamb averred that seeing "these *things in books' clothing* perched upon shelves, like false saints, usurpers of true shrines, intruders into the sanctuary, thrusting out the legitimate occupants" offended his eyes (Lamb 190). Lamb listed "Court Calendars, Draught Boards bound and lettered at the back" and other examples of "books that are no books—*biblia a-biblia*." Crewe attributed Lamb's omission of the inn album to Lamb's generous disposition toward the volume's inscribers, however insipid their entries. Yet Crewe assigned those volumes to the same body of *biblia a-biblia* for which Lamb reserved such scorn.

For his part, Crewe evaluated visitors' books from a unique vantage point: he possessed perhaps the most famous page ever torn from such a volume—one whose columns bore an 1816 inscription by the celebrated Romantic Percy Bysshe Shelley. The contents of that single leaf fuelled decades of speculation over their inspiration, their inscriber, and the motivations behind apparent interventions in the text by an equally famous traveller, Lord Byron. Shelley's autograph, and the bold sentiments it proclaimed, made the page a subject of intense scholarly and antiquarian interest, defying the stigma of *biblia a-biblia* that otherwise attended many inn albums (or hotel albums or visitors' books, as they were also commonly known). By the time Crewe wrote his appraisal of the leaf in his possession, it had already passed through many hands and entered into lore. Its meaning and value were shaped by assessments of the hotel album as a text in the years since Shelley's famous journey. For in contrast to the intrinsic value attributed to this single leaf, the vast number of inscriptions found in Victorian hotel albums were dismissed in print as fripperies.

https://doi.org/10.7330/9781646422302.c009

In the discussion that follows, I will explore close readings and interpretations of the single leaf inscribed at Montenvers and situate it within the context of wider, inferiorizing discussions of the album genre in the nineteenth century. In particular, I will focus on how reading and writing in a hotel album were entwined with the iteration and reiteration of the social role of the hotel guest, as the genre's conventions became ritualized. Like other contributions in this volume that explore the relationship between text and social practice, whether manuscript letters or print manuals, I treat *inscribing* in these texts as acts of social production and self-fashioning, in this case as part of the choreography of a guest's departure centered on a particular set of objects (the book, the pen, the desk on which it was inscribed). *Reading* the inscriptions might occur in other physical contexts (a parlor, or even a bedroom—for the book was moveable within the walls of hostelry) and could also respond to different incentives. Very often, the two acts entwined as reader-inscribers fashioned social identities through creation of a textual form that was, by virtue of its collective authorship, a social production. This approach to exploring how inscribers and readers made sense of the albums is informed by Carolyn R. Miller's assertion that genre does not structure expression as much as it is created through the iteration and reiteration of social actions that stabilize particular forms of communication in specific contexts (1984). What Cydney Alexis (2016) describes as the writing habitat—a matrix of materials and of rituals—was a critical shaper of reading and inscription within the walls of the hotel. The writing habitat was prescribed by the affordances of the building but offered much scope for acts of furtive reading (there was general licence to steal away with the books to a parlor corner and even to a private room for the night), conspicuous writing (at the desk, upon departure), or more clandestine inscription (while reading in comparatively private spaces), as well as for dissemination of the book's contents far beyond the hostelry's walls (though transcription in private notebooks, which sometimes then found their way into print). Ownership of the book by inn- or hotel-keepers meant that access to the volume was ultimately at their discretion, and many bore evidence of excised pages—perhaps containing offending comments, or perhaps prized autographs. Outside the confines of the hostelry, the book was treated in a constellation of printed texts in which it figured as a tool for another agenda of authorial self-fashioning. Scripts that guided "proper" hotel-album inscription and reading were expounded in books, periodicals, and columns of newspapers. These texts largely treated inn albums as specimens of generic decline and offered offending excerpts as egregious examples of insipid album culture. Excerption and publication had other aims, too—to entertain readers, to magnify the authority of the writer, and to stabilise meanings of the visitors' book as *biblia a-biblia* in the public mind. Yet, however often they were derided in print, or, when lacking the mark of a famous traveler such as Shelley, dismissed as inconsequential texts, these books were critical tools in the development of in nineteenth-century travel culture.

The Montenvers leaf was an enduring exception to the denigrating assessments of the hotel album, and it attracted sustained and serious attention for more than a century. Poring over the inscriptions of Romantic travelers on the single, surviving page, writers offered divergent opinions that were often entwined with fierce personal antagonisms amongst critics and literary luminaries (New Ivey White; R. Glynn Grylls; Hopps). Famous figures engaged in exegetical exercises that affirmed the page's status as evidence not only of a celebrated early-nineteenth-century journey but also of the dynamics of Romantic travel culture. What piqued interest in this album, beyond the famous personalities whose names it immortalized? Partly it inspired the imagination of a fragment of an episode—because it took the form of a single leaf of paper, physically extracted from the album in which it was initially bound. Such material and textual decontextualisation invited speculation as to its original material and textual contexts and heighted interest in its origins, its circulation, and its value as a window onto a stormy and scandalous Romantic world. In order to understand the exceptional character of this page, we must explore the evolving relationship between social and textual practices centered on the visitors' album, how contemporaries structured its textual value through the long lens of generic history, and how acts of hotel-album inscription and reading were conventionalized and depreciated in the Victorian era.

Let us return to the debates that surrounded the single page that came into Lord Crewe's possession and his reflections on the leaf in 1898. By that time, most commentators accepted an established narrative of events that had brought Romantic luminaries together under one roof. During an 1816 summer tour, Percy Bysshe Shelley, in the company of Mary Godwin and her half-sister, Jane, encountered Lord Byron in Switzerland at Diodati near Lake Geneva and on Lake Leman, before Shelley's party proceeded to Montenvers, in Chamonix, France, a region near the border with Switzerland and Italy. They reached it late in July (Crewe 336). Shelley, after apparently recording his name in a Montenvers hotel visitors' album, offered his address as "Supex," his destination as "L'Enfer," and entered his occupation (in Greek) as

"Democrat, philanthropist, atheist"—evoking an earlier, infamous claim that led to his expulsion from Oxford. The names of his traveling companions were recorded beneath Shelley's, in his hand. Godwin claimed the same infernal destination. Shelley's early biographer, Edward Dowden, wrote that a traveler later added "fool" to the poet's "occupation." Lord Byron, subsequently visiting the same hostelry, declared to a companion, John Cam Hobhouse (later Lord Broughton), that it would be advisable to efface the recorded occupation. Hence Byron scratched out both the words "atheist" inscribed by Shelley and the anonymously appended "fool" (Dowden 30). Dowden's account of these acts of inscription and alteration led to diverse speculations over the motivations behind Byron's putative interventions, as critics, antiquarians and scholars attempted to reconstruct the contexts of inscription. Fierce debates centered on the page's contents as it was torn from the volume and made its way, as a leaf within the pages of *The Revolt of Islam*, into the possession of the collector Rev. John Mitford, and then to Lord Houghton—who was later raised to the earldom of Crewe. It was subject to critical scrutiny by leading members of the literati, in some of their preeminent print forums, from an assessment proffered by Algernon Charles Swinburne, who condemned the mangled Greek of the inscription (Rossetti 64), to Lord Crewe's short essay in *Literature*.

In final possession of the leaf, Crewe offered a detailed description of the page that lay before him: a "rough, blue-grey paper, foolscap size," which "shows evidence of having been cut from a book, as a word or two is missing from each line on the inner margin." The page was ruled by hand into vertical divisions headed respectively "jours, mois, noms des voyageurs, lieu de naissance et profession, d'ou ils viennent, ou ils sont dirigé, observations" [days, month(s), names of travelers, place of birth and occupation, origin, destination, observations] (336). Noting that both sides of the paper were filled with names and observations in many languages, Crewe asserted that there was "nothing very striking in this list" (336). Indeed, it resembled many contemporary visitors' books found in hotels in Switzerland, throughout the United Kingdom, and farther afield, with the singular exception that it immortalized the presence of illustrious Romantic travelers and also bore the mark of Shelley's scandalous impieties.

Efforts to reconstruct the motivations and mind-sets of its inscribers involved imaginative immersions in Shelley's world and encompassed close material and textual analyses of the page. Crewe, noting that the names of the Highland magnate The Mackintosh and his wife immediately followed those of Shelley's party, speculated as to what such distinguished travelers would have made of the inscriptions of the "poet and his compatriots" (336). Casting their eyes over the entire leaf for clues to decipher the contexts of the inscription, Dowden and Crewe postulated that Shelley's disavowal of religious faith may have been formulated in playful response to an earlier anonymous inscriber who displayed a "well-intended but tasteless exhibition of conventional piety" at the top of the page. Crewe, like Algernon Charles Swinburne, dissected the Greek inscriptions and also contended that there was no trace of Byron's alleged effacement. Rather he recorded that a "tolerably successful effort has been made to efface the entry of Claire Clairmont's initials and to an extent the place of birth, 'Clifton,' so that it is only just possible to make out the 'Madlle. C.C.'" (337). Piecing together evidence from the page, Crewe imagined how the scene had unfolded: Byron was little troubled by his fellow Romantic's atheistic declaration. But, seeing on the same page the name of Claire (a woman, there identified as "Madlle," with whom Byron had an affair, and who was soon to bear his daughter, Allegra), he was moved to "erase anything that reminded him of a disagreeable and discreditable episode, in which he had played, not merely a loose, but a heartless part" (337). "Such," Crewe remarked, "was Shelley's foolish, bitter jest—bad Greek, and bad taste" (337).

The analysis of this page as an artifact of Romantic culture did not end with Crewe's speculations. In 1958 Gavin de Beer offered another interpretation of the inscription. He reviewed the long history of the debate and mapped out the parties' routes of travel, discussed sites and surfaces of inscription, and assessed the metrical and other qualities of the inscriptions. De Beer challenged the conventional view that only one visitors' book was implicated in this controversy (2). He contended that four separate inscriptions proclaiming Shelley's atheism in Greek, at four separate sites, all featuring rebukes, had given rise to a century and a half of confusion. One book lay at the Hôtel de Londres at Chaminox and was inscribed on 23 June 1816; the page from this volume had come into Lord Crewe's possession, with the famous rebuke by an unknown hand, which Byron had seen. A second book was inscribed at the Hôtel d'Angleterre on an unspecified date, with a similar rebuke. A third book was found at a hut on Montenvers on 25 July 1816, with yet another rebuke. The last visitors' book was found at an inn on the road between Chaminox and Geneva around 26 July of that year (11). It contained yet another reproach, redacted by Byron. After extensive review of the "first-hand evidence from the chief actors in this comedy and from others who saw the inscriptions, either *in situ* or on the torn-out leaf," and then a survey of later, apparently inaccurate, writing on the subject (13), de Beer repudiated Dowden's claims that Byron had defaced Shelley's comment at Montenvers and questioned the Earl of Crewe's speculations, too. De Beer contended that Shelley had been more promiscuous in his atheistic claims than heretofore believed and asserted that through his close analysis of many manuscript and print sources he had settled the matter.

What is striking about this case is just how much ink was metaphorically spilled over the one leaf from a hotel album at a time when, we shall see, the genre had been widely depreciated in many circles. Yet the treatment of the Montenvers page affirms the intense interest in celebrity inscription that endured over decades—the autograph of a monarch, or a literary figure such as Sir Walter Scott, could elevate a book into a treasured object, with corresponding cachet accruing to the hostelry. This valorisation of the hotel album's role in memorializing the presence of eminent travelers contrasted sharply with, and indeed was a corollary to, the denunciation of the Victorian hotel album that played out on the printed page.

MAKING MEANINGS OF THE ALBUM: HISTORICAL GENEALOGIES OF THE VISITORS' BOOK

Few inscriptions were treated with such interest and indeed such reverence by some as those on the Montenvers leaf, especially as the hotel album as a type came to be lodged within public consciousness in print culture as a compendium of banality and self-indulgence (Durie; James; Michalkiewicz and Vincent). To many Victorian critics who offered their assessments of the books in print, the books appeared to constitute little more than a compendium of dross in which Britons spilled out effusive prose and poetry in unoriginal, sometimes pseudo-Romantic forms at the end of a hotel stay. The Montenvers page, by contrast, bore the mark of true Romantics—indeed the autographs of literary luminaries—and furnished tantalizing, allusive evidence of their exploits. To the legions of critics who found in the Victorian visitors' book a subject of humorous denigration, as well as a tool to stake claims to discernment, their age offered nothing to posterity that would rival the mysteries of the Montenvers page and the celebrity of its cast of characters. Indeed, the comparatively banal inscriptions of an expanding number of unknown tourist-scribes seemed to affirm the distance between them and the elite Romantic fraternity whose adventures and inscriptions enthralled Victorians and Edwardians. The Montenvers leaf reminded them of a world that had been lost—and this nostalgia also informed many generic genealogies that traced the album's history to Antiquity.

From the first years of the nineteenth century, the album's history became the subject for much meditation and exposition. In an exploration of the album form, the French writer Victor Joseph Étienne de Jouy, writing under the name of "L'hermite de la Chaussée-d'Antin," offered a mildly facetious textual genealogy. In his narrative, the genre assumed three distinct but related forms: *l'Album à plein vent* [open air album], *l'Album des murailles* [wall album], and *l'Album vulgaire* [vulgar, or popular, album]. In Jouy's narrative, the first inscriptions compiled in recognizable album form had been made on walls by invalids in Ancient Greece. Hippocrates had subsequently transcribed the inscriptions. Antiquity conferred, one source declared, "great dignity and antiquity" on the genre ("A Library Antiquary," "Albums" 131). From that point, the album, in proliferating forms, captured and preserved humanity's *cacoethes scribendi*. In short time, Jouy's playful account of the album became the received historical narrative of the album's development.

In 1823, *The Mirror* abbreviated the history of the album from antiquity to the present day in a few short paragraphs, contending that "albums are now usually kept by ladies, and consist of original contributions, drawings, music, scraps of poetry, autographs, fragments of prose, sentiment, wit and no wit at all, written either by the possessor or such of her friends and acquaintances as she can press into the service" ("S.N." 466). Indeed, in the first few decades of the nineteenth century, sentiment and autograph albums came to be regarded as the most common album types, in place of the esteemed commonplace book. The commonplace book was an early-modern indexed volume of extractions from other texts that was accorded great esteem as an instrument of education. Early-nineteenth-century commentators believed that they were poised at a moment of decisive change in the genre's status, as technology and social change produced new material forms, new inscribers and readers, and new potentialities for the album. Indeed, the 1820s witnessed the expansion of print and manuscript albums, fuelled by interrelated developments. Literacy increased. Paper production was mechanized. There were improvements in volume design: innovations in bindings and in embossing techniques produced resulted in a growing variety of forms, including the "sewn book structure" often associated with the visitors' book (Rutherston 15–19). As the manufacture and distribution of these books expanded, critics alleged that their contents yielded to a morass of jottings that was unmoored from priorities of meticulous curation and literary character of its storied antecedents. Some claimed that it was impossible to make sense of the amalgam of materials contained between the covers of a "lady's album:" an 1823 exposition, invoking Milton, declared that the volume "is a micro-chaos, where all manner of humours contend for mastery 'light armed, or heavy, sharp, smooth, swift or slow.' It is a Noah's ark, in which odd fish, and strange animals are jumbled together by sixes and sevens, and not arranged by twos" (*Mammon in London*, 12–13). Here the album found its historical foil in the commonplace album and is associated with the careful indexation of "useful knowledge." By contrast, popular private albums were mere miscellanies associated with female custodianship, sociability, and frivolity.

It was clear to contemporaries, as it is to modern scholars, that there was a distinctively gendered hue to album culture (and responses to it), with masculine and feminine scribal practices embedded within different social and cultural networks and expressed in different album types (Di Bello; Dickinson; Harris; Kunard). Patrizia Di Bello contends that the album's compilation of miscellaneous printed and manuscript material furnished a textual vehicle through which women participated in wider cultural, social, and political activities, while partially reaffirming conventions of the female private sphere and customary networks of personal exchange. Autograph books could become tools with which women transcended the domestic sphere, enjoyed new opportunities for leisure, and engaged in inventive rhetorical practices (Ricker 2010). But these practices and potentials also generated wider cultural anxieties over the status of the texts, particularly over their place within a private/public binary (231–22). This anxiety was compounded by concern that the "album craze" of the early nineteenth century—personified by the predatory autograph-hunter—undermined the "culture of politeness" and taste with which it was initially associated, disrupting associations between the album form, the original, elite coterie of its creators, and their meticulous scribal practices. An extensive textual field propounded the protocols of proper albuming—the very codes that were now widely transgressed. In 1824, for instance, the London-published *Catholic Spectator* printed a letter, "To a Lady on Albums," advising ladies that convention required the insertion of full names and dates, with comments in English, French, or Italian (Latin inscriptions to be accompanied by translation). Finally:

> A Lady, who contemplates possessing one, should reflect, whether her acquaintance is likely to consist of persons sufficiently numerous, distinguished, and informed, to render it probable, that it will be well filled with insertions of the nature which has been mentioned. ("S." "A Letter" 62)

In this formulation, a properly maintained album was a marker of gentility and social exclusivity. But as the album "epidemic" ["Further Gossip" 13] took hold, "friendship" albums percolated down the social order in the Victorian period, from famous salons to a much broader population of possessors. Denunciations of a new album culture marked by saccharine inscription and predatory autograph hunters articulated entwined assessments of class and gender. The formulaic pedestrianisms of the sentiment album signalled this decline. At the same time, a new transatlantic community of albumers asserted its utility as a tool for receiving, organizing, and retrieving personal reminiscence: Jane E. Locke declared in the American periodical *The Casket* in 1833: "Let those who may, ridicule the custom of collecting a choice selection of pages, from various friends, on the leaves of an album; let them pronounce it the mere flummery of idle love-sick girls, or of more silly and affected men; my album I would not part with for a shekel of gold" (272). When another species of album—the hotel visitors' book—fell under the eye of the album's critics, their evaluations echoed disparagements of the album's insipidities—and often reached new rhetorical heights.

THE VISITORS' BOOK AND ALBUM CULTURE

Where did the hotel album figure into constructions of, and responses to, these narratives of generic decline? As part of the culture of travel writing, albeit connected to an institution associated not with movement as much as repose, the visitors' book was an important commodity within the hotel stationery market, where it joined hotel letterhead, account books, and other specialized products manufactured for the sector. But the book attracted much more popular interest as a textual artifact of travel culture. When Victorian critics and writers turned their attention to the hotel book's origins, they did so in breezy tones. By then more widely known as the visitors' book (though Robert Browning's 1875 *The Inn Album* had kept the nomenclature fresh in popular consciousness), it figured as a subject of tangential reflection in wider travelogues or popular local, regional, and national studies of the inn as an institution. "The Visitor's Book is no new thing," Charles G. Harper asserted in his survey *Old Inns of Old England* in 1906:

> In 1466, when a distinguished Bohemian traveller, one Baron Leo von Rozmital, dined with the Knights of Windsor, his hosts, after dinner, produced what they called their "missal," and asked for his autograph "in memoriam" of him. A little daunted, perhaps, by so ill-omened an expression, but still courteous, the Baron complied with the request, and wrote,

"Lwyk z Rozmitala a z Blatnie." This uncouth autograph was not unnaturally looked upon with suspicion, and the Baron, on leaving Windsor, found himself followed by the Knights, who make inquiries of his retinue as to his real name. They suspected him to be some imposter, or at the least considered him guilty of that kind of foolishness which nowadays induces a certain class of visitor to sign himself "Kruger" or the "King of the Cannibal Islands," or, worse still, to write down the name of the latest notorious criminal. (291)

These printed evaluations of the visitors' book identified the apotheosis of the book's putative literary merit in a distant past, when monasteries such as the Grande Chartreuse outside Grenoble in France boasted storied tomes in which celebrated writers had left their mark. By contrast, the modern visitors' book entry followed a supposedly tedious template—usually praising the host and cuisine in florid prose or (less occasionally) verse, and sometimes featuring anonymous, mischievous critiques of other entries, penned as part of the ritualized departure of a guest.

It is impossible to penetrate the logic behind most nineteenth-century print assessments of the hotel visitors' book, and its entwined social and generic conventions, without querying wider evaluations of the album genre that nourished them. Purportedly banal hotel book inscriptions were presented as indices of the demotic character of travel, and the effusive tone of entries were denounced as manifestations of the general effeminacy of album culture. Writers derided as insincere the flatteries that filled ladies' albums. Indeed, while contemporaries queried the origins of the visitors' book, they also asked the wider question "What is an Album?" as "Tom Folio" did in 1872. He proceeded to quote excerpts from some of the most famous and diverse nineteenth-century writings on the subject—repeating a claim that Robert Southey and William Wordsworth had, like Sir Walter Scott, proposed to form an "anti-album society," in frustration at the endless stream of "gay and gaudy scrap-books that found their way to the Cumberland Mountains" (57). As this contention suggests, the proliferation of albums was concomitant with social and technological changes that assigned new uses and values to the album form and also linked it to a more demotic, and mobile, body of users. This appraisal highlighted the expansion of tourism: indeed the hotel visitors' book became a textual marker of popular tourist culture.

In the expansive constellation of album types, the hotel album occupied space between the visitors' books in public spaces such as museums, those which were sited in private homes, and the autograph and personal albums that were associated with the 'album epidemic' of the early nineteenth century. They also occupied a distinctive place in the expanding specialized hotel stationery market, many of whose bound volumes were designed for the purposes of hotel management, such as internal recordkeeping: the very name of the "visitors' book" telegraphed the degree to which guests participated in textual and social production on its pages. When writers put pen to paper, they participated in the stabilization of a genre that united objects, environments, and the performances governed by specific codes. Hewing to conventional content—mainly laudatory comments on hospitality and scenery, expression of frustrations with the weather, or mischievous annotation of previous inscription, and to familiar prose and verse forms and styles, writers' enactions signalled their entry into the social world of travel. That travel, whether motivated by business or pleasure, united inscribers in moments of repose within the walls of a hostelry. Inscription and reading were often bound with conspicuous and collective acts of rest, however fleeting—and travelers used the hotel book in ways that stabilized these communicative purposes and inscribed their identities in hotel space. For inscribers, the conventions of open display of the books in hotels' public rooms, and the sense of guests' collective identification with each other as travelers through the books, scripted their participation in social production in specific places and at specific moments—especially upon departure, when guests chose to add their names to the community of inscribers. These iterations and reiterations of their social identity were highly contingent on context: whereas in Britain, the hotel book often boasted doggerel and anonymous sparring amongst guests, in nineteenth-century continental Europe, hotel books had a legal status as documents of record, and were incorporated within formal systems of registration that tracked the movement of people. "Registration" was compulsory. This contrasting legal status underscored the degree to which the visitors' authority over inscription in the visitors' book was at least partially contingent on the legal regimes that governed inscription. Even so, British travelers apparently found ways to reiterate familiar conventions when traveling abroad and thereby resist prescriptive codes that governed the continental texts. The prominent Alpinist writer Albert Smith (1850, 82), noting that although once-unstructured pages had yielded to "regular ruled column . . . supplied with matter-of-fact headings," they nonetheless tempted the British traveler to engage in customary, free-form expositions, or factious responses more typical of codes in Britain. Lord Crewe avowed that the visitors books' pages revealed that about one person in five believes that he or she is capable of some form of literary composition worthy of being set down and preserved. Allowing for a little modesty in the remaining four, one is tempted to wonder if there is any man or woman alive who is not the author in secret, and to thank Heaven that in literature free coinage is unknown, and that only these humble mints, the Visitors' Books, remain always open. And though the better educated of these *commis-voyageurs* Troubadours would not admit it, they are but the genteeler cousins-german of those travellers who carve their names on the temple of Luxor, or treat Vatican statues in a manner which argues a contempt for graven images worthy of Shadrack, Meshach, and Abednego. (336)

Inscribers, then, used acts of inscription to stake out their identities as hotel guests, to affirm their membership in a community of travelers and, outside Britain, to sometimes articulate a national identity as well, as the album entry became a conventionalized means of participating in a social manuscript culture centered on the spaces of the hotel. These acts of inscription were deeply entwined with acts of reading, and readers approached the texts from several stances, including: (1) as readers of the text *in situ*, many of whose discursive practices as inscribers in the book were conditioned by the form and content of entries they read; (2) readers-cum-commentators, who read the texts *in situ* and conveyed elements of the manuscript texts beyond the hostelry's walls to a wider readership in print; (3) and readers of these print evaluations, who encountered the excerpted inscriptions *ex situ*, mediated by the commentators' dispositions towards the culture of the visitors' book. This analysis now turns ways that the visitors' book figured into these print evaluations and to a specific set of incentives through which it became a tool for authorial self-fashioning.

Printed textual productions built a meta-analysis of hotel albums that shaped attitudes toward visitors' book reading and inscription. For these commentators, the albums also furnished a tool for identity building, and very often this end was achieved through jaundiced evaluations of the volumes as *biblia a-biblia*. To this end, their acid remarks framed a tactic "manual" for readers on how to encounter the books on their travels. Above all, readers were advised to maintain a calculated distance from their temptations, while recognising their instrumentality under specific circumstances. Reading, for instance, might be authorized when superior literary or travel pursuits became temporarily unavailable. In such cases, the book supplied a time-honored "stand-by" ("The Visitors' Book," 1). As one writer opined, the visitors' book, "like the cold roast, may always be resorted to. One advantage it has over the Dryden; under the same title everywhere its contents are everywhere different.

Generally they are very human; sometimes they are topographical; not infrequently they are funny; and frequently they are melancholy moments of would-be-wit" ("The Visitors' Book," 1). Another writer in the Bangor-based *North Wales Chronicle*, providing specimens of visitors'- books inscriptions, averred:

> such books as the one from which we propose to give a few extracts, ought to be named "Albums," rather than visitors' books; for they often contain effusions quite as sincere and as fully poetic, too, as those to be found in those little square books, which used to be poked by young ladies into the hands of every "talented" friend, with a request that he would fill a page with "something pretty." ("Hotel Albums" 6)

Indeed, the author declared that "we should have no objection to see these albums of the hotels supersede the others; for they have one merit—they will beguile an hour of tedium, when the unfortunate guest is house-bound by untimely showers; and may often provoke a laugh, which, after dinner, is said to be highly promotive of digestion" (6). Here the author explicitly subsumed the hotel book within the constellation of album types and accorded it merit for rainy day distraction and post-prandial entertainment.

In such print narratives, inscription constituted a much riskier affair than reading. Critics of the volumes' tortured verse and florid prose lamented that writers had not paused before dipping pen into ink and reflected on the likelihood they would bequeath an undistinguished text for posterity. As one writer cautioned in 1896, "Since the Young Ladies'Album has fallen into desuetude and the Inn Album now provides the cheapest outlet for effusive rhyming, it does seem more than a little odd that passable verse should be so rare in Visitors' Books" ("A.T.Q.C." 146). Albert Smith, in his periodical *The Month* in 1851, lambasted the practice of album writing, the historiated initial of his first sentence depicting an ass, quill in hand, seated at a table and inscribing in a volume (203). Inscribers became object of satire: they gravitated to the book merely because it was there and, worse still, injudiciously spilled out effusions that immortalized their folly. C. Hill Dick in 1894 depicted circumstances that would promote such vanity and reckless participation in the culture of *biblia a-biblia*. Dick offered a vivid depiction of the weary traveler's arrival at a country inn:

> after a disagreeable journey through uncomfortable weather in a mood of dissatisfaction with the defectiveness of human affairs in general and the seasons in particular, not unmixed with a concealed contempt of your own character for ever trusting yourself abroad after previous experiences which you might have learnt from, had you been a wiser man. (263)

In such a doleful and restive state, Dick wrote that "providence has mercifully provided an antidote for your spirit of dejection in the form of a quasi-literary collection of opinions and records made by previous occupants on the inn and known as the Visitors' Book" (263). Here materials that produced the inscription and constituted elements of the habit of writing were distinguished: the book, if read with some care before inscription, might entertain, and could also restrain, a predilection to inscribe. The pen, however, like the serpent in the Garden of Eden, could tempt the hotel guest into incautious acts. Nothing good would come of yielding to its seductions. In remote hostelries, guests were especially unrestrained in their "violent out-pourings of spirit or enthusiastic terms of description." Dick wrote that if they afforded any benefit, poring over such embellishments, the traveler apprehended that "from despising yourself, it teaches you to despise others." For "in no other place can a man show himself to such disadvantage as in a Visitors' Book. He simply scribbles according to the inflated whim of the present." The visitors' book bore more visible evidence to such proclivities than other albums. When impromptu recklessness attended private albums, it remained largely shielded from public view, but the visitors' book laid bare the imprudence of improvisational scribes before a wider community of readers. It became a conspicuous exemplar of the album's general decline into insipidities: "people, however, will always immortalise themselves by their folly, if by nothing else, and a Herostratus may be found any day of the week." Dick also underscored how the act of inscription was guided by acts of reading preceding entries:

> When you are about to leave the inn, you take up the Visitors' Book and finger it uneasily. Then you look at the last page that has been written on and the last few entries. You give a feeble smile and feel for your pencil. Then you write, and you think you have done something sober and sensible; but do not delude yourself! [I]t is only tame and uninteresting, and perhaps foolish. So you go on your way—and God rest your conscience! (264)

If guests exercised only a modicum of self-reflection and self-restraint, Dick averred, they might spare themselves the indignity of association with the fraternity of travelers whose banalities were bequeathed to posterity in the leaves of the visitors' book—and, as we have seen often, circulated in print.

There is a paradox in the print space devoted to excerptions and the extensive commentary on their insipidities. As writers circulated morsels of the visitors' book in print, they revealed their own status as readers of these *biblia a-biblia* and affirmed their participation in networks of textual transmission. Even denunciations of the form could not entirely remove commentators from complicity in albuming, for they had opened, and read, the book, and circulated its contents. Even if grandiloquent abjuration of their contents was the *sina qua non* of their reading response, writers engaged in florid, humorous, and occasional lengthy expositions that betrayed their close relationship to it and the social identity that they fashioned through it. Indeed, if the visitors' book was a critical material of social textual production for hotel guests *in situ*, baroque rebukes of the book in print had their own authorial instrumentality.

CONCLUSION

Lord Crewe's 1898 analysis of the leaf from the Montenvers album departed from these Victorian denigrations of the manuscripts and seemed in many respects to uphold it as an exception to the banality of the Victorian form. Yet Crewe's own words reveal a calculated ambivalence toward even this famous leaf: had even he perhaps devoted too much energy to *biblia a-biblia*? In the end, in tones of seeming mock exasperation, Crewe advised that the wisest course was to read Shelley's celebrated poem " 'Mont Blanc' and to forget all about the Inn Album" (337). Crewe facetiously ended his short essay with the contention that such a conclusion "seems to show that this paper had better not have been written" (337).

If the visitors' book furnished some writers an opportunity to stake out their literary taste vis-à-vis *biblia a-biblia*, there was a shift in such appraisals in the interwar period that offers as a provocative coda to this analysis and affirms the ways in which the genre's status and uses evolved. In a 1937 publication, Fitzwater Wray proclaimed himself the sole historian of the visitors' book (ix). Perhaps this was because his relationship to the book was framed by personal and cultural incentives that distinguished him from the book's Victorian and Edwardian critics: Wray was engaged not in acts of denigration but rather preservation through the medium of print. To him, great reward lay in finding books in out-of-the-way hostelries and transcribing fading inscriptions from their pages. Writing at a time when he believed that the twin "diseases" of the automobile and the Great War had extinguished a distinctly British writing practice, Wray participated in an altogether different project through the medium of the printed word: recording the vestiges of a vanishing manuscript culture. Traveling the length and breadth of Britain and Ireland in search of old volumes, Wray asserted that the earliest surviving British books dated from the 1840s at Tibbie Shiel's Inn in the Borders of Scotland (165). However, Wray contended that "the first *proved* reference to a Visitor's [*sic*] Book comes from abroad," when Lord Byron, traveling in Greece around 1810, came across an anonymous rhyming entry in such a volume, to which he had appended a mischievous rejoinder gently mocking the quality of the verse (xvi). Wray enfolded the book within a wistful narrative of lost travel practices and a nostalgic assessment of the decay of a British travel form. To him, inscriptions that had once been dismissed as trite, penned by anonymous hands, were now emblems of a creative travel culture that preceded from, rather than violated, Byronic inspiration. The hotel album, then, had multiple instrumentalities, to the inscriber, the reader, and the print commentator, which were shaped by their stances toward, and participation in, changing travel cultures—as readers and inscribers, and also as commentators on, and chroniclers of, the form. Attention to these actors and the interweaving of their manuscript and print productions reveals the iteration and reiteration of social identities centred on these albums and underscores the valuable evidentiary status of neglected travel texts for exploring dynamic, historical generic creations.

WORKS CITED

Secondary Sources

Alexis, Cydney. "The Material Culture of Writing: Objects, Habitats, and Identities in Practice." *Rhetoric, through Everyday Things*, edited by Scot Barnett and Casey Andrew Boyle, U of Alabama P, 2016, pp. 83–95.

de Beer, Gavin. "An Atheist in the Alps." *Keats-Shelley Memorial Album*, edited by Dorothy Hewlett, no. 9, Keats-Shelley Memorial Association, 1958, pp. 1–15.

Di Bello, Patrizia. "Mrs Birkbeck's Album: The Hand-written and the Printed in Early Nineteenth-Century Feminine Culture." *Interdisciplinary Studies in the Long Nineteenth Century*, vol. 1, 2005, n. pag., http://doi.org/10.16995/ntn.435.

Dickinson, Cindy. "Creating a World of Books, Friends, and Flowers: Gift Books and Inscriptions, 1825–60." *Winterthur Portfolio*, vol. 31, no. 1, 1996, pp. 53–66.

Durie, Alastair. "Tracking Tourism: Visitors' Books and Their Value." *Scottish Archives*, vol. 17, 2011, pp. 73–84.

Grylls, Rosalie Glynn. *Mary Shelley: A Biography*. Folcroft Library Editions, 1938.

Harris, Katherine D. "Borrowing, Altering, and Perfecting the Literary Annual Form—or What It Is Not: Emblems, Almanacs, Pocket-books, Albums, Scrapbooks, and Gift Books." *The Journal of the Initiative for Digital Humanities, Media, and Culture*, vol. 1, no. 1, 2010, pp. 1–30, https://journals.tdl.org/paj/index.php/paj/article/viewFile/23/21. Accessed 5 Apr. 2018.

Hopps, Gavin. "Religion and Ethics: The Necessity of Atheism, A Refutation of Deism, on Christianity." *Oxford Handbook on Percy Bysshe Shelley*, edited by Michael O'Neill and Anthony Howe, with the assistance of Madeleine Callaghan, Oxford UP, 2013, pp. 117–31.

James, Kevin. "'[A] British Social Institution': The Visitors' Book and Hotel Culture in Victorian Britain and Ireland." *Journeys*, vol. 13, no. 1, 2012, pp. 42–69.

Kunard, Andrea. "Traditions of Collecting and Remembering: Gender, Class and the Nineteenth-Century Sentiment Album and Photographic Album." *Early Popular Visual Culture*, vol. 4, no. 3, 2006, pp. 227–243.

Michalkiewicz, Katarzyna, and Patrick Vincent. "Victorians in the Alps: a Case Study of Zermatt's Hotel Guest Books and Registers." *Britain and the Narration of Travel in the Nineteenth Century: Texts, Images, Objects*, edited by Kate Hill, Routledge, 2017, pp. 75–90.

Miller, Carolyn R. "Genre as Social Action." *Quarterly Journal of Speech*, vol. 70, no. 2, 1984, pp. 151–167.

Ricker, Lisa Reid. "(De) Constructing the Praxis of Memory-Keeping: Late Nineteenth-Century Autograph Albums as Sites of Rhetorical Invention." *Rhetoric Review*, vol. 29, no. 3, 2010, pp. 239–256.

Rutherston, Jane. "Victorian Album Structures." *The Paper Conservator*, vol. 23, no. 1, 1999, pp. 13–25.

White, Newman Ivey. *Shelley*, vol. 1. Octagon, 1972.

Primary Sources

"A Library Antiquary." "Albums." *The History of Origins: Containing Ancient Historical Facts, with Singular Customs, Institutions, and Manners of Different Ages*, Sampson Low, 1824, pp. 131–136.

Cook, Mrs. E. T. "Visitors' Books." *Good Words*, edited by the Right Rev. Donald MacLeod, vol. 36, 1895, pp. 334–339.

Crewe, Earl of. "A Leaf from an Inn Album." *Literature*, vol. 1, no. 2, 1 Jan. 1898, pp. 336–337.

Dick, C. Hill. "Concerning Visitors' Books." *The Treasury: An Illustrated Treasury of Old-Time Literature*, Elliott Stock, 1894, pp. 262–264.

Dowden, Edward. *The Life of Percy Bysshe Shelley*, vol. 2. Kegan Trench Paul, 1887.

"Folio, Tom" [pseud.]. "What Is an Album?" *The Atlantic Almanac for 1872*, James R. Good and Company, pp. 57–58.

"Further Gossip from London. June 1846." *Chambers's Edinburgh Journal*, vol. 6, no. 131 (new series), 4 July 1846, pp. 11–14.

Harper, Charles G. *The Old Inns of Old England: A Picturesque Account of the Ancient and Storied Hostelries of Our Own Country*, vol. 2. Chapman and Hall, 1906.

"Hotel Albums." *North Wales Chronicle, and Advertiser for the Principality*, 20 July 1850, p. 6.

Jouy, Victoire Joseph Etienne de. "Recherches sur l'Album et sur le Chiffonnier Sentimental." *L'hermite de la Chaussée-d'Antin: ou, Observations sur les moeurs parisiens au commencement du xixe siècle*, 6th ed., vol 1, Pillet, 1815.

Lamb, Charles. "Detached Thoughts on Books and Reading: An Essay." *Essays of Elia, to Which Are Added Letters, and Rosamund, a Tale*, Paris: Baudrys European Library, 1835, pp. 189–194.

Locke, Mrs Jane E. "My Album." *Atkinson's Casket, or Gems of Literature, Wit and Sentiment*, n.v., no. 6 (June 1833), pp. 272–275.

Mammon in London; or, the Spy of the Day, vol 1. Printed for W. Sams, 1823.

Rossetti, William Michael. *A Memoir of Shelley (with a Fresh Preface)*. 2nd ed. Printed by Richard Clay and Sons for the Shelley Society, 1886.

"S." "A Letter to a Lady on Albums." *The Catholic Spectator and Selector; or Catholicon*, 3rd series, vol. 2, Keating and Brown, 1824, pp. 60–62.

"S.N." "The Editor's Album." *The Mirror of Literature, Amusement, and Instruction*, vol. 1, no. 30 (supplementary number), 17 May 1823, pp. 465–467.

Smith, Albert. "Travellers' Albums." *The Miscellany: A Book for the Field or the Fire-side. Amusing Takes and Sketches*, David Bogue, 1850.

[Smith, Albert.] "The Latest Chronicle of Fools." *The Month. A View of Passing Subjects and Manners, Home and Foreign, Social and General*, by Albert Smith and John Leech, Sep. 1851, pp. 203–210.

"The Visitors' Book." *The Globe and Traveller*, 5th ed., no. 31, 097, 5 Feb. 1895, pp. 1–2.

Wray, Fitzwater ("Kuklos"). *The Visitor's Book*. J. M. Dent and Sons, 1937.

10
GENDERED LETTERWRITING IN RENAISSANCE ENGLAND
Genre as Sociomaterial Action

Keri Epps

> *My good Watt; I have received your letter, and give God thanks for your good health and safety in your journey. You writ to me to send you a black box of writings, which I have sent you by this bearer having in these parcels, 2 fines, one feoffment and one exemplification, which I found at Blythefield my self in your study this day, and by chance knew them without any help.*
>
> (Folger MS L.a.48)

The above excerpt comes from a letter Elizabeth Bagot writes to her husband Walter Bagot in July of 1614. In it, Elizabeth delights in her husband's safety and responds to a request for some documents Walter needs to conduct business. Significantly, Elizabeth notes her ability to navigate Walter's study and identify the requested documents "without any help."

I open with this excerpt from Elizabeth's letter because it offers a snapshot of a Renaissance woman performing her family duties in a household space—with many documents and writing objects—that required knowledge beyond her typical domestic duties. Rebecca Laroche comments on the significance of Elizabeth's letter in her article for the Folger Shakespeare Library's *Manuscript Miscellany*:

> Lady Bagot's pride in knowing these documents "without help" hints that she has had some exposure both to the space of the study and to such documents but was expected not to be comfortable when confronted with either. One can imagine, however, that Walter Bagot's absence from the household puts much of the estate affairs in the hands of his wife. (n. pag)

Here, then, Elizabeth assumes the role of business manager in Walter's absence and a more authoritative position in a space that is ordinarily Walter's domain. Elizabeth's letter also catalogues the included materials—a "black box of writings" associated with family business matters, including fines, deeds for land, and a copy of a document (not specified) stamped with an official seal—that are in some ways of more importance than the accompanying letter's written, alphabetic content. I have also introduced this chapter with Elizabeth's letter to illustrate its complex intersections of material space and rhetorical genre awareness that reveal tensions among genre, materiality, and prescribed roles for Renaissance women. Such tensions are also present in the letters of two other women included in the Family Archive—Ursula Wardwicke and Lettice Kynnersley—whose letters are analyzed in the chapter's final sections.

The Bagot family was one of the most prominent families in England during the late sixteenth and early seventeenth centuries. The family's place in the upper social class was largely due to the family's patriarch, Richard Bagot (c. 1530–1597), who served as the sheriff and deputy lieutenant of Staffordshire, and who in addition to these duties was also known for having a number of responsibilities to the Crown. After his death in 1597, his son, Walter Bagot, received many of these civic and royal duties—in addition to his father's patriarchal responsibilities. In assuming the patriarchal role, Walter was not only responsible for his mother and his siblings (including his sister Lettice Kynnersley) but was also responsible for overseeing their children and spouses, making sure that all of the Bagot family, and those members connected to it (including Ursula Wardwicke), were provided with appropriate care. Walter's multiple responsibilities—to the Crown, to Staffordshire, and to his family—emerge in nearly all of his letters curated in the extensive Bagot family letter collection, and the women's letters included in this study were directed to Walter because of his role as the family's patriarch.

The Bagot family archive was additionally an ideal site for a genre analysis because it offers a unique glimpse into a close-knit epistolary community over the span of 114 years. Housed at the Folger Shakespeare Library in Washington, DC, the collection's 1,016 total papers range from secret, personal letters about domestic disputes to land transactions and business dealings with members of the royal family and cabinet. This collection remains one of the largest preserved collections from the period and offers a salient and insightful example of how this everyday genre was central to the family's daily lived experiences (O'Day). Although the majority of the Bagot letters are male-authored, the collection does have sets of letters from many of the female family members, including the women named above, that make studying the complex interrelationships among genre, materiality, and gender possible.

When I use the term *material/ity* in this study, I am referring to the manuscripts' physical materiality *and* the social implications and realities that result from writers' material uses. To define *materiality*, I borrow from Renaissance historian James Daybell who states that materiality is

> defined first in terms of the physical characteristics of manuscript letters and the meanings generated by them: for example, the significance of handwriting, the size and quality of paper used, the layout of the manuscript page and the significance attached to seals. Such forms were imbued with social signs and codes that affected meaning. . . . Indeed, the material rhetorics of the manuscript page were central to the ways in which letters communicated. (11)

Daybell's attention to the rhetorical and communicative significance of the manuscripts' materiality, then, offers a direct point of intersection for writing studies (WS) and material culture studies (MCS), and as James (previous chapter) also highlights, material signs and symbols give us more insight into how genres are created, circulated, and sustained. Even more specifically, identifying the rhetorical effects of material signs can help us see the importance of *everydayness* and the significance that everyday objects, including genres of writing, have on shaping our beliefs, values, and daily lived realities *and* on creating (or blocking) pathways to social power and individual agency that current studies in Rhetorical Genre Studies (RGS) and MCS otherwise might miss. In the opening letter, for instance, based on the wax seal and the handwriting of Walter's original request, Elizabeth would have been able to confirm Walter's safety before reading the letter's message. Additionally, and most importantly for my discussion, Elizabeth's navigation of the writing *spaces*, including both Walter's office space *and* the space of the page, offers a glimpse into how writing spaces and objects could provide agentive moments for women in Renaissance England who were not authorized participants in the discourse communities where those documents circulated. Ultimately, Elizabeth's letter and the letters of other Bagot women demonstrate how an everyday letter might not only be a genre of social action but also one of *sociomaterial action* that activates and shapes writers' and readers' responses *and* shows writers' rhetorical aptitude and awareness of the range of a genre's material affordances.

My support for a sociomaterial genre framework results from the following study of how the Bagot women participated in personal and business communication in agentive ways, even while not having the same positions of power as their male counterparts. The letters discussed here illustrate a complex interrelationship among a rhetorical everyday genre (the letter), a physical and material medium that was the most accessible and rhetorically effective in the English Renaissance (the manuscript), and the objects (including ink from different substances, varied types of quill pens, colored wax, watermarks, and embroidery thread) that were used to create and circulate the letters. By examining a combination of genre conventions and material means that Renaissance women used in discrete examples of letters, I contend that Elizabeth, Ursula, and Lettice's material uses of their letters exemplify how genres instigated action in ways that go beyond language and discourse.

The chapter begins by exploring what the materiality of genres would add to longstanding conversations of genres as social action in RGS. Then, I explain the methodological choices for the selected excerpts from the Bagot collection and analyze how Elizabeth, Ursula, and Lettice interacted with and drew from varied material resources to meet their rhetorical goals. Ultimately, the analysis demonstrates how gendered authority, as represented in the selected letters, is dependent on interrelationships between rhetorical genres and material culture, and the chosen examples depict instances of texts and objects mediating who can/does exercise authority—a significant takeaway from joining WS and MCS as noted by Alexis and Rule in the collection's introduction. While the chapter's scope only allows me to introduce these concepts through selections from a single case study, I conclude with a call to apply a similar sociomaterial framework to other rhetorical genres to examine how ideologies and power manifest in genres as objects.

THE RENAISSANCE LETTER AS A MATERIAL GENRE

In his book *The Culture of Epistolarity: Vernacular Letters and Letter Writing in Early Modern England*, Gary Schneider aptly assesses early modern letters: "Although letters were present everywhere, they seem to exist nowhere: they were frequently the 'invisible' means of a great portion of sociocultural interaction, yet are rarely analyzed in and of themselves" (286). Similarly, on letterwriting more broadly, David Barton and Nigel Hall contend:

> that the most revealing way of investigating letter writing is to view it as a social practice, examining the texts, the participants, the activities and the artefacts in their social contexts. The aim [of their collection and introductory chapter] is to understand more about the phenomenon of letter writing and, more broadly, about the role of literate activity in society. (1)

In this section and the subsequent analyses, I provide examples of the letter genre as sociomaterial action in an effort to expose some of the "invisible" practices that have much to tell us about literate activity and how it mattered to individuals in a single Renaissance family unit. In doing so, I emphasize material aspects, such as the tactile components of the paper and seals *and* the visual elements of the participants' interactions with the letters, including stray marks and unconventional uses of marginal space. Such examples demonstrate that materiality is an important, yet undertheorized, aspect of rhetorical genres that has the potential to help scholars of MCS and WS more clearly see and understand who writes, why, and what resources make those circumstances possible or not.

Even in its seeming invisibility, the letter has been deemed the most important genre of the English Renaissance (Stewart and Wolfe). Renaissance scholars have examined the letter closely to uncover some of the tacit social practices that are a part of letterwriting performance, including the material features of the manuscript and other writing tools that similarly carried social and ideological meaning. Daybell has specifically discussed the letter's material meaning-making potential, contending that the Renaissance letter's materiality should be prioritized in letterwriting studies to enlighten us on the larger contexts in which letters were composed. Daybell calls this concept "social materiality," a concept that "contextualises epistolary practices, establishing the conditions of writing and reading, the range of literacies (written, visual, and oral) associated with letter-writing, the role of secretaries, amanuenses, servants, and bearers, the environments and spaces in which letters were composed, received and read" (16). For Daybell, then, acknowledging social materiality helps give us a more comprehensive view of letterwriting practice, including the people behind writing, sending, and receiving letters and the actual spaces and contexts in which writing was happening. As I elaborate on later, I see Daybell's argument as one point of intersection for RGS and MCS, and I draw on this understanding of letters' social materiality to make the argument that materiality is a necessary component of rhetorical genre study.

Letters' material features, such as those delineated in Daybell's definition of *materiality* included in the chapter's introduction, have also been discussed in relation to their ability to make individuals present to their readers even in their absence. The letter, in fact, has a long-accepted tradition of recreating the writer's presence to the reader in her physical absence, stemming from the medieval *ars dictaminis* tradition, or the art of composing letters, and becoming revitalized with Erasmus' humanist instruction during the Renaissance (Daybell, *The Material*; Henderson; Schneider). For this reason, I argue that the letter is a productive site to study how genre conventions and material characteristics come together to create a surrogate for the human author, or at the very least *extend* the writer's presence, particularly for women writers whose everyday lives were not documented as extensively as those of their male counterparts.

The material manuscript was a site where many women represented their lived experiences through the bodily interactions that they had with the text, as shown through the sometimes erratic traces of the pen and the personal handwriting inscribed in some of the letters, all of which have rhetorical meaning-making potential.

Responding to Schneider's call and Daybell's understanding of social materiality, I have selected the genre of the letter for several reasons that align with my three-pronged focus on genre, gender, and materiality: the most significant being the genre's codependence on multiple modes of meaning-making, including writing materials and tools, *and* the genre's potential to allow unauthorized or marginalized writers to communicate across prescribed hierarchies because of the genre's quotidian nature. Making these practices and uses of writing materials more transparent is particularly significant in our efforts to value and understand the *human* writer and her everyday lived experiences—a value that RGS and MCS share through numerous calls to make the objects and/or writing artifacts three-dimensional, as Alexis and Rule highlight in the collection's introduction.

RHETORICAL GENRE STUDIES AND MATERIAL CULTURE STUDIES

Analyzing a letter's rhetorical and generic conventions—including its themes, structure, *and* the visual and material elements of and around the page—open up opportunities for seeing how prescribed gendered power dynamics might be reinscribed or circumvented. Here, I show Renaissance women's letters as a few examples of a genre as sociomaterial action by investigating how material components can show how genres work outside of forms and symbols. In this section, I outline some key RGS theories that invite intersections with MCS scholarship and illustrate how genres are *things* in and of themselves, and their materiality and *everydayness* deserves attention in RGS and MCS, as both disciplines value how writing and things activate, shape, and infuse human experience (Bazerman; Prown). In the case introduced below, the sociomaterial dimension of genres can provide a lens to discover material resources marginalized writers used to access social power—or in this case, agency in a family unit—that a broader historical or textual analysis might not capture.

First, *genre* as defined in RGS scholarship is largely attributed to Carolyn R. Miller's widely used definition from "Genre as Social Action" in which she argues that genres are "typified rhetorical actions based in recurrent situations" (159). In Miller's definition, actions within situations that continue to occur over time can become *types* (and are thus *genres*), but not concrete, stable groups or labels for types of texts; rather, they are types of responses that adapt to social exigencies and can incite action. Building on Miller's understanding of genres as "typified rhetorical actions," Charles Bazerman adds that the genre is a "central nexus of human sense-making" and explains the genre as a type that is flexible enough to meet the rhetor's needs in an individual utterance (in Bawarshi and Reiff, xi). Bazerman's view emphasizes rhetorical genres as central to how individuals or communities make sense of their worlds—through being able to make rhetorical decisions based on the "typified responses" that have preceded them and the constraints of the distinct situation to which they are responding. In several Bagot family letters analyzed below, for example, the family members (at least partially) reject formal letterwriting conventions encouraged in contemporary letterwriting manuals to respond more appropriately to the situation at hand; the degree to which the writer adheres to or manipulates genre conventions depends largely on his or her audience. When Walter writes to members of the Crown, for instance, he uses the formal secretary hand, a type of handwriting that was adopted for business matters and for recipients of a higher social standing and was often used by male secretaries who transcribed what the letterwriter dictated to him. In many of Walter Bagot's extant letters, the level of formality aligns more closely with model letters included in prescriptive letterwriting literature than his more nuanced letters to his wife or other family members. The variation in Walter's letters alone—in style, theme, format, and more—serve as evidence that letters changed, often drastically, depending on the rhetorical contexts and rhetorical exigencies of a particular moment. Such moments exemplify the simultaneous flexibility and stability of writing genres that Miller and Bazerman put forward and, if examined closely, can give us deeper insight into the complex meaning-making and negotiations of power, agency, and action that underlie each use of the genre.

To examine the Bagot letters, I use RGS scholar John Frow's framework of genre dimensions to identify specific points where gendered power is reinscribed or subverted in ways that display the Bagot women letterwriters' intellect, creativity, and rhetorical savvy. Frow's genre dimensions include formal features, thematic structure, a situation of address (or speaking position), the structure of implication (or, an implied shared knowledge), the rhetorical function, and the physical setting. Frow elaborates on the physical setting, stating that "the generic structure of [the] text is established, and many of these other dimensions activated, by a physical *setting* that takes on the force of a regulative *frame*. This frame differentiates the genre of this text from other possible genres, alerts us to the way it works (its rhetorical function), and draws our attention toward some of its features and away from others" (73). Frow argues, however, that *physical setting* is not part of the genre; rather, the setting *frames* the genre performance.

Frow's argument provides an entry point for MCS. By adding *materiality* to Frow's already-robust framework, we see more clearly how investigating writing materials and spaces, as inscribed or referenced in historical documents, can help us draw conclusions about how a genre's materiality created or prohibited pathways to social authority and power. Toward this point, Frow describes how power becomes bound in genres. He states that knowledge of genres and the information they generate are "bound up with the exercise of power, where power is understood as being exercised in discourse, as well as elsewhere, but is never simply external to discourse" (2). As power gets reinforced in particular discourse communities, the boundaries between the insiders and the outsiders continue to deepen, making genre participation for those writing from the margins all the more difficult. In short, Frow considers power and genre to be inextricable, and given the interventions this edited collection makes, I argue that examining genres as sociomaterial action can illuminate *how* and *why* power gets *materially* reproduced (or not) in specific writing contexts.

THE BAGOT FAMILY LETTERS: METHODS AND ANALYSIS

My study of this corpus of letters follows Miller and Kelly's 2017 call in *Emerging Genres in New Media* to dive deeply into single historical moments to understand how genres and media circulate and instigate action in those moments. Toward this point, Miller writes that "we can understand [genre emergence] processes best by an empirical, case-based approach, being sensitive to the breadth and depth of specific historical, cultural, economic, structural, ideological, and psychological conditions" (26). Since both RGS and MCS are invested in studying how writing genres *and* objects are intimately tied to ideology and cultural values in specific historical moments, I heed Miller's call for intensive case studies here by selecting a single collection of family letters to study Renaissance women's negotiations of a genre, writing objects, and power dynamics that are materially bound in these texts.

The Bagot collection, while beneficial to this study in its copious amount of material, also posed methodological challenges for the same reason and required that I narrow my sample significantly. To meet my goals for this chapter, I selected ninety-four letters from the Bagot family of Staffordshire, England, with dates from 1570 to 1623. After identifying the women's letters and transcribing each one, I coded the letters based on particular words or phrases that revealed genre awareness, using Frow's dimensions of genre. Specifically for this project, I coded the material elements of the text, including the style of handwriting, the use of space on the page, and other characteristics of the manuscript medium that could shed light on the writer's gendered position of authority and her relationship with the recipient. I also identified the recurrent theme of the *petition* in the selected women's letters. This thematic approach also corresponds to Frow's dimension of "thematic structure" that uncovers some ways that positions of power become sedimented in genres over time (2). The situation of address, another of Frow's dimensions, also guided me in selecting the following examples, as the included letters demonstrate women navigating multiple positions in relationship to the speaker and using the manuscript and other writing materials to do so. The focal letters analyzed below, then, rose to the surface when applying Frow's framework and represent some ways Renaissance letters served as sociomaterial action in theme, structure, and physical setting.

First, Ursula Wardwicke, a female correspondent included in the Bagot Family archive, wrote several letters that provide evidence of how one Renaissance woman materially represented her existence and her need for help. Ursula's letters include themes and rhetorical functions that characterize letters of petition, a type of letter described in contemporary letterwriting manuals. Ursula has two existing letters in the collection that, when juxtaposed, show several distinctions in her genre performance of the same letter type: the theme and content of the letters, her situation of address, the physical setting in which she wrote, and the material components of the manuscript itself (see figs. 10.1 and 10.2). Examining each of these genre dimensions provides more insight into how Ursula was materially and rhetorically resourceful in navigating genre conventions that she may or may not have received formal instruction in.

In the first of her letters, Ursula informs Walter of a canceled business meeting he was scheduled to attend. She writes:

> Good cousin, These [letters] are to advertise to you that Sir Thomas Wolseley cannot meet you upon Thursday as was appointed but on Friday next he promiseth not to fail. Therefore I would desire you to meet him there and my husband and myself will be there hoping that by your good means there will be some order take for our good. Thus with my kind

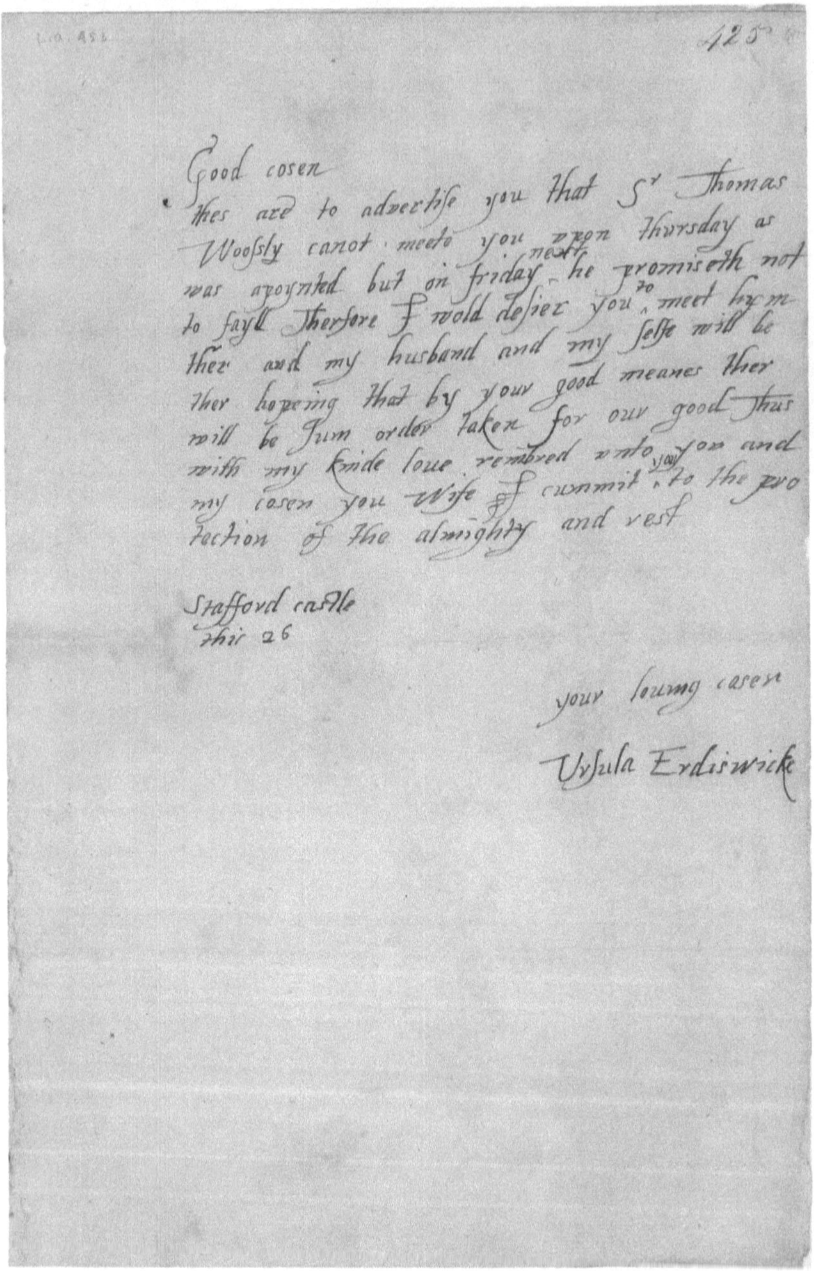

Good cosen
thes are to advertise you that Sr Thomas
Woosly canot meete you vpon thursday as
was apoynted but on friday next he promiseth not
to fayll therfore I wold desier you to meet hym
ther and my husband and my selfe will be
ther hopeing that by your good meanes ther
will be sum order taken for our good Thus
with my kinde loue remembred vnto you and
my cosen your wife I cummit you to the pro
tection of the almighty and rest

Stafford castle
this 26

your louing cosen
Ursula Erdiswicke

Figure 10.1. Ursula (Stafford) Erdeswicke. Letter from Ursula (Stafford) Erdeswicke, Stafford Castle, to Walter Bagot *(Stafford Castle, 1618)*. L.a.453. Used by permission of the Folger Shakespeare Library under a Creative Commons Attribution-ShareAlike 4.0 International License.

love remembered unto you and my cousin your wife I commit you to the
protection of the Almighty and rest your loving cousin, Ursula Wardwicke.
(Folger MSS L.a.453)

Ursula starts with a generic formal feature establishing the letter's audience: a salutation. She also establishes the situation of address by marking her speaking position; notably, she removes herself from the agentive position in the first sentence, making the *letter* the agent rather than herself. She does not introduce herself as the agent until the second sentence, when she directly asks Walter to meet with them at an alternative time. Yet, even in the same line, Ursula relies on her husband's authority and credibility by mentioning his intention to join her at the requested meeting. By varying the subjects of her sentences and referencing her husband's presence, Ursula distances herself from a position of authority, even as she is tasked with making this request.

Importantly, the material aspects of Ursula's letters include her handwriting *and* the use of writing space on the page. Handwriting practices alone can lead to many conclusions regarding a writer's positionality. Styles of handwriting in the Renaissance were also *gendered*, as men knew and often wrote in the secretary hand, and women wrote in the italic hand, a style most comparable to our modern-day print. The styles of handwriting also visually represented social hierarchies that letterwriters would have been expected to represent in their writing. Significantly, too, the ability to break the rules or bend genre conventions was largely determined by the writer's social standing and gender. Daybell writes, for instance, that "it was perfectly acceptable for noblemen and noblewomen to write with scrawling almost illegible hands, a mark of their aristocratic reserve. . . . Women and children in particular often received censure for their poor handwriting and orthography" (89). Put another way, neat handwriting and handwriting of the correct *style* were sociomaterial signs of respect and subservience. Furthermore, whether or not the letters were written in the author's own hand or not could signal the writer's position and/or the urgency with which the letter was sent. Gary Schneider comments that "the hand was . . . associated with authenticity and authorization, and could likewise represent intimacy and demonstrate emotion. Both the handwritten letter and one's signature, therefore, were socially significant" (121). The nuanced ways the letterwriter made her handwriting her own and added particular flourishes or other markings were thus additional ways the writer could present herself, unmediated by others, to her reader. Her script was a visual imprint of her identity and representation of her own interaction with the letter, as opposed to being dictated to and transcribed by an amanuensis. Significantly, both of Ursula's existing letters have been identified as "autograph" letters, meaning they were written in her own hand, thus making the differences between the two all the more telling.

In addition to the handwriting's type and legibility, space on the page was another marker of social standing and respect for one's reader. The period's letterwriting manuals prescribed such uses of the paper. Borrowing much of his material from slightly earlier French epistolography manuals, William Fulwood, author of the manual *The Enemy of Idleness*, comments on specifics such as leaving significant space between the body and the signature, which should be placed at the "right side in the nether end of the paper," to show one's utmost deference to the reader (qtd in Gibson). On this topic, Jonathan Gibson, summarizing the significant conventions espoused in William Fulwood, Angel Day, and contemporary French manuals on epistolography, argues, "All of these regulations amount effectively to the same thing: the requirement that socially superior addressees be honoured with as much blank paper as possible" (2). Such references to space demonstrate how the writers' and recipients' social standings were materially inscribed into their manuscripts; yet when seeing contrasting uses of material space from the same letterwriter, we can begin to identify intentional disruptions in letterwriting practice that deviates from the writer's other letterwriting performances *and* from the technical letterwriting manuals. In the photo of MS L.a.453 (see fig. 10.1), we can see the significant amount of space that Ursula allocated, presumably for the purpose of signaling her deference to Walter. Furthermore, her placement of her signature leaves ample space between the message, her signature, and the bottom of the manuscript. In sum, Ursula's letter adheres to generic conventions of the theme (a petition), situation of address (a subservient position to Walter), and material components (handwriting and space on the page) to serve her rhetorical purpose. Ursula not only recognizes that her message should be concise and deferential but also carefully writes the letter in her own hand and leaves enough space for Walter to recognize her respect for him before he even reads the letter's message.

Contrasting her first letter in subject matter, subject position, and material inscription, Ursula's second extant letter communicates a matter of domestic strife that requires immediate attention and action from Walter. In this letter, Ursula reports that she has been wronged by her husband and must write quickly to Walter to receive his assistance—specifically, she asks Walter to have his wife send for her and her servants and have her neighbors testify on her behalf. She writes:

Good Cousin Bagot, my miserable state that I am forced to make my complaint unto so good a friend and kinsman as yourself hoping you will take some compassion of me now in my misery. My husband doth greatly wrong me in such a manner. . . . *I am sorry to trouble you with this rude letter being so badly written which was written in no small haste* but I hope you will bear with my boldness and remember your promise to the Countess of Essex in her chamber when we were there . . . [that] you would stand my friend [if] my husband should ever wrong me. (emphasis mine, Folger MS L.a.454)

As in her first letter, Ursula begins with the generic salutation "Good Cousin." In contrast to the first letter, however, Ursula places herself in a more agentive subject position more quickly, presumably because of her time-sensitive situation, using first person pronouns and highlighting *her* "miserable state" in the first line of the letter. Ursula's rhetorical choices automatically place her in the subject position, and she further demonstrates her agency by addressing Walter as a "good friend and kinsman" whom she trusts and who she expects will show her compassion. By explicitly stating what she expects Walter's response to be, Ursula reinforces her agentive role even as she finds herself in a vulnerable position in her own household. Moreover, later in the letter, Ursula emphasizes her authority once more when she calls attention to the promise Walter made to her to protect her from her husband. Ursula relies on this shared knowledge, what Frow might call the "structure of implication," to strengthen her plea for help. Ursula's established speaking position, while still respectful, carries more authority through her subtle uses of pronouns, subject positions, and implied shared knowledge with her reader: all of which would be considered generic features of a petition letter that bear some similarity to the previous letter, but also vary enough to be considered a distinct generic performance that showcases this vulnerable letterwriter's agency in ways that might not be expected.

While these semantic aspects of her writing offer productive insights into Ursula's shifting subject position and nuanced uses of this letter type, her uses of material resources are most compelling in this example and support the need for *materiality* to be included in our understanding of genres as social action; the second letter represents one of the clearest examples of social position, authority, and agency being bound in, and in this case limited by, material resources. For instance, Ursula writes the letter in the italic hand, but her handwriting here drastically differs from that of the previous letter. As shown in figure 10.2, her handwriting in the second letter is very lightly penned, almost to the point of being illegible.

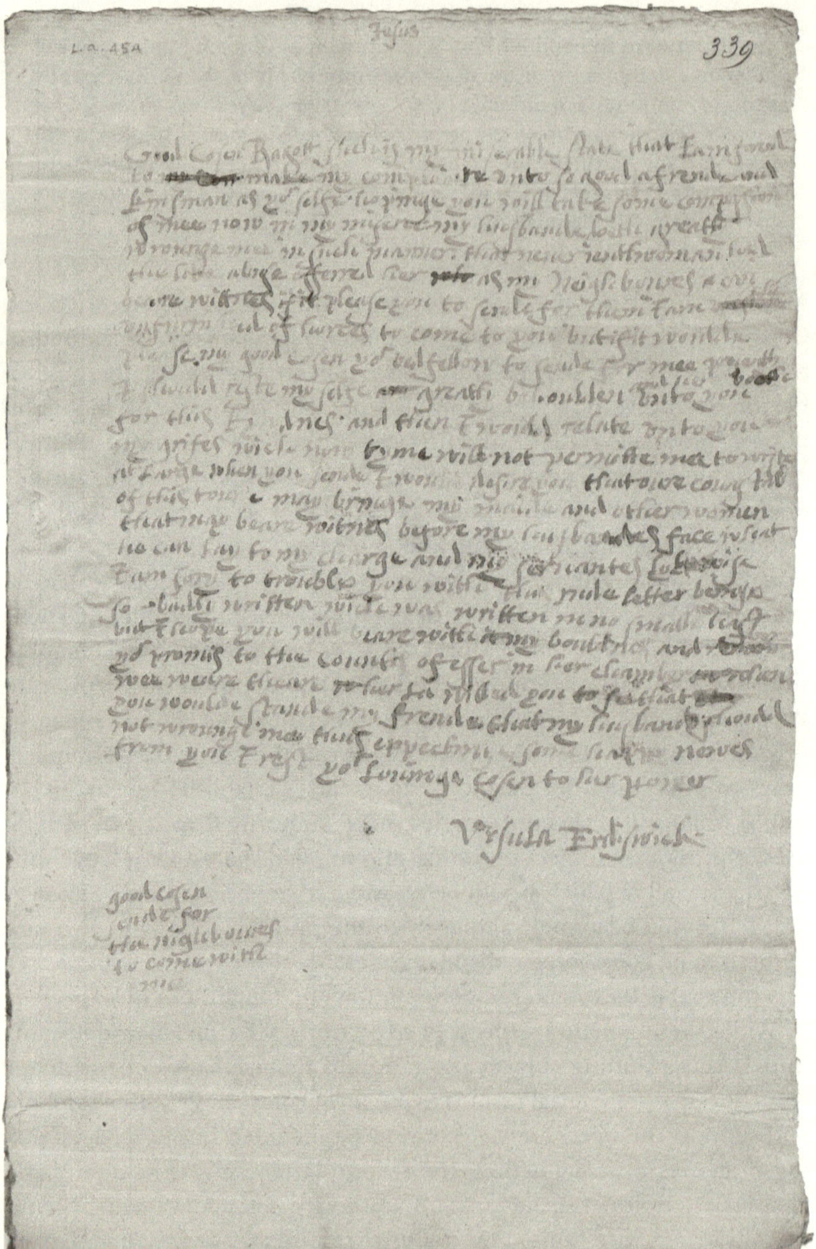

Figure 10.2. Ursula (Stafford) Erdeswicke. Letter from Ursula (Stafford) Erdeswicke to Walter Bagot? (ca. 1618). L.a.454. Used by permission of the Folger Shakespeare Library under a Creative Commons Attribution-ShareAlike 4.0 International License.

Yet Ursula explicitly addresses her knowledge of this "flaw" when she says, "I am sorry to trouble you with this rude letter being so badly written which was written in no small haste." Her poor handwriting thus reinforces the desperation that undergirds the letter's content and points to another material condition that was valued by early modern epistolographers: time. Limitations of time become materially and visually apparent through her several extraneous markings on the page and revisions to her text, and all of these markings offer visual evidence that Ursula did not have the typical writing tools available that she appears to have had used in her former letter. The usual materials—a goosefeather quill and ink made from iron gall nuts—do not appear to be the tools that Ursula used in this particular instance (Stewart and Wolfe 13). In handling Ursula's manuscripts at the Folger, I was able to see the visible differences more clearly—the ink bled and smeared causing the alphabetic letters to lose their form; the blotting was heavier; and the manuscript itself was more fragile than the previous letter. In addition, what this visible and tangible evidence suggests is that the second letter may not have been treated or stored properly, highlighting once more that this letter was not written under normal circumstances.

By analyzing Ursula Wardwicke's two existing letters through Frow's generic dimensions and the additional dimension of materiality, I aimed to demonstrate how this one female letterwriter harnessed multiple resources of meaning-making in two distinct letterwriting performances. As noted above, I understand materiality to be an integral, not an extratextual or idiosyncratic, component of the genre. Ursula's letters demonstrate how the manuscript's materiality can signal the writer's positionality and the overall rhetorical function of her letters. Significantly in this case, the material uses of the letter differed in the two examples. In the first, the material components reinforced the writer's message and the speaking position that she assumes; however, in the second example, the material components of the letter contradict some of the more agentive moves the writer performs, particularly the authoritative use of Walter's previous promise to protect her. In either case, the expanded framework offers us a more comprehensive view of the rhetorical range that this material genre offered writers from marginalized and vulnerable positions.

I conclude this analysis of genre and materiality with a brief examination of a letter from another woman in the Bagot family: Walter's sister Lettice Kynnersley. The Bagot collection includes approximately fifteen letters from Lettice Kynnersley, and based on the coding practices described briefly above, I have selected one salient example of Lettice assuming an authoritative role in the text through traditional genre conventions and rather unconventional material uses of the page that allow her to insert her voice in the document's margins. In Folger MS L.a.606, Lettice Kynnersley writes to her brother to describe a detailed legal matter regarding a potential fine that involves her husband and a man referred to as Vaughn. The letter begins with a traditional salutation, "Good Brother," and then immediately launches into a detailed description of the matter at hand, a description that consumes nearly the entire body of the letter. In fact, the letter's body never actually includes an explicit request for Walter's counsel on the matter, though the reader can assume that this request is implied.

What I have not yet mentioned about this letter, however, is that the letter's body was not written by Lettice. In fact, two hands are present in this letter: the family's male secretary's hand, who likely transcribed Lettice's dictation, and Lettice's own handwriting which appears only in her signature and in a marginal note in the left-hand margin (see fig. 10.3).

During the sixteenth and seventeenth centuries, the secretary often was a third-party male writer who "physically penned, and possibly authored" many letters and was an "integral part of letterwriting in the Renaissance," especially for members of the royal family and/ or families occupying the upper ranks of society, as the Bagot family did (Stewart and Wolfe 55). The secretary often wrote letters for the family's female members who did not know how to compose a letter in secretary hand. Here, Lettice's use of a secretary in this scenario conformed to traditional letterwriting practices that required letters regarding legal or formal business matters to be written in the formal secretary hand, but importantly, it is Lettice's handwritten marginal note that includes the explicit request for Walter's guidance. She writes, "Good brother will you write unto me: what you give me counsel to do. I will be directed by you: but I have no reason to pass away any of my estate to pay him: for I have been used with all cruelty." In examples like this one, we see the letterwriter's text contradicting the manuals' prescription that space "should" be left as a sign of deference to the reader, and we can see her own handwriting contrasting the secretary's hand. What this signifies is that the letterwriter valued authenticity, and perhaps knew her brother would also, to the extent that the desire for authenticity overruled formal genre conventions that were being followed in the letter's body.

Without even reading the letter, Walter would have recognized the authenticity of Lettice's marginal note—a distinct handwriting that is present in the other fourteen of her existing letters—in contrast to the

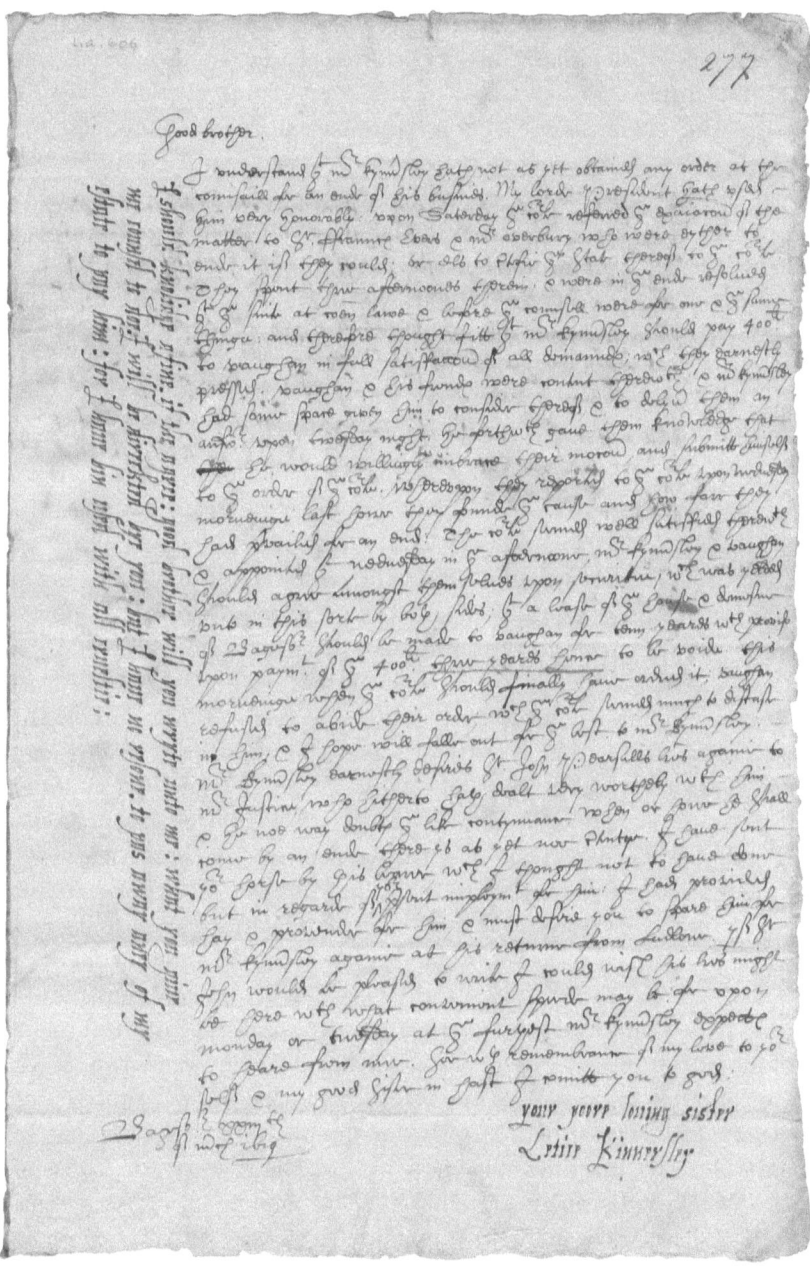

Figure 10.3. Lettice Kynnersley. Letter from Lettice Kynnersley, Badger, to Walter Bagot and Letter from Richard Weston to Walter Bagot, March 25, 1620 (1619/1620 March 23). L.a.606. Used by permission of the Folger Shakespeare Library under a Creative Commons Attribution-ShareAlike 4.0 International License.

letter's body. Such tensions productively show how the written generic conventions—disseminated through formal letterwriting manuals that were not written for women as their audience—could be pushed against through the ways the letterwriter chose to manipulate the material space. As with the analyses of Ursula's letters, if we disregard the important visual and physical characteristics that are part of the genre's makeup, we risk missing several elements of the writer's textual performance that, as Daybell argues, point us toward important issues of authenticity, secrecy, and the writer's duty to the recipient—a relationship that reveals the power dynamics at play in this gendered genre.

CONCLUSION: A CALL FOR FURTHER MATERIAL GENRE STUDIES

The letterwriters presented in this chapter make some of the invisible practices of letterwriting more visible and accessible, allowing us the opportunity to draw conclusions about complex negotiations of the letter as a genre and a material object. By combining the frameworks of RGS with the values of MCS, we are better able to see the letter's potential for providing resources for women to balance socially accepted roles with more agentive, autonomous roles in their writing.

It is worth repeating here that both RGS and MCS value how the object of inquiry (either a genre or a material object) carries ideology, cultural assumptions, beliefs, and values—all which relate to how power and authority are exercised and exchanged in specific cultural moments. MCS scholar Jules David Prown, for instance, writes in "Mind in Matter" that "material culture is the study through artifacts of beliefs—values, ideas, attitudes, and assumptions—of a particular community or society at a given time" (1). Describing similar values to those of the RGS scholars referenced earlier in the chapter, what Prown identifies as most important is that the *objects themselves* carry cultural and historical values and ideologies that are essential to studying any community.

Yet another exigence for this interdisciplinary study is represented in Edith Mayo's comment that "word people," such as historians or compositionists, often do not know how to "handle *images* and *icons*" (596). While WS scholars certainly have become much more invested in *visual* rhetoric, as the field's direction toward multimodal composition and digital publishing attests, Mayo's argument still holds relevance for the limited ways that we "word people" have handled other modes of meaning-making, such as material objects. Mayo adds, "The use of material culture, then, should become an important resource and tool, either as an adjunct to or on a part with, more traditional history methodologies. The past, as seen through the written record, can be confirmed and enriched by artifactual evidence" (597).

In this chapter, I have attempted to respond to this call by identifying how we can study writing and objects together—and study genres *as material objects*—namely through valuing writing materials as "on part with" rhetorical genres that facilitate action and human sense-making. If we accept the preceding theories of genre, power, and materiality, we can better understand individuals' sense-making through genres and objects, as they use both to alter their positions of power and make their lived realities known to those around them. The framework introduced necessarily adds materiality to an existing list of dimensions that help us analyze a genre's fuller context and the human lives that are represented and circulated through those genres. Combining the foundations and values of RGS and MCS as I have done above only *begins* to make some of the important "invisible" interactions, meaning-making, and potential for social mobility more visible. In the case of the Bagot women's letters, the analyses of the language and generic conventions used in conjunction with manuscripts' material features show how the women carefully positioned themselves to their readers in any given moment. For those in WS and other disciplines who value the study of writing genres and material objects, seeing genre as social *and material* action might help them answer their own research questions that attend to shared disciplinary values of seeing how cultural and historical values become bound and circulated in iterative performances of a single genre.

WORKS CITED

Barton, David, and Nigel Hall. *Letter Writing as a Social Practice.* John Benjamins Pub., 1999.
Bawarshi, Anis S., and Mary Jo Reiff. *Genre: An Introduction to History, Theory, and Pedagogy.* Parlor Press and WAC Clearinghouse, 2010.
Daybell, James. *The Material Letter in Early Modern England.* Palgrave Macmillan, 2012.
Daybell, James. "Material Meanings and the Social Signs of Manuscript Letters in Early Modern England." *Literature Compass*, vol. 6, no. 3, 2009, pp. 647–667.
Frow, John. *Genre.* Routledge, 2006.
Gibson, Jonathan. "Significant Space in Manuscript Letters." *The Seventeenth Century*, vol. 12, 1997, pp. 1–9.
Henderson, Judith Rice. "Defining the Genre of the Letter." *Renaissance and Reformation*, vol. 7, no. 2, 1983, pp. 89–105.
Kvande, Marta. "Printed in a Book: Negotiating Print and Manuscript Cultures in Fantomina and Clarissa." *Eighteenth-Century Studies*, vol. 46, no. 2, 2013, pp. 239–257.
Laroche, R. "Gendering Hands, Gendering Business: A Letter from Elizabeth Bagot." *A Manuscript Miscellany*, Folger Shakespeare Library, 2014.
"Letter from Elizabeth (Cave) Bagot, Bromley Pagets, to Walter Bagot, 1614 July 7." Papers of the Bagot family of Blithfield, Staffordshire, 1428–1671 (bulk 1557–1671), Folger MS 48, Folger Shakespeare Library, Washington, DC.

"Letter from Lettice Kynnersley, Badger, to Walter Bagot, [1619/20] March 23." Papers of the Bagot family of Blithfield, Staffordshire, 1428–1671 (bulk 1557–1671), Folger MS 606, Folger Shakespeare Library, Washington, DC.

"Letter from Ursula (Stafford) Erdeswicke, Stafford Castle, to Walter Bagot, [1618?]." Papers of the Bagot family of Blithfield, Staffordshire, 1428–1671 (bulk 1557–1671), Folger MS 453, Folger Shakespeare Library, Washington, DC.

"Letter from Ursula (Stafford) Erdeswicke, to [Walter Bagot?], ca. 1618." Papers of the Bagot family of Blithfield, Staffordshire, 1428–1671 (bulk 1557–1671), Folger MS 454, Folger Shakespeare Library, Washington, DC.

Mayo, Edith. "Introduction: Focus on Material Culture." *Journal of American Culture*, vol. 3, no. 4, 1980, pp. 595–604.

Miller, Carolyn R. "Genre as Social Action." *Quarterly Journal of Speech*, vol. 70, no. 2, 1984, pp. 151–167.

Miller, Carolyn R., and Ashley R. Kelly, editors. *Emerging Genres in New Media Environments*. Palgrave Macmillan, 2017.

Mitchell, Linda C. "Entertainment and Instruction: Women's Roles in the English Epistolary Tradition." *Huntington Library Quarterly*, vol. 66, no. 3/4, 2003, pp. 331–347.

O'Day, Rosemary. *The Family and Family Relationships, 1500–1900: England, France, and the United States of America*. St. Martin's Press, 1994.

O'Neill, Lindsay. *The Opened Letter: Networking in the Early Modern British World*. U of Pennsylvania P, 2015.

Perry, Ruth. *Women, Letters, and the Novel*. AMS Press, 1980.

Prown, Jules David. "Mind in Matter: An Introduction to Material Culture Theory and Method." *Winterthur Portfolio*, vol. 17, no. 1, 1982, pp. 1–19.

Schneider, Gary. *The Culture of Epistolarity: Vernacular Letters and Letter Writing in Early Modern England, 1500–1700*. U of Delaware P, 2005.

Steen, Sara Jayne. "Reading beyond the Words: Material Letters and the Process of Interpretation." *Journal of the Rocky Mountain Medieval and Renaissance Association*, vol. 22, 2001, pp. 54–69.

Stewart, Alan, and Heather Wolfe. *Letterwriting in Renaissance England*. Folger Shakespeare Library, Distributed by U of Washington P, 2004.

AFTERWORD

Kate Smith

Published in 2005, as material culture studies became an established area and method of enquiry, Leora Auslander's seminal article "Beyond Words" remains prescient. It argues that historians should move beyond texts and embrace the opportunities offered by material culture sources. Reaching out to a wider diversity of source types and the new questions they prompted would allow historians to explore a broader range of past human experiences. One of Auslander's most compelling arguments for the inclusion of objects within historical analysis was that "most people for most of human history have not used written language as their major form of expression" (Auslander 1018). By including artefacts in their analysis, historians could make another important move toward realising more diverse histories. Objects were held to provide a conceptual space in which previously marginalised and unstudied histories could emerge with greater force. In this volume, the embrace of material culture studies by both material culture and writing studies scholars demonstrates how far the field has come. The chapters included within *The Material Culture of Writing* take Auslander's call to move beyond words full circle by examining the very objects, spaces, and practices that create and have created texts. The volume reveals these objects, spaces, and practices as deeply meaningful and impactful. By unearthing their centrality in the production of writing, texts are made fully material. Despite the move toward material culture and materiality across a range of disciplines and fields over the last thirty years, Auslander's arguments remain key. Issues of power, authority, and marginalisation continue as crucial elements in understanding human expression and they are acutely invoked by the study of things.

Writing and reading cultures have long been understood as central to the formation of self and the construction of identities. The growing popularity of and access to forms of writing from the seventeenth century onwards, including letter writing, diary entries, commonplace books, and account books fostered new spaces in which individuals reflected on and recorded their daily interactions (Mascuch; Smyth). These forms of writing and reading are understood as crucial to the emergence of interiority, individualism, and identity in the modern period. *The Material Culture of Writing* prompts us to consider how such practices continue in the contemporary world, but significantly it looks to the specific tools, bodily gestures, and spaces of production that shape them. As Cydney Alexis and Emilie Merrigan's chapters show, alongside the writing produced, the tools, spaces and gestures used in acts of writing impact the identity formations that take place as a result. In the case of the Moleskine, investigated by Alexis, the weight of the object's meaning raises questions for their users. It can facilitate their ability to identify as writers (as in the case of Fiona) and challenge such claims (as in the case of David). Yet the weight of certain objects and the established nature of their particular meaning can also provide users with foils against which they can form "alternative" identities as writers or practitioners. Alexis found that one respondent, Lily, used Moleskine notebooks but resisted identification with them. She challenged the value of their meaning, particularly their perceived links to and celebration of male writers, by instead stressing their functional value and her lack of loyalty to that specific brand. Similarly, Merrigan's analysis of Jessie Grabel's copy of *The Book of Baby Mine* demonstrates how in 1930s America, writing allowed women to resist the "scientific motherhood" such books sought to promote. Mothers demonstrated resistance by completing (or not completing) the sections in ways other than those prescribed by the book's printed headings and instructions. As with Moleskine notebooks, baby books acted as surfaces upon which individuals encountered, questioned, and navigated their writing and identities. Merrigan's chapter shows how a refusal to write within the parameters prescribed by an object can be a powerful and meaningful act.

Outside of individual identity formation, writing and reading objects also provide important sites upon which collective identities can coalesce. Jenny Krichevsky's chapter on indexical heirlooms demonstrates the important roles objects, such as books and encyclopedias, play across time and space in anchoring cultural identities. Following migrations, which involved leaving book collections behind, Krichevsky's respondents worked to obtain copies of the books they once owned. They placed value on "reclaiming" these physical objects. Similarly, recent work in anthropology has underlined how absent objects can have as much impact as those which are present (Bille et al. 10). Sociologists have also shown how, when absent, the traces of past objects can linger on, keeping imaginative holds on their past possessor (Hetherington

167). The objects that shape writing and reading cultures then, are not necessarily those which are present when writing and reading take place. Rather, we also need to take into account the absent objects and tools, whose traces might shape writing. Krichevsky's respondents felt the traces left by absent objects and the holds they had across time and space. Locating copies of their old books in a bookshop in Cambridge, Massachusetts, afforded Krichevsky's respondents a means of reinstating important cultural connections, thus revealing the centrality of (absent and present) material culture to such processes.

Writing objects can be sites that allow cultural imaginings of belonging to take place, but they can also be appropriated as sites upon which cultural negotiations about writing and reading can happen. Desirée Henderson's chapter demonstrates how objects connected to writing have provided cultural spaces within which people have sought to talk about who has "permission" to write and who does not. Henderson shows how ink proved to be a particularly important symbolic object in the nineteenth century. Cultural commentators focused on ink to discuss the roles and activities of white women writers. Ink stains and spills "served as evidence of women's inability to combine authorship with housekeeping responsibilities or with protocols of feminine self-presentation" (24). Writing was thus conceived as a threatening and problematic activity for women to engage in. The seeming colour contrasts of black stains on white hands caused by writing or ink spills were also heightened in arguments about racial purity and white women's often fragile relationship to respectability. Similarly, Henderson shows, African American authors also interrogated associations between ink, paper, and skin color to "imaginatively overcome or to outright condemn the racist ideologies that transformed writing instruments into emblems of white supremacy" (39). Writing materials offer fertile ground upon which to discuss the power embedded in writing practices.

In these analyses of use and access, writing objects, even mundane writing objects such as notebooks and ink, are found to be deeply meaningful and powerful things. At the same time, *The Material Culture of Writing* also engages with recent shifts in material culture studies to explore what writing objects and environments do and how they effect change: they themselves are actants operating in networks and assemblages (Latour; Deleuze and Guattari). Actor network theory and more recent moves within object-oriented ontologies have placed new emphasis on how things exist outside of subject/object relations and have the ability to effect change. Such work has also reconceived "the social" in flatter terms. Rather than privileging human agency, it seeks to include a range of nonhuman actants with "the social," opening up our understandings of social interactions. In thinking through writing, we begin to see writing objects as tools, collaborators, or extensions that help people to complete tasks but also contain material restrictions, limitations, and opportunities which shape the writing that is produced (Hayles 287). Questions of materiality and identity come together in Diane Ehrenpreis's chapter on Thomas Jefferson's writing suite. It shows how Jefferson constructed his identity as a man of letters, not only through writing copious correspondence but also by designing furniture which allowed him to work through his letter reading and writing tasks with greater efficiency. We might go further in our reading of the role of such things. Through the elaborate redesign of everyday objects—a desk, a chair—Jefferson made claims to the enormity of his task and his proficiency in completing it. These objects were crucial in the projection and demarcation of power within his household. The intricate nature of these objects demonstrates the value Jefferson placed on the workings of *his* writing tools and their relationship to *his* writing body, as opposed to the enslaved labour of others that afforded him the time to complete these tasks. Yet, as Ehrenpreis reveals, the suite displayed significant inefficiencies. Positioned as it was in a room that was too hot in the summer and too cold in the winter, Jefferson failed to consider the broader environment in which he worked (158). Rather than the complete and all-encompassing system of efficiency he imagined then, here we further see how Jefferson only focused on those objects in direct contact with his body or the reams of paper he sought to tackle. These objects and their environment speak to the hierarchy of values at stake within Jefferson's household. Analysing the material cultures of writing reveals how writing practices can work to foreground and legitimate the labour of certain people, while obscuring the violent exploitation of others.

Deborah C. Andrews's chapter on the writing practices active in academic makerspaces considers broader questions of environment and shows how people write in complex "social" spaces. Rather than the lone writer or the trope of the lone literary writer, by focusing on makerspaces we see writing as an everyday and collaborative activity that takes place in relationship with complex networks of people, things, spaces, and practices. Andrews' piece utilizes a more diverse conception of "the social" (described above), to examine the significance of interactions between people, things and spaces, and how they shape practices. Similarly, Anne MacKay's chapter examines a different "space": the conservation file. Here again, we encounter an assemblage of things, from a folder to documentation and the original components of an object. MacKay also reminds us of the importance of recognising the vibrancy of the matter at stake in the material world (Bennett). Matter is constantly fluid and open to changes, such as decay. From the founding of public national museums in the eighteenth century, museums have sought to stave off the loss of objects, maintaining them for posterity. Yet as the growth of conservation practices in the nineteenth century demonstrated, curtailing the vibrancy of matter and stopping the slow decay of material objects is a difficult task. Alongside conservation practices, focusing on the conservation file shows us how the bureaucracy and material culture of conservation is also an important part of the apparatus used as ballast against loss. Nevertheless, even here, matter is vibrant. Writing cultures rely on material reactions, such as ink on paper and rubber on pencil lead. Documentation designed to record and identify slow material change is itself slowly changing. Similarly, such documentation often silently contains loss through its inability to fully render the complex stories of objects and how they came to be in the museum at all.

The final two chapters of the book also underline the importance of examining socio-material actions. They show how genres are constructed through the constant reiteration of socio-material actions: the signature in the hotel book, the comment in the margin of the letter. These actions can only be unveiled through a rich understanding of the social, which sees people as active agents within networks of objects and spaces. These chapters underline the importance of the thinking through assemblages and interrelationships more broadly. No writing practice takes place with one object alone, but rather it is enacted through interactions between objects, spaces, and people. In our contemporary world of laptops and phones, a world in which we constantly type, it is not only the Moleskine that acts as a "facilitating artifact" but also the pen or pencil that is used to write in it. The act of *hand*writing is a material practice that is made meaningful by the long history of writing cultures—letter writing, hotel book signing, and life writing—that it draws from.

Nevertheless, as Auslander reminds us, historically the written language has not been *the* major form of human expression (Auslander 1018). Instead it is material culture that opens up our understanding of human expression in broader terms. It is important then to consider how, even though access to writing has been and is limited, writing as a form of expression has been consistently shaped by the material objects that have made it possible. We might pause then to consider the makers of pens, notebooks, paper, and books. These people create (and created) forms of expression through the materials, skills, tools, and time they utilised and utilise to make writing objects (Ko). Whether engaged in or excluded from writing practices themselves, their *making* practices contain significant histories and meanings.

The Material Culture of Writing insists on taking seemingly mundane and ubiquitous writing materials seriously. It has unpicked some of the ways in which paper and pens have had and continue to have the ability to exclude. But it also suggests at the need for further work in this area. In the past and present, the material culture of writing has proved important in providing writers with authority and excluding others (Dierks). The politics of writing is played out in material culture in both material and cultural terms. The meanings understood to be embedded within particular objects, such as Moleskines, can provoke questions and anxieties in people, an inability to live up to or to want to live up to the demands such meanings can make. That those meanings are culturally produced and enforced, as in the case of ink, shows how culturally powerful they are deemed to be. Access to the material cultures of writing has long been policed and regulated. Yet, it is also difficult to do the work of unpicking the structural ways in which exclusion works and the role material culture plays in such exclusions. As Auslander asserted, when using the historical record, it is difficult to "see" those excluded from writing cultures, or those who utilised different forms of expression. As this volume shows, however, it is crucial to switch our understanding of writing cultures. We need to fully materialise them and consider the full range of expressions included within them. Everyday writing practices—notes, lists, accounts—are important, even as they are incomplete and fragmentary in nature. Such practices can be further understood, not only by seeing them alongside other texts, however, but also by fully understanding the material cultures and networks that facilitated the production of such writing. The ink that allowed a note to be included in the margin of a letter, the paper and printing that created the page of a baby book, and the cardboard that formed a conservation folder provide important clues in fully understanding the authority, power, and meaning at stake in acts of writing.

WORKS CITED

Auslander, Leora. "Beyond Words." *American Historical Review*, vol. 110, no. 4, 2005, pp. 1015–1045.

Bennett, Jane. *Vibrant Matter. A Political Ecology of Things*. Duke UP, 2010.

Bille, Mikkel, et al. "Introduction: An Anthropology of Absence." *An Anthropology of Absence: Materialization of Transcendence and Loss*, edited by Mikkel Bille, Frida Hastrup, and Tim Flohr Sørensen, Springer, 2010, pp. 3–22.

Deleuze, Gilles, and Felix Guattari. *A Thousand Plateaus: Capitalism and Schizophrenia*. U of Minneapolis P, 1987.

Dierks, Konstantine. *In My Power: Letter Writing and Communication in Early America.* U of Pennsylvania P, 2009.
Hayles, N. Katherine. *How We Became Posthuman: Virtual Bodies in Cybernetics, Literature, and Informatics.* U of Chicago P, 1999.
Hetherington, Kevin. "Secondhandedness: Consumption, Disposal, and Absent Presence." *Environment and Planning D: Society and Space,* no. 22, 2004, pp. 157–173.
Ko, Dorothy. *The Social Life of Inkstones: Artisans and Scholars in Early Qing China.* U of Washington P, 2017.
Latour, Bruno. *Reassembling the Social: An Introduction to Actor-Network-Theory.* Oxford UP, 2005.
Mascuch, Michael. *Origins of the Individualist Self: Autobiography and Self-Identity in England, 1591–1791.* Cambridge UP, 1997.
Smyth, Adam. *Autobiography in Early Modern England.* Cambridge UP, 2010.

INDEX

ableism, 9
access, viii, 6, 10, 12–13, 22, 44, 51–52, 55, 61, 63, 73, 117, 193, 216, 233, 236
academic makerspaces, x, 119, 120–22, 127; community ethos, 121, 130–32; and entrepreneurship, 134–37. *See also* Stanford University Hasso Plattner Institute of Design (d.school); University of Delaware Design Studio
actor-network theory (ANT), 8, 182–83, 233
Adams, John, 146, 163–64
African-American authors, vii, 50–51, 60–61; interrogations of race/racism, 22, 51, 61; literacy, 51, 61, 62–63, 66*n17*. *See also* Chesnutt, Charles; Fern, Fanny; Forestier, Auber; Gillette, Israel; Morrison, Toni; Ward, Jesmyn
Alexis, Cydney, vii–viii, xiii, 7–9, 19, 22, 73, 85, 109, 142, 176, 195, 214, 216, 232
Allen, Chris T., 39
Andrews, Deborah C., x, 234
anti-Semitism, 74, 85
artifacts, vii–viii, xi, xiii, 3–13, 22, 27, 33, 43–44, 73, 78, 89–90, 92–93, 95–97, 101, 104–108, 110–11, 117, 141, 166, 184, 191–92, 198, 202, 216, 228–29, 235; cultural artifacts, 78, 92; facilitating artifacts, 22, 27, 43–44, 73, 235; material artifacts, 90, 92, 95–97, 105, 110–11, 191. *See also* writing objects/artifacts
assemblage, 174–75, 180
Auslander, Leora, 231, 235
autograph albums/books, 200–201, 204

baby books, vii, 8, 12, 22. *See also Book of Baby Mine, The*; motherhood; scientific motherhood
Bacevice, Peter Anthony, 128
Bacon, Francis, 144
Bagot, Elizbeth, 191, 211, 213–14, 217, 222
Bagot, Richard, 211
Bagot, Walter, 211–13, 217, 219, 222–23, 226
Bakhtin, Mikhail, 74

Ball, Cheryl E., 129
Barnett, Scot, 117, 126
Baron, Denis, 4
Bartlett, Lesley, 10, 71
Barton, David, 214
Bazerman, Charles, 14*n1*, 20, 192, 217
Beecher, Henry Ward (Mrs.), 54
Beert, Dan C., 129
Belk, Russell W., 8, 25, 33, 35, 84
Bemer, Amanda M., 129
Bennett, Jane, 185
Berlin, James, 131
Bih, Herng-Dar, 79
Black Art Speaks, xi–xii
Black disenfranchisement, 64
Black Lives Matter (BLM), xi; murals, xi–xiii, xii
Black/white binary, 50, 55–56, 63–64
blackface minstrelsy, 59, 63, 66*n16*
Blackness, 50, 56, 59–60
bluestockings, 53, 58, 66*n6*
Book of Baby Mine, The, 89, 94, 232; as artifact, 95–98, 100; advertising in, 100–101, 103, 106; childrearing advice, 89–90, 94, 101, 110, 111*n3*; history of, 93–96; illustrations, 89, 99–100; materiality, 89; memory records, 89–90, 105–106; photographs, 90, 106; singularization of, 89, 95–96, 101, 104–105, 108, 111, 111*n1*
bookcases/bookshelves, vii, 22, 75–76, 80
bookstores, 32, 74–75
Bourdieu, Pierre, 126
Bowman, Leslie Greene, 141, 166*n1*
Bowser, Muriel, xi
Boyle, Casey, 117, 126
Brand, Stewart, 121, 128
Brandt, Deborah, 4, 10, 19, 21, 76
British Museum, 172
Brown, William Wells, 60
Browning, Robert, 202
Buchanan, Richard, 131
Buckley, Jenni, 122, 137

INDEX

Bunin, Ivan, 74
Burstein, Andrew, 163
Byron, George Gordon (Lord Byron), 194, 196–99, 209

Caldor, M. T., 56, 60, 66*n13*
Canagarajah, Suresh, 193
Carlone, Heidi B., 21
Cary, Amelia Fitzclarence, 177
Chatwin, Bruce, 30, 32
Chesnutt, Charles, 51, 62–64
Chuikina, Sof'ia, 72
Clairmont, Claire, 198
classroom design, 129–31, 133
collaboration: learning, 127, 132; writing, 120, 122, 129, 132
colorism, 63
Colter, Mary Ann, 161
Conquergood, Dwight, 62
conservation files, 170, 172, 179, 186; material fragments, 170, 177–79, 184–86; object documentation, 170–76, 181; visual references, 170, 178–80
conservation, vii, 171, 173, 181–82, 234; breakdown, 183–84; ethical practices, 171, 173; history of, 172–74; professionalism, 171, 173–74, 180–81, 186
consumer culture theory, 3, 11, 14–15*n3*
consumerism, 180
Cook, Devon, 137
cookbook writers, 12
Coolidge, Ellen Randolph, 158, 160, 165
Coppage, Michael, xii
copresence/coawareness, 133
COVID-19, ix, x, xi, 12, 115
creative improvisation, viii, 22
Crewe-Milnes, Robert (Earl of Crewe), 194, 196–98, 204, 208
Csikszentmihalyi, Mihalyi, 8, 26, 84, 98
Curasi, Folkman, 71–72

d'Alembert, Jean Le Rond, 146
Day, Angel, 222
Daybell, James, 213, 215–16, 221, 228
de Beer, Gavin, 198–99
de Bello, Patrizia, 201
Declaration of Independence, 140, 145
decommodification, viii, 71–72
Deetz, James, 6–7, 12
DeJean, Joan, 158
de Jouy, Victor Joseph Étienne, 200
Denny, Melcena Burns, 96, 111*n2*
Devitt, Amy, 192
Diderot, Denis, 146
Dierks, Konstantine, 51–52
Dick, C. Hill, 206–207

Digital: communication, ix, 30, 129, 132, 135; devices, ix–x, 8, 42, 116, 124–25, 130–31; and materiality, 31–32, 37, 45*n4*, 126, 187, 228, 155; objects, 8. *See also* laptops; mobile technology; screen readers
disability studies, 9. *See also* ableism
discursive heirlooms, 22, 72; attachment to, 71, 73, 75; and cultural literacy values, 71, 74, 76–78, 85; disposition of, 71, 76; of familial endurance, 71, 76–82; and literary practice, 75, 86; of national belonging/alienation, 71, 82–85
Dolmage, Jay, 9
Douglass, Frederick, viii, 61–62, 66*n17*
Dowden, Edward, 197–99
Dropbox, 132

eBay, 89
Ehrenpreis, Diane, viii–ix, 9, 120, 234
Elbow, Peter, 19
embroidery, 55, 214
environmental structuring, 120, 176
Epp, Amber M., 8, 71–72, 77
Epps, Keri, 191–93
Erasmus, 215

face masks, 13
Faraday, Michael, 173
Farrell, Thomas, 95
Fern, Fanny, 53, 66*n5*
Flickr, 30
Floyd, George, xi
Forestier, Auber, 57–58, 60, 66*n14*, 66*n16*
fountain/reservoir pens, 52, 54
Frow, John, 217–19, 225
Fulwood, William, 222
Fuss, Diana, 8–9, 141, 158

Genre, vii, 11–12, 37, 93, 95, 105, 108, 109, 111, 115, 132, 136, 191–93, 195, 199–200, 203–204, 208, 212–19, 221, 223, 225–26, 228–29, 235
Gensler, 130
Gerasimova, Ekaterina, 72
ghost writers, 12
Gibson, Jonathan, 222
Gillette, Edward, 161
Gillette, Israel (I. Jefferson), 9, 117, 161–62, 166
Gillette, Jane, 161
Glassie, Henry, 5–7, 10, 12–14
global trade, 180
Godwin, Mary, 196–97
Golden, Janet, 93–94, 105
Goldhagen, Sarah, 126

Goodman, Dena, 52, 165n4
Google Classrooms, ix
Google Docs, ix, 132, 135
Gouge, Catherine, 9, 13
Grabel, George, 108
Grabel, Jessie, 92–93, 105, 108–10, 232
Grabel, Mary Louise, 92–93, 101, 103, 107–109
Gray, Francis C., 160
Grayson, Kent, 80, 86n3
grocery lists, 8, 73
Grulke, Eric A., 129–30
Gurova, Ol'ga, 72, 75

Hall, Nigel, 4–5, 214
Haltman, Kenneth, 7
Hamilton, Alexander, 163–65
handwriting/penmanship, 146, 221–23, 225–26, 228
Harper, Charles G., 202
Harper, Frances Watkins, 60
Heath, Shirley Brice, 4
heirlooms, vii, 22, 71, 73, 79, 82. *See also* discursive heirlooms
Hemingway, Ernest, viii, 30–32, 40
Henderson, Desirée, vii, 21–22, 233
Henry, Jim, 130–31
Herndl, Carl, 126
Hillier, Bill, 127–28
Hobhouse, John Cam, 197
Holland, Dorothy, 29, 44–45n3

identity, vii–ix, xiii, 8, 11–13, 19–21, 25–29, 31, 34, 37, 39–44, 44–45n3, 53, 59, 62–63, 71–73, 76–77, 79, 82, 86, 90–93, 109–11, 116, 120, 126, 134, 142, 170, 176, 191, 204–205, 208, 221, 232, 234; and motherhood, 90–93, 98, 105, 108–10; writing identity, vii–ix, xiii, 3, 22–23, 25, 27–29, 34, 37, 39–44, 73, 92–93, 142, 232
industry-sponsored projects, 122
Ingold, Tim, 185
ink pots, vii, 12, 65
ink powder, 51, 65n2
ink/ink stains, vii, viii, 12, 50, 54–55, 225; and gender, 53–54, 57–58; racialization of, 56, 58, 61–65, 66n11; removal of, 54–55
inkstands, 51
inkwells, 51
Instagram, 30
interdisciplinary collaboration, 121, 123, 127

Jack, Jordan, 9–10
Jackson, Steven, x, 183–84
Jacobs, Jane, 128

James, Kevin, 191–92
James, William, 8
Jefferson, Thomas: correspondence, 140–41, 143–44, 146–47, 156–62, 164–65; revolving chair, 142–44, 159–60, 163–65; reading stand, 143, 149, 151, 155, 165; and slavery, 140–41, 144, 158–59, 161–62, 165–66, 234; writing practice, 140, 143–45, 149, 156–59, 161, 165; writing suite, vii, 9, 141, 143–44, 148–52, 155–65, 234; writing stand, 120, 140, 143, 145–46, 149, 151–52, 155–59, 165
Jim Crow/segregation, 61, 63
Johnson, Angela, 21
Johnson, Nan, 52
Johnson-Sheehan, Richard, 137
Jones, Hannah, xii
Jones, John, 9, 13
journaling, 28, 32–33

Katriel, Tamar, 95
Keller, Helen, 9
Kelley, David, 120
Kerschbaum, Stephanie L., 9
Kirkland, Caroline, 53–54
Kleine, Robert E., III, 39
Kleine, Susan Schultz, 39
Komsomol (USSR), 77
Kopytoff, Igor, 27, 181
Kostelnick, Charles, 131–32
Krichevsky, Jenny, vii, 22, 232–33
Krupskaya, Nadezhda, 76
Kuprin, Aleksandr, 74–75, 80
Kynnersley, Lettice, 212, 214, 225–26

Laing, Andrew, 128
Lamb, Charles, 194
Lane, Derek R., 129
laptops, ix, 8, 116, 125, 131, 235
Laroche, Rebecca, 211
Latour, Bruno, 182
Lave, Jean, 29, 44–45n3
Lavin, Joe, 32
letter writing: gendering of, 191, 211, 215, 217, 226, 228; genre conventions, 215–19, 221–22; manuals, 52, 217, 219, 222, 226, 228; in Renaissance England, 214–16, 226; social materiality of, 215, 223, 225–26. *See also* Jefferson, Thomas: correspondence
literacy, vii, 4, 10, 12–13, 19, 22, 26, 51–52, 61–63, 65, 69–86, 117, 200; and enslavement, 22, 26, 117; and materiality, 4, 11, 13, 71; and race, 22, 51, 61–63, 65, 117
literacy narratives, 22, 61, 70–71, 73, 75–77, 79, 82–83, 85

literacy studies, 4, 11, 19, 73
Locke, Jane E., 202
Locke, John, 144
Lorimer Leonard, Rebecca, 86*n1*
Lott, Eric, 59
Louvre, 172

MacKay, Anne, x, 116, 234–35
manual writers, 12
market capitalism, 14*n3*
Marxism, 71, 76
material culture studies (MCS), viii, 3, 5, 10, 13, 14*n2*, 14–15*n3*, 73, 89–90, 193, 213, 218; intersection with Rhetorical Genre Studies (RGS), 215–16, 218, 228–29; intersection with writing studies (WS), 11–12, 21, 116, 214–15
material goods, 11–12, 37, 39, 75
materialism/materiality/new materialism, vii, 5, 15*n4*, 108, 119, 126, 180, 185, 187*n2*, 212–13, 223. *See also* new materiality
Mayo, Edith, 228
McCord, David Ross, 176
McCord Museum, 176, 187*n1*
Mehta, Raj, 84
Merrigan, Emilie, vii, 7, 22, 232
meta-cognition, 127
Mi'kmaq community, 176–77, 180, 182–86, 187
Micciche, Laura, 4, 13, 175
military medals, vii, 71, 82, 84–85
Miller, Carolyn R., 192, 195, 216–18
Miller, Daniel, 8, 126
Miller, Herman, 128
Miller, Susan, 14*n1*
miscegenation, 22, 50, 57
Mitford, John, 197
mobile technology, 129–31, 134
Modo & Modo, 30, 32
Moeller, Ryan M., 129
Moleskine notebooks, vii, viii, 9, 30–32, 34, 45*n5*, 109, 232, 236; attachment to/fixation, 28–29, 32–33, 37; as cultural symbols, 29, 34; as facilitating artifact, 22, 27, 31–33, 37, 40–42, 43; hacking of, 34–35; popularity of, 29–30, 45*n4*; and writerly identity, 25, 29, 31–34, 37–40, 43, 44–45*n3*
Monticello: museum, 141–44, 147; and slavery, 140–42, 159, 161–62; Thomas Jefferson's writing suite, viii–ix, 9, 117, 156–63, 165, 234
Morrison, Toni, 56, 64
motherhood, vii, 22, 72, 90–91; mothers' identities, 90–93, 98, 105, 108–10; nostalgic/romantic outlook, 94, 96–98, 101, 105, 108–10. *See also* scientific motherhood
Muñoz-Viñas, Salvador, 184
museum and conservation studies, 11

Nail, Thomas, 175
National Gallery (London), 173
New Literacy Studies, 10, 70
new materiality, 172, 185–86
Newcomb, Mathew, 131
Newton, Isaac, 144
nibs, 51–52, 54

object-oriented ontology, 5, 15*n4*
open-plan workplaces, 119, 130, 133–34
Ozturk, Aysel, 7

Pahl, Kate, 10
paper, vii, 50–52, 61–62, 66*n10*, 214
Pascali, Lara, 92, 95, 108, 110
passports, vii, 71, 82–84
patriarchy, 59–60, 111, 141, 212
pencils, 4, 51
penknives, 51
pens, 50, 61–62. *See also* fountain/reservoir pens; quills/quill pens
pianos, 22, 73, 80–81
Picasso, Pablo, 30, 40
police brutality, 12, 13
pounce pots/blotters, 51, 52
Powell, Alandes, xi, xii–xiii
Price, Linda L., 8, 71–72, 77
print culture, 63
Prior, Paul, 4, 119–20, 176
privilege/cultural power, ix, 14; gender, ix; and objects, viii; race, ix
problem-based learning, 127–28
Prown, Jules David, 7–8, 22, 93, 106–107, 143, 164, 228
Purdy, James P., 131
Putzi, Jennifer, 59

quills/quill pens, 51–52, 54, 214, 225

racism, xi–xiii, 12–13, 21, 22, 51, 56; racist violence, 61–63, 65. *See also* Black disenfranchisement; Black Lives Matter (BLM); blackface minstrelsy; Black/white binary; Floyd, George; ink: racialization of; Jefferson, Thomas: and slavery; Jim Crow/segregation; paper: racialization of; privilege/cultural power; white supremacy ideology; writing implements: racialization of
Randall, Henry, 165

Randolph, Thomas Mann, 159
Reither, James, 132
restoration, 172–73
Reynolds, Nedra, 119
Rhetorical Genre Studies (RGS), 192, 213; intersection with material culture studies (MCS), 215–16, 218, 228–29
Roberts, Dustyn, 121–22
Roberts, W. O., 121
Rochberg-Halton, Eugene, 8, 26, 84, 98
Rule, Hannah J., vii–viii, xiii, 214, 216
Russian literature, 74–75
Russian-speaking immigrants, vii

Saunders, Tamia, xii
Schneider, Gary, 214, 216, 221
scientific motherhood, vii, 8, 90–96, 98–99, 104–105, 108, 110–11, 111n1, 111n3, 232
Scott, Walter, 199, 203
scrapbooks, 94–95
screen readers, 8
Senchyne, Jonathan, 55
sexism, 21
shared possessions, 8
Shelley, Percy Bysshe, 191, 194, 196; atheism, 198–99; Montenvers inscription, 195–200, 208
Shipka, Jody, 4, 119–20, 176
shopping lists, 8
Shulman, David, 80, 86n3
singularization, 71–72. *See also Book of Baby Mine, The*: singularization
Slack, 132
Slack, Jennifer, 126
Smith, Albert, 204, 206
Smith, Margaret Bayard, 158, 161, 165
Smith, William Loughton, 164
social writing, 133–34, 136–37
Society for College and University Planning (SCUP), 128
Southey, Robert, 203
Spartz, John M., 136
spatial configuration, 80, 127–28
Spinuzzi, Clay, 132, 136
Stanford University Hasso Plattner Institute of Design (d.school), 120, 125, 131
Stockton, Frank, 155–56, 165
Swinburne, Algernon Charles, 197–98

technical communication, 11, 116, 129
textbooks, 22
Thoreau, Henry David, 4
tourism, 203
Townsley, Bartley, 61–62
transnational literacy, 10
transnational migration, 70

Trapper Keepers, 25
Trist, Nicholas, 145
Turgenev, Ivan, 74

Ulrich, Laurel Thatcher, 144
Union of the Soviet Socialist Republic (USSR), 86n2; commodified objects/consumer culture, 72–73, 75; encyclopedias, 78–79; literacy, 69–71, 73–76, 80, 86; novels/poetry, 69, 74–75; textbooks, 69–70, 76, 81; writers, 70. *See also* discursive heirlooms; Komsomol; Krupskaya, Nadezhda; Marxism; Russian literature
University of Delaware Design Studio, 119–20, 121–23, 125, 127–28, 130, 133–37

Van Gogh, Vincent, viii, 30
Vickery, Amanda, 145
Victorian visitors' books, vii, 11, 191–92, 195–96, 199–209. *See also* Shelley, Percy Bysshe: Montenvers inscription
Vieira, Kate, 10–11

Walsh, Robert, 147
Ward, Jesmyn, 64
Wardwicke, Ursula, 212, 214, 219, 221–23, 225
Warner, Susan, 51
watermarks, 214
Weber, Ryan P., 136
Weiner, Lynn, 93–94, 105
white supremacy ideology, viii, 51, 61–63, 233
White-Farnham, Jamie, 73
whiteness, 56–57, 59, 60, 62. *See also* women: whiteness
Wi-Fi access, ix
Wilson, G. S., 163
women writers: cultural challenges, 50, 54, 56–59, 64, 65n1; stories about, 56–59
women: civic power, 192; domestic lives/power, 50, 53–54, 60, 192; femininity, 50–51, 53, 60, 64; in Renaissance England, 192, 212–13; self-representation, 50, 64; whiteness, viii, 22, 64; writing practices, 201–03. *See also* motherhood; scientific motherhood
Wordsworth, William, 203
workplaces, 12, 115, 128, 130, 133
Wray, Fitzwater, 208
writing desks, 3, 11, 52, 65n2
writing furniture, vii, 12, 117, 140, 166n4
writing implements, 12; as consumer goods, 52; and gender, 52; racialization of, 51, 55–56; and social status, 52. *See also* fountain pens; ink; inkstands; ink-

wells; nibs; paper; pencils; penknives; pounce pots/blotters; Moleskine notebooks; quills

writing objects/artifacts, viii–ix, xi, xiii, 4, 7–12, 22, 25, 33, 109, 117, 143–44, 166, 171, 211, 216, 218, 233–35

writing studies (WS), vii, ix–x, 8, 12, 19, 14$n1$, 211, 213; genre as social action, 191–93; material culture, 3–5, 26–27; intersection with material culture studies (MCS), 11–12, 21, 116, 214–15, 231

Wyche, Susan, 4

CONTRIBUTORS

Cydney Alexis is Associate Professor of English at Kansas State University where she directed the writing center for five years. Her qualitative research interrogates the complex relationships between writing, identity, people, and material goods. Her long-form scholarship, both individual and with frequent coauthor Dr. Eric Leake, can be found in *Composition Studies* and various edited collections, including *Bad Ideas about Writing* and the forthcoming *Style and the Future of Composition Studies*. Her short piece "Stop Using the Phrase Creative Writing" was reprinted in *Slate* after initial publication in *Inside Higher Education*.

Deborah C. Andrews is professor of English, Emerita, and former director of the Center for Material Culture Studies at the University of Delaware. She has published several articles, book chapters, and texts on technical and professional communication, especially in an international context. These include *Technical Communication in the Global Community* and *Management Communication: A Guide*. A researcher, consultant, and speaker, she is the former editor of *Business Communication Quarterly*. More recently, she has integrated her communications interests with research in material culture studies. She coordinated and edited an anthology, *Shopping: A Material Culture Perspective*. Her latest research project is a broad study of how the physical environment of twenty-first-century workplaces fosters or constrains collaborative communication. Her most recent co-authored book is *Designing Technical and Professional Communication: Strategies for the Global Community*.

Diane Ehrenpreis, associate curator of decorative arts, Thomas Jefferson Foundation at Monticello, is responsible for the collections and material culture encompassing Thomas Jefferson's diverse interests and his family's activities including fine and decorative arts, historic interiors, and social history. Since 2010, she has coordinated new initiatives and research reflecting domestic life at Monticello, leading to the reinterpretation of numerous public and private rooms in the house. She has published on various topics including the reinstallation of the upper floors at Monticello and the Campeachy chair and Jefferson's association with its popularization. Most recently she co-authored *Enlightened Networks: Thomas Jefferson's System for Working from Home* and a forthcoming article *"Threads and Clues of It": Thomas Jefferson's New York Furniture*.

Keri Epps is assistant teaching professor of writing at Wake Forest University. Her research and teaching lie at the intersection of rhetorical genre theory, media studies, and community-engaged and social justice research. She received her PhD in English—Rhetoric and Composition—from the University of Louisville in 2018. Her dissertation titled *Pens, Print, and Pixels: Gendered Writing and the Epistolary Genre in Transitional Eras* has provided opportunities for continued research to understand how genres and media transition and evolve together to offer opportunities for marginalized writers' voices to be heard, shared, and valued over time. In addition to this work, she has received numerous fellowships and grants for her work in community-based research projects and teaching, such as her work with community members to develop literacy programs in the Winston-Salem area for middle-school girls in underperforming schools.

Desirée Henderson is professor of English at the University of Texas at Arlington where she specializes in American literature, life writing, and women's writing. She is the author of two books: *Grief and Genre in American Literature, 1790–1870* (Ashgate, 2011) and *How to Read a Diary: Critical Contexts and Interpretive Strategies for 21st-Century Readers* (Routledge, 2019). She has published numerous essays including in the edited collections *A History of Nineteenth-Century American Women's Poetry* and *The New Dickinson Studies*, and in journals such as *a/b: Auto/biography Studies*, *American Periodicals*, and *Legacy: A Journal of American Women Writers*.

Kevin James is Scottish Studies Foundation Chair and professor of history at the University of Guelph, with research interests in the history of tourism and the nineteenth-century hotel, in each case with a focus on Scotland and Ireland. His most recent books are *Histories, Meanings and Representations of the Modern Hotel* (2018) and *Tourism, Land, and Landscape in Ireland: The Commodification of Culture* (2014). His current research explores hotels and resorts in Britain and Ireland during World War I and the hotel visitors' book as an artifact of travel in Victorian Britain. Kevin collaborates with Patrick Vincent of l'Université de Neuchâtel on the Swiss Guestbook Project. Their work is supported by the Swiss National Science Foundation, and Kevin's research programs on tourism and travel history have been supported by grants from the Social Sciences and Research Foundation of Canada. He has also appeared on television and served as a consultant to media and galleries.

Jenny Krichevsky is assistant professor of English and directs the Writing Across the Curriculum program at California State University, Fresno. She specializes in multilingual writing, immigrant family literacies, and Writing Across the Curriculum. Her research looks at the ways in which transnational and multilingual families transmit literacy and language values across space and time, through generations and geopolitical boundaries.

Anne MacKay was the head of conservation at the McCord Museum in Montreal from 1997 to 2021. She also worked as a conservator at the National Gallery of Canada, the Canadian Museum of History, the Museum of Anatolian Civilisations, and the Metropolitan Museum. She has published and lectured widely on conservation issues, is an associate editor of the *Journal of the Canadian Association of Conservation*, and has taught courses on the history and theory of art conservation at Concordia University and the Université de Montréal in Montreal. She is a member of the Canadian Association of Professional Conservators, accredited in the conservation of sculpture.

Emilie Merrigan holds an MA in English Composition, Rhetoric, and Literature with a Certificate in Technical Writing from Kansas State University. She also holds a Masters in Teaching English and English as a Second Language from Hastings College (NE) and previously taught high school language arts. Her research and writing interests include sociolinguistics in education, rhetorics of motherhood, and intercultural technical communication. She is currently a technical writer for a software company that specializes in public administration asset management.

Laura R. Micciche is professor of English at the University of Cincinnati. Her research focuses on feminist and affective approaches to writing and teaching practices. Her books include *Failure Pedagogies: Learning and Unlearning What it Means to Fail*, coedited with Allison D. Carr (2020), *Acknowledging Writing Partners* (2017) and *Doing Emotion: Rhetoric, Writing, Teaching* (2007).

Hannah J. Rule is associate professor of composition and rhetoric in the department of English at the University of South Carolina. Her teaching and research focuses on the teaching of writing in postsecondary contexts, composition theory, and disciplinary histories. She is the author of *Situating Writing Processes* (2019), a novel take on the trajectories of the process paradigm in composition studies and a reimagination of contemporary process teaching as material, embodied, and improvisatory. Her scholarship also appears in *College Composition and Communication, Composition Studies, Composition Forum*, as well as edited collections including *Best of the Journals in Rhetoric & Composition 2018* (2019).

Kate Smith is associate professor in eighteenth-century history at the University of Birmingham, UK. She researches eighteenth- and nineteenth-century Britain and empire and studies how material cultures have been shaped by flows of knowledge, imperial connections, and global trade. Kate's recent books include *Material Goods, Moving Hands: Perceiving Production in England, 1700–1830* (Manchester University Press, 2014), *New Pathways to Public Histories* (coedited with Margot Finn for Palgrave Macmillan, 2015), *The East India Company at Home* (coedited with Margot Finn for UCL Press, 2018), and *British Women and Cultural Practices of Empire, 1770–1940* (coedited with Rosie Dias, for Bloomsbury, 2018). Kate is currently working on her next monograph project, provisionally entitled *Losing Possession in London's Long Eighteenth Century*.

www.ingramcontent.com/pod-product-compliance
Lightning Source LLC
Chambersburg PA
CBHW020522080526
44583CB00013B/700